Sanctuary cities and urban struggles

MANCHESTER
1824

Manchester University Press

Sanctuary cities and urban struggles

Rescaling migration, citizenship, and rights

Edited by Jonathan Darling and Harald Bauder

Manchester University Press

Published by Manchester University Press
Altrincham Street, Manchester M1 7JA
www.manchesteruniversitypress.co.uk

British Library Cataloguing-in-Publication Data
A catalogue record for this book is available from the British Library

ISBN 978 1 5261 3491 2 hardback
ISBN 978 1 5261 5599 3 paperback

First published 2019

Typeset
by Toppan Best-set Premedia Limited

Contents

Figures

Notes on contributors

Idil Atak is an Associate Professor and the Graduate Program Director in the Department of Criminology of Ryerson University, Toronto. She is a member of the International Association for the Study of Forced Migration's executive committee and a past president of the Canadian Association for Refugee and Forced Migration Studies. She is currently conducting research funded by the Social Sciences and Humanities Research Council of Canada on the intersection of security, irregular migration, and asylum.

Jen Bagelman is a Lecturer in Geography at Newcastle University. Her academic and activist work critically examines how displacement is produced through exclusionary citizenship and bordering practices. She is also deeply interested in how people mobilise to enact more loving geopolitics. In particular her research explores how anti-colonial sanctuary movements challenge (and sometimes inadvertently reproduce) the hostile treatment of refugees and other displaced peoples. Her book *Sanctuary City: A Suspended State* (PalgraveMacmillan, 2016) explores this topic.

Harald Bauder is Professor in the Department of Geography & Environmental Studies at Ryerson University, Toronto. He is the director of the MA Program in Immigration and Settlement Studies and the founding academic director of the Ryerson Centre for Immigration and Settlement. He has edited five volumes and published four monographs, 72 articles in peer-reviewed journals, and multiple book chapters, reports, and op-eds in the popular media. In 2015 he received the prestigious Konrad Adenauer Research Award from the Royal Society of Canada and the A. v. Humboldt Foundation.

Jonathan Darling is Associate Professor in Human Geography at Durham University. Prior to this he was Senior Lecturer in Human Geography at the University of Manchester, and the director of the Cities, Politics, Economies Research Group. His research focuses on the spatial politics of asylum, sanctuary, and the urban dynamics of forced migration. He has co-edited two volumes and published 18 articles in international journals, alongside numerous book chapters and public commentaries. In 2012 he was awarded an ESRC Future Research Leaders Award to conduct research on the UK's dispersal system of housing and support for asylum seekers and refugees.

Graham Hudson is an Associate Professor in the Department of Criminology at Ryerson University, Toronto. He holds a BA (Hons) in History and Philosophy from York University, a JD from the University of Toronto, an LLM from Queen's University, and a PhD from Osgoode Hall Law School. His current research includes the sanctuary city movement in Canada, the criminalisation of (irregular) migration, national security law and policy, and the judicial administration of secret trials in Canada and the UK.

Janika Kuge is a PhD candidate in political geography at the Institute of Human Geography in Freiburg, Germany. She has a state's degree in geography, German linguistics and philosophy and is now working in the Department of Sustainable Development and Geography of Economy. Her special interest in the geographies of marginalised groups in society and critical theory was sparked by a long history of activism in refugee solidarity alliances.

Valeria Raimondi is an urban geographer with a background in political science. In 2019 she was awarded a joint PhD degree in Urban Studies from the Scuola Universitaria Superiore Sant'Anna di Pisa and the Gran Sasso Science Institute in Italy. Her research is characterised by an interdisciplinary approach at the crossroad of urban geography, critical migration and border studies, and critical citizenship studies. As an activist researcher, she is part of an international network of scholars engaged in the study of transnational migrant solidarity, state repression, and resistance to criminalisation.

Ben Rogaly teaches in the Department of Geography at the University of Sussex. He has a long-standing research interest in migration in England and India and is author of *Stories from a Migrant City: Living and Working Together in the Shadow of Brexit* and co-editor of *Creativity and Resistance in a Hostile World* both published by Manchester University Press in 2020.

Sheryl-Ann Simpson is an Assistant Professor in the Department of Geography and Environmental Studies at Carleton University. Her work focuses on the production of place, the ways in which state and resident actions interact in and on places and landscapes, including built environments. She focuses these broad questions through an examination of immigration and settlement in Canada, the US, and northern Europe. She also works in the area of spatial methods more broadly, linking qualitative, quantitative, visual, and participatory methods.

M. Anne Visser is an Associate Professor of Community and Regional Development in the Department of Human Ecology at the University of California, Davis. Her research interests include the socio-economic implications of the informalisation of work and employment, low-wage and informal labour markets, and the impact of state policy and socially based labour-market interventions on economic opportunity. This research specifically includes a focus on policies related to migrant workers in the global informal economy. Her research has recently been published in *Urban Geography, Journal of Ethnic and Migration Studies,* and *Work Employment & Society.*

Acknowledgements

First and foremost, we would like to thank each of the authors who have contributed their work to this book. It has been a pleasure working with so many committed and insightful scholars. Most of the essays collected together here were first presented as part of a series of sessions on 'Rescaling migration, citizenship, and rights' at the Association of American Geographers Annual Meeting in Boston, in April 2017. We thank all of those involved in these sessions, both panellists and audience members, for some fruitful discussions and for getting us thinking about this book. At Manchester University Press, we thank Tom Dark and Rob Byron, who have supported, encouraged, and helped us in translating our proposal into this book. Thanks to Humairaa Dudhwala who managed the typesetting process, and Martin Hargreaves who compiled the index. Thanks also to the anonymous reviewers, whose careful reading and feedback has been invaluable in sharpening the arguments behind this book. Lorelle Juffs helped format the chapters prior to submission to Manchester University Press. Finally, we would like to thank our trusted colleagues who have supported and encouraged us throughout this project. In particular, Jonathan would like to thank Martin Hess, Colin McFarlane, Kevin Ward, and Helen Wilson for their generous support, insight, and guidance. Harald thanks his colleagues at Ryerson University for providing a stimulating and collegial working environment.

Introduction – Sanctuary cities and urban struggles: rescaling migration, citizenship, and rights

Jonathan Darling and Harald Bauder

Migration, and the attendant questions of rights, entitlements, and citizenship that emerge alongside it, is typically positioned as a political challenge for the nation-state. From the perspective of a territorially bound sovereign authority, migration poses fundamental questions of inclusion, identification, and border enforcement. The acceleration of migration, transnational connections, and the hybridisation of identities associated with globalisation has served to further challenge the ability of nation-states to effectively order, sort, and classify migrants according to varying metrics of income, skills, education, and cultural capital. Thus, we have seen increasingly sophisticated attempts to filter migrants through biometric forms of sorting and classification (Amoore, 2006; Vaughan-Williams, 2009), and control their journeys and life chances through the use of enforced and punitive mobility, rerouting them through ever more hazardous channels on the borders of Europe and North America (Crawley, 2016; Doty, 2011, Hess et al., 2017). Importantly, within a policy context that seeks to 'manage migration' in the interests of those most readily able to take advantage of mobility (Bauman, 1998), it is the nation-state that remains the focus of critical attention among policy makers and academics.

We might think here of three high-profile examples. First, in September 2015 the German Chancellor Angela Merkel announced that refugees fleeing the Syrian conflict would be able to remain in Germany after the country briefly suspended the Dublin II agreement and made a commitment to process all asylum claims from this group. Second, in January 2017 President Donald Trump signed Executive

Order 13769 which suspended refugee admissions and entry by nationals of seven Muslim-majority countries to the US, leading to numerous legal challenges and significant political protest. Third, on 29 March 2017 the UK Prime Minister Theresa May signed a letter announcing the British government's decision to invoke Article 50 of the Treaty of Lisbon and thereby set in motion the process of leaving the European Union. One impact of this has been to raise critical questions over the citizenship rights of EU citizens living in the UK, and over the approach to migration and freedom of movement that a post-Brexit Britain will take. Each of these three cases illustrates how the nation-state is the focal point of political attention in trying to manage migration to address questions of rights and entitlements, solve problems of security, and tackle geopolitical challenges. Treaties are signed, executive orders issued, and summits convened to discuss migration and deliberate responses to mass population displacements from conflict, persecution, and economic hardship, all based upon the presumption that it is the nation-state that is uniquely placed to respond to migration. Yet this presumption overlooks other sites of activity, other scales of analysis, and other political possibilities. The chapters of this book are devoted to these actors, actions, and possibilities to explore how migration, rights, and citizenship might be understood beyond the limits and demands of the nation-state system. The value of doing so, we argue, is not just in illuminating elements of the politics of migration that are often overlooked, but in offering perspectives that may reorient how we understand migration, citizenship, and rights.

We are not suggesting that the nation-state is no longer a significant force within the politics of migration. Far from it, as numerous bodies of literature have illustrated: the nation-state remains central to the production of border control, the definition, processing, and categorisation of different forms of migrant status, and the securitisation of migration (Mavroudi and Nagel, 2016; Walters, 2004). However, the expansion of border enforcement technologies and techniques to new sites, from policing and legislation within the nation-state (Coleman, 2012; Walters, 2006), to the growth of processing and detention in extraterritorial locations (Collyer and King, 2015), has led growing critical attention to ask how such spaces of migration can be understood in their own terms. The chapters in this book examine ways to advance such work: they ask how migration is experienced, politicised, and policed when framed as a concern for cities, communities, and everyday life, rather than purely for the policies, rhetoric, and imaginaries of the nation-state. As Prem Kumar Rajaram (2013: 693) argues in the context of asylum, such discussions are conceived 'from within the limits of a particular society, often a society imagined by a state', and are thus subject to the limits of imagination associated with a purely statist perspective (Balibar, 2004). To move beyond this narrow perspective, we might ask how we can think about Germany's suspension of Dublin II, Trump's exclusionary executive orders, and the uncertainties of citizenship during Brexit in ways that foreground non-national scales, lived experience, and diverse political imaginaries of possibility.

In making this case, *Sanctuary cities and urban struggles* draws upon recent debates over migration, refuge, and citizenship that are challenging the assumed primacy of the nation-state as the key guarantor of rights and entitlements. This critical inquiry is centred upon two developments. On the one hand, a growing body of literature has considered how bordering processes and functions are performed at urban, regional, and local scales, viewing each as a site of exclusion and for the reproduction of state power. For example, Varsanyi (2008a) highlights how local land-use ordinances and zoning regulations in a number of US states have been co-opted to exclude migrant workers and to increase the precarity of undocumented migrants. Similarly, Walker and Leitner (2011) illustrate the diverse geography of anti-immigrant legislation across the US, arguing that national policies are refracted through state and local forms of governance and enforcement to produce often radically different outcomes for migrants on the ground. On the other hand, critical scholars have also pointed to the opportunities that exist for political contestation and claims-making when concerns with rights, citizenship, and political subjectivity are articulated beyond the nation-state. Here, we might consider the growth of work on claims-making centred around 'acts of citizenship' (Isin, 2008) that may be directed towards audiences other than national governments and authorities, including fellow migrants and citizens (May, 2010), urban authorities (Uitermark et al., 2012; Swerts, 2017), and transnational networks of activists in search of solidarity (Featherstone, 2012). In this context, there is both an empirical and an analytical importance in exploring migration, citizenship, and rights beyond the nation-state. Empirically, the chapters in this book unveil novel evidence of the politics of migration as they assume perspectives beyond the nation-state. Analytically, there is an opportunity to explore other forms of politics if we refuse 'seeing like the state' (Scott, 1998), and examine additional ways in which social movements, activists, migrants, and others are imagining relationships to place, rights, and belonging.

If questioning the primacy of the nation-state represents the initial driving force behind this book, the second orientation point is to examine the role of the city as an actor within the politics of migration. On the one hand, recent work seeks to expose a 'methodological nationalism' (Wimmer and Glick Schiller, 2002) that arguably has dominated discussions around migration, citizenship, and rights. Our intention is not to replace the nation-state with the city, but rather to offer alternative political narratives. The move from a centralised governmental form associated with the modern state, to the fragmented and decentred governmentality of urban authorities that demand compromise, contingency, and incomplete claims to authority – a move that Magnusson (2011) typifies as a shift from 'seeing like a state' to 'seeing like a city' – is indicative of this analytical framing (see also Amin and Thrift, 2016). Indeed, a focus on epistemological practices of apprehending the world is important because it illustrates that a growing concern with the city is not purely an empirical consideration born of a growth in urban movements around migrants rights (although this is clearly significant), but also points to an open-ness to interrogating incomplete claims to control and sovereignty (Darling, 2017a). Alongside such epistemological claims for the category of the urban has been work that sees the city as a space that challenges the exclusions perpetrated at the scale of the nation-state. This work explores the city as a politically charged arena where 'state borders are being produced and contested' in multiple ways (Lebuhn, 2013: 39). From migrants' rights-organising in cities, through sanctuary ordinances, and the networking of migrant struggles with other contested claims to citizenship, the urban has emerged as a terrain through which political claims to rights are being articulated (Bauder, 2016a). This is not a new phenomenon. Cities have often played defining roles in creating forms of membership, belonging, and identification that respond to mobility in novel ways (see Brett, 2011; Isin, 2002; de Graauw and Vermeulen, 2016). However, contemporary discussions point to the centrality of mobility to the urban, whereby urbanism is 'characterised by movement, flux, restlessness ... [and] the politics of urbanism is a politics of movement' (Magnusson, 2000: 298), and to the role that cities may play in countering the exclusions of the nation-state. At a time when the demands of the supposedly sovereign nation-state for ever greater control over mobility appear to be meeting their limits, the pragmatism of urban networks may offer a point of hope for the future (Barber, 2013).

Sanctuary cities and urban struggles responds to both of these areas of debate: first, critically questioning the limits of the nation-state as a primary site of rights and citizenship, and, second, exploring the roles cities play in relation to those rights and claims to citizenship. We do not seek to romanticise the city in doing so. Indeed, a number of the chapters are explicitly cautious of a turn to the urban (see Bagelman in particular). Rather, we ask what opportunities open up if we think migration, citizenship, and rights at political sites and scales other than the nation-state alone. In doing so, we turn to the urban as a key scale of both analysis and political activity. In this way, the city presents a contested and ambivalent socio-spatial formation. This formation is, on the one hand, a site through which regimes of border control, securitisation, and legal exclusion are enforced in everyday life (Coleman, 2009; de Graauw, 2014; Ridgley, 2008; Yuval-Davis et al., 2018). On the other hand, it is a space in which networks of political solidarity, organising, and mutual support give presence to the claims of illegalised migrants and refugees (Bauder, 2016a; Darling, 2017b). Many of the chapters in this book explore how an urban context can offer a space for experimenting with different forms of political enactment and claims-making, while they acknowledge that this space is always highly constrained, open to governmental subversion and co-option, and, crucially, that these forms of experimentation carry risks unequally borne by those involved (see Raimondi and Darling).

With this agenda in mind, in the remainder of this introduction we briefly outline three areas that have emerged in recent work seeking to reconsider migration beyond a national perspective. Each of these areas reflects some of the chapters brought together in this book.

Within this discussion we also give a brief overview of the chapters to come.

Scalar relations: policy, governance, securitisation

The first key development in the literature around the rescaling of migration and its political expression has involved detailing how practices of border control and securitisation are increasingly 'local' activities. In this literature, a concern with the diversification of borders into everyday life (Gilbert, 2009; Sassen, 2013; Varsanyi, 2008a) has led to the exploration of how the devolution of policies and enforcement measures from the nation-state to specific urban contexts translate into modes of 'local border control' (Lebuhn, 2013: 38). For example, Graham (2010) contends that today borders have become a 'ubiquitous' part of urban life, and that such ubiquity is central to producing conditions of insecurity and precarity for irregular migrants (Coleman and Kocher, 2011). Similarly, Coleman (2009, 2012) shows how the enrolment of an expanded array of authorities, services, and professionals into the practice of immigration control and border enforcement serves to extend responsibility for border policing, while simultaneously spreading migrant insecurity. In this sense, the nation-state 'literally takes place in the everyday spaces of the city, which means its exclusions are also worked out there' (Young, 2011: 542).

Of course, the transfer of policies around immigration enforcement is not a binary process that assumes the centrality of the nation-state. Rather, as Steil and Ridgley (2012) show in the context of municipal ordinances that restrict migrant rights in the US, such ordinances have often acted as forerunners to legislation at federal and state levels. The rescaling of immigration control in evidence here is not simply about the transferral of authority down a scalar hierarchy, but rather involves 'true grassroots efforts at immigration control' alongside 'efforts emerging from a devolution of immigration powers by the federal government' (Varsanyi, 2008b: 892). The process of developing and enacting migration policy involves the mobility of ideas, practices, and processes of learning from different contexts, such that experiments with forms of control, selection, and categorisation of migrants through different legislative mechanisms are translated between sites and scales (Jamison, 2016). Indeed, as Coleman (2012) and Walker (2014) note, the ways in which enforcement practices are produced and enacted in US cities is highly dependent on local negotiations of policy, biography, and the nuances of electoral politics. These elements of localised context and knowledge condition how policies are enacted (see also de Graauw and Vermeulen, 2016).

Discussions around migration policy and the governance of mobility have thus neither sought to deny the authority of the nation-state, nor to underplay its role in establishing the conditions in which many policies are conceived and enacted. However, critical scholarship has begun to unpack how policy is implemented, translated, and remade when put into practice through different spatial contexts. This scholarship has also explored possibilities for policy and governance to be both conceived and practised differently. It is here that *Sanctuary cities and urban struggles* makes a key conceptual contribution to work on migration, citizenship, and rights, through foregrounding the political negotiations and mobilisation of different spatial scales within both the governance of migration and the contestation of citizenship regimes. For example, Anne Visser and Sheryl-Ann Simpson's chapter discusses how a range of sub-national actors define the politics of migration and immigration enforcement in the US. Critically, they illustrate disjunctures between federal, state, and municipal scales of jurisdiction and action, such that regularisation becomes a complex process of negotiating varying authorities, policies, and sites.

Beyond this chapter, the book also contributes to thinking through the significance of negotiating scales of policy through chapters that reflect on how local contexts of municipal governance shape practices of sanctuary (see Atak, Bauder, and Kuge), and through exploring the securitisation of cities via the enrolment of municipal governance and the co-option of sanctuary (Hudson). In doing so, the book advances two conceptual insights. First, many of the following chapters address how spatial scales are politically mobilised for various, often contradictory, purposes. Thus, while the book focuses on the city, it shows that political campaigns and enactments performed in cities often make claims on discourses, legislatures, and publics situated beyond cities. This 'trans-scalar' outlook, as Graham Hudson terms it, reorients work on sanctuary cities away from a reification of the city and towards understanding urban struggles as *both* urban *and* outward looking. Jonathan Darling's discussion of the 'Dignity not

Destitution' campaign in the UK illustrates this reorientation. Second, the book foregrounds a series of more intimate scales of political mobilisation, thus drawing attention to the social and cultural relations that emerge from, and at the same time help to reproduce, modes of governance and contestation. In this vein, Jen Bagelman's concern with sanctuary as an intimate expression of refusing authority focuses on the cultural possibilities of sanctuary itself. Similarly, Ben Rogaly's discussion of how forms of convivial culture can serve to foster prosaic 'acts of citizenship' highlights the need for 'trans-scalar' analysis to consider how intimate and seemingly mundane relations, and locations, can profoundly shape experiences and understandings of rights and positions within regimes of citizenship and belonging. In drawing out some of these scalar relations and complexities, *Sanctuary cities and urban struggles* makes a first significant contribution to these current debates.

Sanctuary: movements, cities, intimacies

The second area of significant work on rescaling migration, citizenship, and rights are the growing discussions of sanctuary. To date, such work has focused on either how sanctuary has been understood as a practice associated with the suspension of particular sets of normative rules around mobility (see Lippert and Rehaag, 2012), or the creation of sanctuary movements that seek to protect the rights of migrants and refugees who have been illegalised by the nation-state (Bauder, 2016b). Genealogical work has argued that sanctuary has long been associated with a spatial practice of setting a specific territory, location, or building outside the bounds of sovereign authority and legal redress, albeit in often temporary ways (Bagelman, 2016). One manifestation of this suspension is the historical role of religious buildings in offering refuge (Just, 2012), while another is the example of the six biblical 'cities of refuge' that have inspired some contemporary sanctuary movements in their invocation of faith to welcome strangers. From this latter lineage we might see the rise of the 'sanctuary city' as a space often positioned as at odds with exclusionary migration control. This connection between sanctuary and the city has diverse roots in different contexts, and has led to significant variations in how urban sanctuary is practised, as Harald Bauder illustrates in his chapter. What binds work on sanctuary together, however, is a recognition that sanctuary is often sought and practised *within* the nation-state, but that it is rarely practised or performed *by* the nation-state. Instead, sanctuary is most often articulated as an oppositional practice to nation-state authority. This opposition can be observed in the US, where New York City's mayor Bill de Blasio (Robbins, 2017) proclaimed that 'we're going to defend all of our people, regardless of where they come from, regardless of their immigration status', in response to Donald Trump's attempt to withhold federal funds from sanctuary cities. In this way, sanctuary is not only an urban phenomenon but also an important political critique of the nation-state from within.

Three trends are evident in this respect. First, a body of work has examined the history and current practice of the New Sanctuary Movement across North America, a network of social movements with roots in faith-based communities that focus on offering protection from deportation to individual refugees and undocumented migrants (Caminero-Santangelo, 2012). While these immigrant rights organisations seek ways to practise sanctuary in response to anti-immigrant sentiments and legislation, critical studies have highlighted how, in doing so, they can also reiterate distinctions between 'deserving' and 'undeserving' migrants through the selective application of sanctuary to some but not others (Houston and Morse, 2017; Yukich, 2013). Second, also in the context of North America, there has been a growth in work that examines the rise of 'sanctuary cities' as municipalities that have passed various forms of pro-immigrant ordinances in order to protect the rights and presence of undocumented migrants (de Graauw, 2014; Ridgley, 2008, 2012; Young, 2011). Of these, San Francisco was an early exemplar (Mancina, 2012), but the sanctuary city designation has grown considerably over the last decade and has taken on an increasingly contentious political position since the Trump administration's threat to de-fund such municipalities. This work has highlighted the opportunities to establish rights through restricting the reach of federal immigration enforcement and offering services based on residency rather than status (Nyers, 2010; Varsanyi, 2008a). It has also critically reflected upon the political possibilities that arise from embedding sanctuary within the legal and social fabric of a city. In this sense, as Ridgley (2008: 56) argues, the sanctuary city 'is not only a space of protection from an increasingly anti-immigrant national security agenda, but also a potential line of flight out of which alternative futures can be materialized'. Finally, discussions in a European context have drawn attention to the growth of sanctuary-oriented movements (see Lundberg and Strange, 2017; Pyykkonen, 2009). From Derrida's (2001) evocative vision of a 'city of refuge' that may challenge the sovereignty of the nation-state, to contemporary anti-deportation activism (Lebuhn, 2013), a history of employing sanctuary as a political claim for migrants' rights is also evident across Europe. Most recently, this has been manifested in studies of the UK's City of Sanctuary movement, a social movement designed to offer conditions of safety and welcome to asylum seekers and refugees in towns and cities across the country (Bagelman, 2016; Darling, 2010; Squire and Darling, 2013). Unlike the sanctuary cities of North America, the UK movement has less legislative authority and focuses instead upon effecting cultural change and shifting attitudes towards refugees.

Within this existing set of discussions, *Sanctuary cities and urban struggles* provides a series of empirical and conceptual engagements with the practice, politics, and spatiality of sanctuary. Chapters by Idil Atak and Graham Hudson explore the urban context in which sanctuary ordinances are established and how articulations of sanctuary interact with concerns over public safety, security, and a desire for forms of localised border enforcement. In situating these cases within the wider field of urban sanctuary, Harald Bauder's chapter explores the scalar and spatial specificity of sanctuary as it is envisaged and practised across a range of sites. Asking what constitutes the 'sanctuary city' in different contexts, this chapter offers a critical account of the political possibilities, and limits, of framing migrants' rights through the lens of sanctuary. In taking seriously these limits, Jen Bagelman's chapter argues for an account of sanctuary that draws on the intimate politics of everyday life, and in doing so questions the turn to the city in much work on sanctuary. Her contribution considers how notions of sanctuary intersect with practices of care, solidarity, and affective intimacy, which may exceed normative ideas of political belonging, but which may also add depth to how we consider the experiential aspects of sanctuary as a felt set of relations. Janika Kuge's chapter explores how sanctuary legislation and movements illustrate a series of shifts in authority and influence from the nation-state to an increasingly interconnected and urbanised world of multiple authorities and political actors. Arguing that sanctuary legislation may serve as either a sign of changing priorities in the management of migration or, in specific political contexts, a marker of changing political relations in which the sovereign presumptions of the nation-state are challenged from within, Kuge's chapter places discussion of sanctuary into conversation with work on migrant activism, contested citizenship, and urban forms of solidarity.

Sanctuary cities and urban struggles thus extends work on sanctuary to consider both the contextual nuances of different sanctuary practices and how models of urban sanctuary are based upon remaking political and social relations at various scales. In this way, the book makes two main contributions to developing debates around sanctuary and its politics. First, it makes the case for a sustained focus on the formation, meaning, and practice of what might be termed the 'sanctuary city'. As Harald Bauder illustrates, this terminology has varying meanings in different international contexts, but what unifies these cases and orients this book is a framing of sanctuary as a practice tied to the negotiations of urban life. Jonathan Darling articulates this link through a concern with urbanism as a 'way of life' associated with proximate diversity, multiple sources of authority, and claims to political presence. Similarly, both Idil Atak and Graham Hudson illustrate how the practice of sanctuary necessarily entails many distinctly urban facets of contested claims to authority, influence, and ultimately rights. From these discussions comes the second main contribution: to focus upon those points where sanctuary as a mode of protection, safety, or refuge intersects with a context of wider urban struggles. Thus, in positioning work on sanctuary alongside discussions of refugee squatting and urban activism (Raimondi) and struggles over equal citizenship rights (Rogaly), the book draws out relations of contention between sanctuary and other diverse forms of political claims to rights. In this sense, we view sanctuary as one articulation of contemporary urban struggles over rights and belonging. Sanctuary movements themselves are often formed and maintained through political contestations and struggles at urban, and at some point national and even transnational, levels, as other chapters demonstrate (see Bauder, Kuge, and Hudson). However, the need to focus attention on the urban scale in exploring the politics of migration and refuge cannot be solely confined to a concern with sanctuary. Rather, as Jen Bagelman and Idil Atak illustrate, sanctuary itself has significant limits and may become removed from a political context of struggle and contestation when co-opted by interests of securitisation and moral closure (see also Darling, 2013). In turning to a broader set of urban struggles for rights to belonging and urban space, we thus highlight how a focus beyond the national scale can bring insight into how regimes of citizenship are contested and solidarities formed in ways that go beyond a concern with sanctuary alone.

Contesting citizenship: solidarity, activism, belonging

The final area of work addressed in this book is a set of debates about challenging forms of migration management. Here again we consider two avenues: first, discussions of political belonging and attachment to spaces and scales of politics, sociality, and interpersonal contact that both transcend, and undercut, identifications of national identity, the possession of formal citizenship, and classifications of status. From the spatially diffuse attachments associated with transnationalism (Leitner and Ehrkamp, 2006; Ehrkamp and Leitner, 2006), to claims for belonging and inclusion in 'local' communities and the 'right to the city' (Varsanyi, 2008a; Williams, 2015), discussions have centred on how belonging is not exhausted by frames of national identity or formal citizenship. The second avenue of consideration is represented by work exploring how forms of activism, protest, and contestation around migrants' rights have centred upon scalar practices beyond the nation-state. Discussions of 'urban citizenship' (Bauböck, 2003; Varsanyi, 2006), and forms of 'urban belonging' (Bauder, 2016a), have highlighted how migrant groups have increasingly appealed to municipalities as guarantors of rights and protections that may be absent at other scales. At the same time, geographers and others have begun to explore how urban networks of political contention have offered contexts in which claims to citizenship and the politics of presence may be articulated in ways not possible elsewhere (Bauder, 2016a; Darling, 2017a; Leitner and Strunk, 2014; Nyers, 2010; Uitermark and Nicholls, 2014). *Sanctuary cities and urban struggles* draws on both of these avenues to explore how the rights claims and politics of presence associated with urban citizenship, solidarity movements, and sanctuary practices all bring to light political opportunities and imaginaries of migration that are easily overlooked when viewed only from the perspective of the nation-state.

A critical question that runs through many of the following chapters is whether refocusing the politics of migration on scales other than the nation-state generates a critique in order to *reform* national-scale migration policy, or to *reject* the nation-state and consider what might emerge 'thereafter' (see Papadopolous and Tsianos, 2013). This issue has been expressed through Cook's discussion of the 'advocate's dilemma'. This refers to the difficulty of seeking to reject state authority and sovereignty, in arguing for migrants' rights to ultimately transcend boundaries, while at the same time appealing to such state authority and sovereignty for compromises and accommodations within its logics for those excluded. As Cook (2010: 160) argues:

> Advocates employing a global frame may find themselves talking past the mass publics they want to influence and unable to counter their opponents effectively. Yet the advocates' dilemma is that those who tackle these arguments head on may find themselves trapped within a national paradigm and unable to lay the discursive groundwork for a significant shift in the way the public views unauthorized migrants.

The challenges of addressing such a dilemma have found expression in recent work around questions of political subjectivity and the insurgent possibilities of acts that trouble, traverse, or reject frontiers and their enforcement (Darling, 2014, 2017b; Isin, 2012; De Genova, 2010; Squire, 2017). Considering this dilemma and its politics of relating to the authority of the state, this book focuses attention on the necessity both to think *within*, and simultaneously *beyond*, current framings of migration, bordering, and sovereign authority. An example of this form of thought might be seen in the practical work of migration advocates in Vancouver and other North American cities who cooperate with agents of the state to achieve practical goals while simultaneously pursuing radical political change (Walia, 2013). Efforts to work with and against the nation-state simultaneously may be compatible, if we conceptualise these efforts as belonging to different kinds of political projects that pursue different political aims (Bauder, 2016b). Another example can be found in 'mesolevel' migration policy (Matheis and Bauder, 2016: 6), referring to a level of political intervention that extends 'beyond the restricted range of policy options that are conventionally presented as "realistic"', but that does not present a radical or revolutionary challenge that can be readily dismissed. The mesolevel denotes interventions that may not be 'revolutionary transformations', but that are nevertheless 'transformative' in reshaping policy in often pragmatic ways (Matheis and Bauder, 2016: 7). Through exploring claims to sanctuary, urban belonging, and practices of refuge and protection, *Sanctuary cities and urban struggles* offers a set of critical reflections on how such pragmatic and transformative claims to political belonging and presence are being made.

In reflecting on these fields of political thought, the book offers a number of important perspectives. The chapter by Valeria Raimondi explores the context of urban claims for belonging and political solidarity associated with responses to the European 'refugee crisis'. In doing so, she questions how alternative forms of citizenship were shaped from the relations of everyday urban life. Alongside the concluding chapter by Jonathan Darling, this chapter advances an understanding of contemporary migration and refuge as critically entwined with the politics of urbanism as a way of life associated with negotiating difference, encountering strangeness, and necessarily forging pragmatic solidarities of interest (Magnusson, 2011). Similarly, Jen Bagelman's reflections on the politics of intimacy within sanctuary, and how intimate socialities are formed through experiences of refuge, speak to the attachments that emerge when we explore refuge as a fragile, everyday accomplishment. Finally, Ben Rogaly's chapter explores how local struggles for belonging are articulated by different urban residents, old and new, all seeking the opportunity to shape and influence local governance. In doing so, Rogaly highlights how the politics of belonging and claims-making extends beyond formal rights and status to encompass a set of negotiated, and often incomplete, positions of authority and influence. While not directed at the formal citizenship practices of the state, such contests are critical in shaping how individuals perceive their political and social position and how a 'right to *the* city' as a right to *their city* is understood and expressed. In this sense, *Sanctuary cities and urban struggles* advances debates around urban contention and the everyday accomplishment of political action, through foregrounding how relations are forged across spatial scales, between political movements, and through practices of mobility in order to sustain critical responses to exclusionary regimes of citizenship. However, the book also reminds us that such relations are made and employed in the service of governing immigration, restricting rights, and reproducing exclusionary citizenship regimes. In this way, this book highlights the entrenchment of established power relations as well as the efforts of those contesting these relations.

Structure of the book

Sanctuary cities and urban struggles explores how the three central themes outlined in this introduction, of scalar relation, sanctuary, and contesting citizenship, each intersect and what can be learned through a focus on migration beyond the nation-state. Following this introduction, the book is divided into two parts, each reflecting different dimensions of the intersection between migration, citizenship, rights, and the urban. Part I focuses on sanctuary cities. It considers how sanctuary has been framed, understood, and practised internationally, and, more specifically, how sanctuary is expressed through the negotiations of urban life in different contexts. Part I opens with Harald Bauder's discussion of how the concept of urban sanctuary has been developed and mobilised, followed by Janika Kuge's analysis of how this concept has been connected to a broader set of concerns in migrants' rights campaigns, extending the reach and depth of what sanctuary might mean. Chapters by Graham Hudson and Idil Atak then funnel this discussion to the concrete context of Toronto, Canada. Here Hudson highlights the tensions of governmentality and regulation that have shaped the limits of what sanctuary can mean, and Atak examines the experiences of those tasked with enacting sanctuary through policy, illustrating the tensions and possibilities in the gap between political aspiration and reality. In the final chapter of Part I, Jen Bagelman examines sanctuary through a more intimate lens, and considers how a variety of creative and cultural practices of 'artivism' convey claims to sanctuary below and beyond the horizon of urban policy making.

Part II then moves on to consider a broader array of urban struggles, often situated alongside, but not necessarily within, discussions of urban sanctuary. The first chapter, by Anne Visser and Sheryl-Ann Simpson, focuses on the development of immigration policy at different spatial scales in the USA. Visser and Simpson show that states, counties, and municipalities develop policies that can promote sanctuary or enact exclusionary measures towards migrants. Sanctuary, in this context, becomes one among a number of policy pathways reflecting struggles over citizenship and rights. The following chapter, by Valeria Raimondi, picks up the theme of urban contests to explore the politics of a self-organised refugee reception facility: the City Plaza Hotel in Athens, Greece. In discussing the squatting of this abandoned hotel by refugees, Raimondi shows how the claims to presence made by urban refugees were met with solidarity from other disadvantaged urban residents and activists. Ben Rogaly's chapter then considers everyday activism and claims-making in the UK. Rogaly discusses how diverse groups of residents assert their ownership over the city of Peterborough, and how a 'right to the city' may be both a progressive and an exclusionary demand in different contexts. Finally, Jonathan Darling reflects upon the links between sanctuary cities and urban struggles more broadly, through discussing how cities have been framed as sites of hospitality for migrants and how diverse forms of political contestation are central to discussions over what constitutes urbanism as a way of life. In discussing how presence may offer alternative orientations for political claims in, and to, the city, Darling argues that cities are often experienced as a necessarily pragmatic, and yet still potentially utopian, ground of negotiation between multiple forms of political struggle and claims-making, including sanctuary movements, calls for human rights, and assertions of belonging.

Finally, a note on language and terminology. We, as editors, worked with the contributors to highlight connections and synergies between chapters, and point them out to the reader. We refrained, however, from standardising terminology between the chapters. As a consequence, contributors use different terminologies to identify a key population discussed in this book: non-status migrants (Hudson), illegalised migrants and refugees (Bauder), irregular migrants (Raimondi), unauthorised migrants (Darling), and undocumented migrants or residents (Atak, Kuge, Visser, and Simpson). Which of these terminologies should be used in which context has been subject to significant debate (Bauder, 2014b; Goldring et al., 2009; Nyers, 2010). The contributors have used the terminology that reflects their own scholarly opinions and rationales. What all contributors agree on, however, is that the term 'illegal migrant' is derogatory, legally inaccurate, and politically manipulative.

References

Amin, A., and N. Thrift (2016) *Seeing Like a City* (Cambridge: Polity).

Amoore, L. (2006) 'Biometric borders: governing mobilities in the war on terror', *Political Geography*, 25:3, 336–351.

Bagelman, J. (2016) *Sanctuary City: A Suspended State* (Basingstoke: Palgrave Macmillan).

Balibar, E. (2004) *We, the People of Europe* (Princeton, NJ: Princeton University Press).

Barber, B. J. (2013) *If Mayors Ruled the World: Dysfunctional Nations, Rising Cities* (New Haven, CT: Yale University Press).

Bauböck, R. (2003) 'Reinventing urban citizenship', *Citizenship Studies*, 7:2, 139–160.

Bauder, H. (2014a) 'Domicile citizenship, human mobility and territoriality', *Progress in Human Geography*, 38:1, 91–106.

Bauder, H. (2014b) 'Why we should use the term "illegalised" refugee or immigrant', *International Journal of Refugee Law*, 26:3, 327–332.

Bauder, H. (2016a) 'Possibilities of urban belonging', *Antipode*, 48:2, 252–271.

Bauder, H. (2016b) *Migration Borders Freedom* (London: Routledge).

Bauman, Z. (1998) *Globalization and its Human Consequences* (Cambridge, Polity).

Brett, A. S. (2011) *Changes of State: Nature and the Limits of the City in Early Modern Natural Law* (Princeton, NJ: Princeton University Press).

Caminero-Santangelo, M. (2012) 'The voice of the voiceless: religious rhetoric, undocumented immigrants, and the New Sanctuary Movement in the United States', in R. K. Lippert and S. Rehaag (eds), *Sanctuary Practices in International Perspectives: Migration, Citizenship and Social Movements* (Abingdon: Routledge), 92–105.

Coleman, M. (2009) 'What counts as the politics and practice of security, and where? Devolution and immigrant insecurity after 9/11', *Annals of the Association of American Geographers*, 99:5, 904–913.

Coleman, M. (2012) 'The "local" migration state: the site-specific devolution of immigration enforcement in the US South', *Law & Policy*, 34:1, 159–190.

Coleman, M., and A. Kocher (2011) 'Detention, deportation, devolution and immigrant incapacitation in the US, post 9/11', *The Geographical Journal*, 177, 228–237.

Collyer, M., and R. King (2015) 'Producing transnational space: international migration and the extra-territorial reach of state power', *Progress in Human Geography*, 39, 185–204.

Cook, M. L. (2010) 'The advocate's dilemma: framing migrant rights in national settings', *Studies in Social Justice*, 4:2, 145–164.

Crawley, H. (2016) 'Managing the unmanageable? Understanding Europe's response to the migration "crisis"', *Human Geography*, 9:2, https://hugeog.com/managing-the-unmanageable-understanding-europes-response-to-the-migration-crisis/ (accessed 18 November 2018).

Darling, J. (2010) 'A city of sanctuary: the relational re-imagining of Sheffield's asylum politics', *Transactions of the Institute of British Geographers*, 35:1, 125–140.

Darling, J. (2013) 'Moral urbanism, asylum and the politics of critique', *Environment and Planning A*, 45, 1785–1801.

Darling, J. (2014) 'Asylum and the post-political: domopolitics, depoliticisation and acts of citizenship', *Antipode*, 46:1, 72–91.

Darling, J. (2017a), 'Forced migration and the city: irregularity, informality, and the politics of presence', *Progress in Human Geography*, 41:2, 178–198.

Darling, J. (2017b) 'Acts, ambiguities, and the labour of contesting citizenship', *Citizenship Studies*, 21:6, 727–736.

De Genova, N. (2010) 'The queer politics of migration: reflections on "illegality" and incorrigibility', *Studies in Social Justice*, 4:2, 101–126.

de Graauw, E. (2014) 'Municipal ID cards for undocumented immigrants: local bureaucratic membership in a federal system', *Politics & Society*, 42:3, 309–330.

de Graauw, E., and F. Vermeulen (2016) 'Cities and the politics of immigrant integration: a comparison of Berlin, Amsterdam, New York City, and San Francisco', *Journal of Ethnic and Migration Studies*, 42:6, 989–1012.

Derrida, J. (2001) *On Cosmopolitanism and Forgiveness*, trans. M. Dooley and M. Hughes (London: Routledge).

Doty, R. L. (2011) 'Bare life: border-crossing deaths and spaces of moral alibi', *Environment and Planning D: Society and Space*, 29:4, 599–612.

Ehrkamp, P., and H. Leitner (2006) 'Rethinking immigration and citizenship: new spaces of migrant transnationalism and belonging', *Environment and Planning A*, 38:9, 1591–1597.

Featherstone, D. (2012) *Solidarity: Hidden Histories and Geographies of Internationalism* (London: Zed Books).

Gilbert, L. (2009) 'Immigration as local politics: re-bordering immigration and multiculturalism through deterrence and incapacitation', *International Journal of Urban and Regional Research*, 33: 26–42.

Goldring, L., C. Berinstein, and J. K. Bernhard (2009) 'Institutionalizing precarious migratory status in Canada', *Citizenship Studies*, 13:4, 239–265.

Graham, S. (2010) *Cities Under Siege: The New Military Urbanism* (London: Verso).

Hess, S., B. Kasparek, S. Kron, M. Rodatz, M. Schwertl, and S. Sontowaski (eds) (2017) *Grenzregmine III: Der lange Sommer der Migration* (Berlin: Association A).

Houston, S. D., and C. Morse (2017) 'The ordinary and extraordinary: producing migrant inclusion and exclusion in US sanctuary movements', *Studies in Social Justice*, 11:1, 27–47.

Isin E. F. (2002) *Being Political: Genealogies of Citizenship* (Minneapolis, MN: University of Minnesota Press).

Isin, E. F. (2008) 'Theorizing acts of citizenship', in E. F. Isin and G. M. Nielsen (eds), *Acts of Citizenship* (London: Zed Books), 15–43.

Isin, E. F. (2012) *Citizens without Frontiers* (London: Bloomsbury).

Jamison, E. C. S. (2016) 'State-based immigration efforts and internally displaced persons (IDPs): an experiment in Alabama', in H. Bauder and C. Matheis (eds), *Migration Policy and Practice: Interventions and Solutions* (Basingstoke, Palgrave Macmillan), 149–174.

Just, W.-D. (2012) 'The rise and features of church asylum in Germany: "I will take refuge in the shadow of thy wings until the storms are past"', in R. K. Lippert and S. Rehaag (eds), *Sanctuary Practices in International Perspectives: Migration, Citizenship and Social Movements* (Abingdon: Routledge), 135–147.

Lebuhn, H. (2013) 'Local border practices and urban citizenship in Europe: exploring urban borderlands', *City*, 17:1, 37–51.

Leitner, H., and P. Ehrkamp (2006) 'Transnationalism and migrants' imaginings of citizenship', *Environment and Planning A*, 38:9, 1615–1632.

Leitner, H., and C. Strunk (2014) 'Assembling insurgent citizenship: immigrant advocacy struggles in the Washington DC metropolitan area', *Urban Geography*, 35:7, 943–964.

Lippert, R. K., and S. Rehaag (eds) (2012) *Sanctuary Practices in International Perspectives: Migration, Citizenship and Social Movements* (Abingdon: Routledge).

Lundberg, A., and M. Strange (2017) 'Who provides the conditions for human life? Sanctuary movements in Sweden as both contesting and working with state agencies', *Politics*, 37:3, 347–362.

Magnusson, W. (2000) 'Politicizing the global city', in E. F. Isin (ed.), *Democracy, Citizenship and the Global City* (London: Routledge), 289–306.

Magnusson, W. (2011) *Politics of Urbanism: Seeing Like a City* (London: Routledge).

Mancina, P. (2012) 'The birth of a sanctuary city: a history of governmental sanctuary in San Francisco', in R. K. Lippert and S. Rehaag (eds), *Sanctuary Practices in International Perspectives: Migration, Citizenship and Social Movements* (Abingdon: Routledge), 205–218.

Matheis, C., and H. Bauder (2016) 'Introduction: possibility, feasibility and mesolevel interventions in migration policy and practice', in H. Bauder and C. Matheis (eds), *Migration Policy and Practice: Interventions and Solutions* (Basingstoke: Palgrave Macmillan), 1–16.

Mavroudi, E., and C. Nagel (2016) *Global Migration: Patterns, Processes, and Politics* (London: Routledge).

May, T. (2010) *Contemporary Political Movements and the Thought of Jacques Rancière: Equality in Action* (Edinburgh: Edinburgh University Press).

Nyers, P. (2010) 'No One Is Illegal between city and nation', *Studies in Social Justice*, 4:2, 127–143.

Papadopoulos, D., and V. S. Tsianos (2013) 'After citizenship: autonomy of migration, organisational ontology and mobile commons', *Citizenship Studies*, 17:2, 178–196.

Pyykkönen, M. (2009) 'Deportation vs. sanctuary: the rationalities, technologies, and subjects of Finnish sanctuary practices', *Refuge*, 26:1, 20–32.

Rajaram, P. K. (2013) 'Historicising "asylum" and responsibility', *Citizenship Studies*, 17:6–7, 681–696.

Ridgley, J. (2008) 'Cities of refuge: immigration enforcement, police, and the insurgent genealogies of citizenship in US sanctuary cities', *Urban Geography*, 29:1, 53–77, DOI: 10.2747/0272-3638.29.1.53.

Ridgley, J. (2012) 'The city as a sanctuary in the United States', in R. Lippert and S. Rehaag (eds), *Sanctuary in International Perspectives: Migration, Citizenship and Social Movements* (Abingdon: Routledge), 219–231.

Robbins, L. (2017) '"Sanctuary city" mayors vow to defy Trump's immigration order', *New York Times*, 25 January 2017, www.nytimes.com/2017/01/25/nyregion/outraged-mayors-vow-to-defy-trumps-immigration-order.html?_r=0 (accessed 23 July 2017).

Sassen, S. (2006) *Territory, Authority, Rights: From Medieval to Global Assemblages* (Princeton, NJ: Princeton University Press).

Sassen, S. (2013) 'When the center no longer holds: cities as frontier zones', *Cities*, 34, 67–70.

Scott, J. C. (1998) *Seeing Like a State: How Certain Schemes to Improve the Human Condition Have Failed* (New Haven, CT: Yale University Press).

Squire, V. (2017) 'Unauthorised migration beyond structure/agency? Acts, interventions, effects', *Politics*, 37:3, 254–272.

Squire, V., and J. Darling (2013) 'The "minor" politics of rightful presence: justice and relationality in City of Sanctuary', *International Political Sociology*, 7:1, 59–74.

Steil, J., and J. Ridgley (2012) '"Small-town defenders": the production of citizenship and belonging in Hazelton, Pennsylvania', *Environment and Planning D: Society and Space*, 30, 1028–1045.

Swerts, T. (2017) 'Creating space for citizenship: the liminal politics of undocumented activism', *International Journal of Urban and Regional Research*, 41:3, 379–393.

Uitermark, J., and W. Nicholls (2014) 'From politicization to policing: the rise and decline of new social movements in Amsterdam and Paris', *Antipode*, 46:4, 970–991.

Uitermark, J., W. Nicholls, and M. Loopmans (2012) 'Cities and social movements: theorizing beyond the right to the city', *Environment and Planning A*, 44:11, 2546–2554.

Varsanyi, M. W. (2006) 'Interrogating "urban citizenship" vis-à-vis undocumented migration', *Citizenship Studies*, 10:2, 229–249.

Varsanyi, M. W. (2008a) 'Immigration policing through the backdoor: city ordinances, the "right to the city," and the exclusion of undocumented day laborers', *Urban Geography*, 29:1, 29–52.

Varsanyi, M. W. (2008b) 'Rescaling the "alien," rescaling personhood: neoliberalism, immigration, and the state', *Annals of the Association of American Geographers*, 98:4, 877–896.

Vaughan-Williams, N. (2009) *Border Politics: The Limits of Sovereign Power* (Edinburgh, Edinburgh University Press).

Walia, H. (2013) *Undoing Border Imperialism* (Oakland, CA: AK Press).

Walker, K. E. (2014) 'The role of geographic context in the local politics of US immigration', *Journal of Ethnics and Migration Studies*, 40, 1040–1059.

Walker, K. E., and H. Leitner (2011) 'The variegated landscape of local immigration policies in the United States', *Urban Geography*, 32:3, 156–178.

Walters, W. (2004) 'Secure borders, safe haven, domopolitics', *Citizenship Studies*, 8:3, 237–260.

Walters, W. (2006) 'Rethinking borders beyond the state', *Comparative European Politics*, 4:2/3, 141–159.

Williams, L. M. (2015) 'Beyond enforcement: welcomeness, local law enforcement, and immigrants', *Public Administration Review*, 75:3, 433–442.

Wimmer, A., and N. Glick Schiller (2002) 'Methodological nationalism and beyond: nation-state building, migration and the social sciences', *Global Networks*, 2:4, 301–334.

Young, J. E. E. (2011) '"A new politics of the city": locating the limit of hospitality and practicing the city-as-refuge', *Acme*, 10, 534–563.

Yukich, G. (2013) 'Constructing the model immigrant: movement strategy and immigrant deservingness in the New Sanctuary Movement', *Social Problems*, 60:3, 302–320.

Yuval-Davis, N., G. Wemyss, and K. Cassidy (2018) 'Everyday bordering: belonging and the reorientation of British immigration legislation', *Sociology*, 52:2, 228–244.

Part I

Sanctuary cities

Part I

Sanctuary cities

1

Urban sanctuary in context

Harald Bauder

Urban sanctuary policies and practices generally serve the purpose of accommodating illegalised migrants and refugees in urban communities. The 'sanctuary city' concept, however, is highly ambiguous. Some commentators critique it for being a 'catch-all phrase' (Chishti and Hipsman, 2015: n.p.) that refers to a variety of different policies and practices; others celebrate the concept and argue that 'Sanctuary City is as much a process as a goal' (Walia, 2014: n.p.) that necessarily responds to a diverse range of social and geopolitical conditions. In this chapter, I examine sanctuary city policies and practices in international perspective to set the stage for subsequent chapters discussing sanctuary policies, the politics of scale, and struggles of belonging.

Sanctuary city policies and practices are reactions to exclusionary national policies and practices. In countries with different national legal and administrative frameworks, sanctuary city policies and practices take on different forms. In addition, historical, geopolitical, and geographical conditions vary between cities. Sanctuary city policies and practices are therefore particular to national context. For example, while sanctuary cities in Canada and the USA seek specifically to protect illegalised migrants from the consequences of lacking national status, in the UK, cities of sanctuary involve a general commitment to welcoming asylum seekers and refugees. In addition, as the following chapters illustrate, sanctuary encompasses complex dimensions and diverse actors (Kuge and Bagelman, this volume), sanctuary city policy intentions and their implementation can differ from each other (Atak, this volume), and urban sanctuary policies and practices respond to policy discourses that permeate various scales of governance (Graham, this volume). Below, I uncover various strategic aspects of sanctuary cities that cut across national contexts. These aspects engage in contextualised ways with the underlying national structures of the social, political, and legal exclusion of migrants and refugees. In this way, this chapter provides an opportunity to discuss the role of the urban scale in mitigating exclusionary national migrant, refugee, residency, and citizenship laws, policies, and practices. One must be mindful, however, as Visser and Simpson demonstrate in their chapter, that the urban scale can also be mobilised to exclude rather than accommodate illegalised migrants.

My use of the term 'illegalised' migrant – rather than undocumented, unauthorised, irregular, or non-status migrant – is intended to draw attention to national laws, policies, and practices that deny migrants full status or legal residency at the national scale (Bauder, 2014b). The use of this term seems particularly appropriate for a discussion of sanctuary cities that focuses attention on the politics of scale. In this case, local authorities, civic society organisations, and activists advocating for the inclusion of illegalised inhabitants in the urban community, as well as illegalised inhabitants themselves who are making claims of belonging, challenge national immigration laws, policies, and practices that deny rights (including the right to belong) to some inhabitants. The tensions between urban and national scales in the way migrants and refugees are treated and claim belonging are a central theme throughout this book.

In what follows, I explore the policies and practices involved in the concept of 'sanctuary city' and investigate how these policies and practices differ between countries. I further examine whether different aspects of sanctuary policies and practices describe a coherent approach towards illegalised migrants and refugees. Addressing these issues is important for several reasons. First, although the concept of the sanctuary city is widely applied in policy debate, planning practice, and activism, its meaning varies between countries. Commentators do not always distinguish clearly between the different urban sanctuary practices in Europe and North America (e.g. Cities of Migration, 2009). This lack of clarity can conceal the variability and contextualised nature of sanctuary city policies and practices. Second, the concept 'sanctuary city' has been critiqued based on policies and practices that are highly context-particular (e.g. American Immigration Council, 2015). Such a critique can lose sight of the structural exclusion at the national scale that migrants and refugees experience and to which urban sanctuary is a contextualised local response. Third, urban sanctuary policies and practices tend to challenge national policies and practices regulating migration and belonging; they reflect a strategy of scale-shifting to mitigate the disenfranchisement of populations in a practical way. Uncovering various aspects of urban sanctuary and how they are applied across national contexts can help overcome what Darling and I called the 'limits of imagination' in the Introduction, associated with national approaches towards migration and belonging.

In the next section, I review the literature on the kinds of policies and practices that the idea of urban sanctuary involves. I focus in particular on how the term 'sanctuary' emerged in the USA, the UK, and Canada in relation to urban practices that mitigate migrant and refugee exclusion at the national scale. Then, I distil this information into several aspects of urban sanctuary. By excavating multiple aspects of urban sanctuary policies and practices, I present the 'sanctuary city' as a concept that can be observed across national contexts. In the discussion, I apply sanctuary city aspects to other, non-English-language national contexts and discuss wider social and political implications, many of which are developed further in later chapters.

Urban sanctuary in the literature

A brief history

The origin of sanctuary is complex. Its history can be associated with various religions, including Buddhism, Christianity, Islam, Judaism, Hinduism, and Sikhism (Bagelman, 2016: 20). The Bible (Numbers 35) mentions six 'cities of refuge' that offered protection to people who had accidentally killed another person, thus articulating sanctuary at the urban scale. Sanctuary, however, is not necessarily a spatially fixed practice of offering protection within a territorial jurisdiction, but can also be understood as a relational and mobile practice (Darling, 2010). Ancient Roman law dating back to 392 CE granted sanctuary privileges to churches rather than gated cities (Lippert, 2005). The practice of church sanctuary continued in medieval Europe, granting protection from worldly authorities to murderers, thieves, and other criminals (Shoemaker, 2012).

Although the term sanctuary was typically not associated with migration or the urban scale in medieval Europe, many European cities at that time did offer the prospect of freedom from serfdom to people who fled from the land to which they were bonded. The medieval saying 'city air makes you free' describes this practice (Schwarz, 2008). This medieval urban practice indeed resonates with the aim of today's sanctuary cities to provide refuge to non-citizens (Bauder, 2016).

With the increasing illegalisation of migrants and refugees through exclusionary national immigration policies in Western countries in the second half of the twentieth century, churches in Denmark, France, Finland, Germany, Norway, Sweden, the United States, and other countries began to offer sanctuary to rejected refugee claimants, asylum seekers, and illegalised migrants (e.g. Caminero-Santangelo, 2012; Loga et al., 2012; Millner, 2012). In 2012 Randy Lippert and Sean Rehaag observed that 'at the centre of contemporary sanctuary activities has been – almost exclusively – immigrants (often asylum-seekers) living without legal status in Western countries' (2012: 3, parentheses in original). Thus, the focus population of sanctuary practices has shifted from criminals to illegalised migrants and refugees – although there continues to be a connection between these two groups in that illegalised migrants have been criminalised in public and political debate and through immigration law. My use of the term 'illegalised' migrant signifies this connection (Bauder, 2014b).

Roughly around the same time as the focus population changed, a shift occurred in the scale of sanctuary practices. The city of Berkeley in the USA is often cited as the birthplace of contemporary sanctuary cities: in 1971 it offered protection on-board the aircraft carrier USS *Coral Sea* to soldiers who resisted the Vietnam War. This urban scale symbolically linked the sanctuary city with the biblical city of refuge, protecting people who kill, i.e. soldiers (Ridgley, 2012).

Today's sanctuary cities offer protection to illegalised migrants and typically follow secular motivations and arguments (Lippert and Rehaag, 2012). Despite their common label, however, sanctuary cities involve a wide range of different policies and practices. Below, I review sanctuary city practices in the USA, the UK, and Canada, where the terms 'sanctuary city' and 'city of sanctuary' have been applied in concrete policy contexts.

United States

An important milestone for the development of sanctuary cities in the USA occurred in San Francisco (Mancina, 2012). In 1985 this city passed the largely symbolic 'City of Refuge' resolution, which was followed in 1989 by the more concrete 'City of Refuge' ordinance. The latter specifically prohibited the use of city funds and resources to assist in federal immigration enforcement, to cooperate with investigations by or surveillance requests from foreign governments (in response to an incident in which a police officer engaged in surveillance activities for the El Salvador consulate (Bau, 1994)), and to request, record, or disseminate information about an individual's immigration status unless required by federal or state law (City and County of San Francisco, 1989). This sanctuary ordinance was intended to end discrimination by the municipal administration and its employees against primarily El Salvadorean and Guatemalan refugees who lacked federal immigration or residency status (CBS SF Bay Area, 2015).

Another milestone was the launch of the faith-based New Sanctuary Movement (NSM) in 2007. This movement shifted focus from newly arrived refugees to illegalised migrants who have been present in the USA for a longer period and now call US cities their home. Thus, urban sanctuary policies and practices in the US increasingly focussed on migrants who seek to maintain the 'quotidian, ordinary life they have built' (Caminero-Santangelo, 2012: 96) rather than refugees fleeing from war, violence, and terror. In other words, the NSM has emphasised the need for safety for individuals and families who already are de facto members of urban communities.

Today, dozens of US cities have passed sanctuary legislation to protect illegalised migrants who are de facto residents of these cities. Concrete policies include Don't Ask, Don't Tell (DADT) policies, which typically prohibit municipal police forces and city-service agencies from requesting, recording, or disseminating status information, and refuse cooperation with federal immigration authorities unless required by federal or state law. Some municipalities, such as San Francisco, have issued municipal identification cards to enable all inhabitants to identify themselves to local authorities, independent of whether they possess federal status documents or a state-issued driver's licence. Other municipalities are accepting *matrículas consulares* issued by the Mexican government to nationals living abroad as means of identification (Varsanyi, 2007).

Some US federal lawmakers have been critical of urban sanctuary policies and practices that challenge national immigration law. The US House of Representatives passed legislation in 2007 that – had the Senate also passed it – would have denied federal emergency funds to sanctuary cities. Federal and state efforts to deny municipal governments the ability to enact sanctuary policies tend to gain momentum and public support in light of sensationalist media reports on crimes committed by illegalised migrants (Chishti and Hipsman, 2015). President Donald Trump vowed to deny federal funding to sanctuary cities – a pledge that sanctuary city mayors, such as New York City's Bill de Blasio, have fiercely defied (Robbins, 2017).

The use of the term 'sanctuary city' has been critiqued for political reasons (American Immigration Council, 2015): it is used 'by immigration opponents to blast … community policing practices' by implying that these cities elevate themselves above national law (Tramonte, 2011: 5). In reality, urban sanctuary policies and practices do not eliminate illegalisation; they merely enable illegalised migrants to better cope with their circumstances. Thus, sanctuary cities do not tackle the root of the problem but rather make life less difficult under the condition of illegality imposed by the nation-state. In fact, the term 'sanctuary city' may evoke a false sense of security among illegalised populations. The American Immigration Council remarks that the term incorrectly suggests that local police can protect illegalised migrants from federal immigration authorities:

> The term 'sanctuary city' is a misnomer when used to describe community policing policies which attempt to eliminate fear from those who worry that reporting a crime or interacting with local law enforcement could result in deportation, (American Immigration Council, 2015)

While urban sanctuary policies and practices in the USA may help solve and prevent crime, they do not prevent federal immigration law-enforcement activities against illegalised migrants. Thus, they cannot guarantee protection from federal authorities. Even in sanctuary cities, illegalised migrants remain vulnerable to detection, detention, and deportation.

United Kingdom

In the UK, the 'City of Sanctuary' movement was established in Sheffield in 2005. Two years later, Sheffield became the first city in the United Kingdom to receive the official title 'City of Sanctuary' when the city council supported the movement's initiatives. Other cities followed suit. By 2011 a network of 17 towns and cities, including Bristol and Swansea, had also achieved official City of Sanctuary status, and over 60 cities and towns across the UK and Ireland have developed sanctuary initiatives (Darling and Squire, 2012; City of Sanctuary, 2016a). In 2016 City of Sanctuary (2016b: 3) reported having 'groups established or starting up in almost 80 cities, towns, and villages'.

Based on interviews with City of Sanctuary organisers and activists, Squire and Bagelman (2012: 155) remark:

> City of Sanctuary promotes a culture of hospitality toward those taking sanctuary across diverse sites, such as local businesses or workplaces, community cafés and religious congregations. This entails a range of practices, such as the placing of signs on the window sills of various community buildings, shops, student unions and offices around Sheffield which bear the words: 'We welcome asylum-seekers and refugees.'

To qualify as a City of Sanctuary in the UK requires support from local groups and organisations, the involvement of the local refugee community, a strategy towards greater inclusion of people seeking refuge, as well as an expression of support from the city council. Darling and Squire (2012: 191) observe that City of Sanctuary involves a 'plethora of localised urban collectives that assert rights to sanctuary within cities'. Along the same lines, Bagelman (2013: 50) notes that City of Sanctuary operates 'as a fluid network of practices aimed at shifting hostile attitudes towards refugees and asylum seekers'.

Unlike in the USA, urban sanctuary initiatives in the UK do not focus on municipal policing practices or the refusal to cooperate with national immigration authorities, and they do not seek ways to protect illegalised migrants and refugees from national immigration authorities.

Rather, these initiatives emphasise 'awareness raising, telling the true stories of refugees to those who never hear them' (City of Sanctuary, 2016a: n.p.). For example, Darling and Squire observe that:

> City of Sanctuary Sheffield does not actively engage in the material or physical provision of accommodation or protection ... It might thus be tempting to suggest that City of Sanctuary represents little more than a collective of organizations and individuals who promote values of hospitality but who do not effectively practice sanctuary. However, this overlooks how the activities of City of Sanctuary both emerge from, and create possibilities for, everyday enactments of sanctuary in a more diffuse sense. (2012: 196, original italics)

The key achievement of sanctuary cities in the UK is not creating legal shelter from national immigration law enforcement to illegalised migrants, but rather intervening in refugee discourse and transforming the geographical imagination of the city.

In respect of refugee discourse, urban sanctuary policies and practices reproduce but also challenge conventional perspectives regarding refugees. On the one hand, City of Sanctuary reproduces the discursive distinction between guests and hosts, 'notions of gratitude and indebtedness' (Darling and Squire, 2012: 194), and images of "good" and "worthy" citizens, as figures "deserving" of sanctuary' (Darling and Squire, 2012: 194). In fact, City of Sanctuary may perpetuate a 'pastoral logic' (Darling and Squire, 2012: 194; Squire and Bagelman, 2012) characteristic of Church sanctuary. On the other hand, urban sanctuary initiatives in the UK also disrupt 'uneven relations between guest and host' (Darling and Squire, 2012: 196) through networking activities that promote everyday encounters between refugees and citizens, and encourage refugees to play an active role in urban life. For example, City of Sanctuary groups across the UK have developed a range of cultural activities, such as exhibitions, music workshops, and dances, to encourage points of contact between citizens and refugees, and have established volunteering opportunities for refugees in a range of charities. In doing so, they challenge conventional views of refugees as recipients of assistance by encouraging refugees to become active participants in the urban community rather than passively awaiting the outcome of the refugee determination process.

With respect to the geographical imagination of the city, Darling suggests that urban sanctuary initiatives in Sheffield 'sought to alter a vision of the city, its identity as a "welcoming place"' (2010: 129). In this way, City of Sanctuary aims 'to alter geographical imaginations – to force a reconsideration of how those in Sheffield view the world and their responsibilities within it' (2010: 129). Urban sanctuary initiatives in the UK thus aim to fundamentally transform the way people think about the city as a space for refugees and asylum seekers, and attempt to draw connections to 'distant' forms of oppression and injustice.

The critique of urban sanctuary initiatives in the UK also focuses on these initiatives' discursive and imaginative effects. In particular, urban sanctuary initiatives may discursively normalise the precarious situation of refugees and asylum seekers, rather than providing tangible and legal solutions. In the context of Glasgow, Bagelman concludes that City of Sanctuary 'regularizes and depoliticizes a violent temporality of waiting' (Bagelman, 2013: 50). While urban sanctuary initiatives claim to promote active citizenship, these initiatives may in fact encourage refugees and asylum seekers to passively endure their situation. Urban sanctuary practices 'fix certain migrants in suspense. In this way, sanctuary does not represent a solution, but a problematic' (Bagelman, 2013: 58). Sanctuary is a 'governmentalizing process' that incites 'a commitment to the rules of the game, where one willingly submits and indeed invests in' the prolonging of the precarious condition in which refugees and asylum seekers are situated (Bagelman, 2013: 56). Bagelman therefore concludes that urban sanctuary practices are a 'gentler' form of control than overtly exclusionary national migration policies. The end results, however, are similar: refugees and asylum seekers remain at the political margins and often in precarious situations.

In addition, the geographical imagination of cities of sanctuary has been criticised. Being a city of sanctuary suited 'Sheffield's image as a cosmopolitan and inclusive city' (Darling and Squire, 2012: 195). In this way, urban sanctuary practices do not radically challenge the imagination of the city as a space of belonging – as envisioned, for example, by Henri Lefebvre (1996) or David Harvey (2012). Rather, the imagination of cities of sanctuary aligns with urban neoliberal politics and can be seen as a means of boosting the reputational capital of a city as 'standing for' particular values and moral imaginaries (see Darling, 2013; Malpass et al., 2007).

Canada

In Canada, urban sanctuary initiatives began as early as the 1980s, when Toronto-based Chilean refugees advocated sanctuary city by-laws (Solidarity City Network, 2013a). An important milestone occurred in 2004: Toronto activists launched a DADT campaign, after which Toronto's city administration and the Toronto District School Board quietly adopted a range of DADT policies (Berinstein et al., 2006; McDonald, 2012). After these policies were either ignored by city staff or only sluggishly implemented, advocacy groups and community organisations formed the Solidarity City Network and began lobbying politicians and city councillors to put a vote in front of Toronto City Council. Corresponding sanctuary city by-laws were passed in 2013 (Solidarity City Network, 2013b). Atak and Hudson in this volume elaborate on the case of Toronto as a sanctuary city. A year after Toronto, the city of Hamilton also voted to become a sanctuary city. More recently, other Canadian cities have followed suit.

Under urban sanctuary policies in Canada, illegalised migrants receive access to municipal services, such as emergency medical services, public health programmes, emergency shelters, fire protection, recreational programmes, and libraries. In spring 2016 Vancouver passed an 'Access to City Services Without Fear' policy. Because this policy excludes many civic services such as police, library, and parks services, and to encourage the future expansion of access-without-fear principles to these services, many advocates refrain from calling Vancouver a 'sanctuary city' (Robinson, 2016). Similar to their US counterparts, urban sanctuary and access-without-fear initiatives in Canada must be seen as acts of defiance by municipal policy makers against exclusionary federal immigration laws and policies.

Municipal police forces in Canada, however, tend not to follow sanctuary practices. Although the Toronto Police Services Board passed a limited DATD policy, it continues to frequently call the federal border enforcement agency to conduct status checks (Keung, 2015). In addition, the training of front-line staff who would implement sanctuary policies has been lacking (Hudson et al., 2017; Atak, this volume). Furthermore, many locally administered services that are funded by the province are excluded from sanctuary policies (Hannan and Bauder, 2015).

Municipal laws and policies that defy federal immigration laws and their enforcement are only one aspect of Canada's urban sanctuary campaigns. McDonald observes that these campaigns also involve practices of identity formation: by presenting 'people living with precarious status as everyday residents of the city' (2012: 137), and including illegalised migrants in the imagined local community, urban sanctuary initiatives disrupt the distinctions created by federal status categories and seek to forge solidarity among all inhabitants of the city. For example, an important aspect of the urban sanctuary campaign in Toronto 'lies in its ability to change the ways in which people interact with one another locally and to develop a shift in ideas around community and belonging' (McDonald, 2012: 143).

In addition, urban sanctuary policies and practices in Canada seek to rescale belonging. In particular, they clearly distinguish between local community and the nation-state and national government. Kamal writes:

> Sanctuary/Solidarity City is about bypassing the ideas behind nation-states and centralized governments. In a Sanctuary/Solidarity City, ideas don't have to get passed at the 'top' in order for them to manifest themselves in our day-to-day lives. Sanctuary City is about building ways of living that allow us to horizontally make decisions with collective communities, on the ground, every day, with or without the approval of a colonial state that we believe is an illegitimate occupying force. (Nail et al., 2010)

Correspondingly, Toronto's sanctuary city activists coined the term 'regularisation from below' to describe their efforts to include illegalised migrants at the local scale and in a non-hierarchical urban community, while rejecting the national-scale policies that renders these migrants 'illegal' (McDonald, 2012).

Aspects of urban sanctuary

The preceding discussion shows that there is a wide range of urban sanctuary policies and practices, and that these policies and practices vary by national context. In this section, I distil the urban sanctuary initiatives I reviewed above into several aspects. In the context of the UK, Darling and Squire (2012) already distinguish between formal aspects, such as requiring support from city councils, and informal aspects, such as social interactions between community members and refugees. The international comparison enables me to obtain a more comprehensive picture of urban sanctuary policies and practices. Altogether, I uncover four distinct aspects, revolving around legal, discursive, identity-formative, and scalar themes.

Legality

The first aspect of urban sanctuary is its legal nature. Sanctuary cities in the USA, the UK, and Canada have in common that the municipal legislative body (i.e. the city council) supports sanctuary initiatives. In the USA, this legal aspect typically involves a commitment by the municipal police and administration to non-cooperation with the enforcement of national immigration law; it also includes municipal DADT policies when requesting, recording, and disseminating personal information about the city's inhabitants. Some cities even issue municipal identification cards or accept identification documents issued by foreign governments to identify de facto city residents irrespective of their federal status in order to deliver city and policing services to them. In Canada, city councils of sanctuary cities also commit to implementing DADT policies, although the municipal police do not fully implement these policies.

Binding municipal DADT policies are not part of urban sanctuary initiatives in the UK. In fact, the focus of urban sanctuary policies and practices in the UK is not on providing protection to illegalised migrants but rather on creating a hospitable urban environment for refugees and asylum seekers. This situation relates to the distinctly centralised nature of government in the UK, which steers policy making from the centre. Nevertheless, despite their lack of legal strength to implement policies in the same way as in North America, municipal lawmakers officially commit to nurturing a local environment of welcome and hospitality. Thus, an overarching characteristic of urban sanctuary across national contexts is the official affirmation of sanctuary initiatives by the municipality's legislative body.

Discourse

The literature on cities of sanctuary in the UK emphasises the discursive aspect of sanctuary initiatives. This aspect can also be observed with respect to urban sanctuary practices in the USA and Canada (Ridgley, 2008). It involves challenging exclusionary refugee discourses that often circulate through national media and national political debate. This aspect connects to a wider literature examining the link between migration and refugee discourses, and the material practices and laws affecting migrants and refugees (e.g. van Leeuwen and Wodak, 1999; Hier and Greenberg, 2002; Riaño and Wastl-Walter, 2006; Bauder, 2011).

The alternative narratives, which urban sanctuary practices present, reflect a range of discursive strategies. For example, urban sanctuary rhetoric and practice can affirm dominant categories of refugee, migrant, and citizen, and reproduce a 'pastoral' logic while presenting some refugees as 'deserving' and 'worthy'. Such narratives often depict the local community as compassionate, affirming this community's morality vis-à-vis illegalised migrants and refugees (Darling and Squire, 2012; Squire and Bagelman, 2012). Other narratives radically dispute the categories of migrant, refugee, and citizen, and fundamentally critique capitalist and neocolonial structures that have given rise to these categories in the first place (Walia, 2014). This focus on being an inhabitant of the city regardless of status links to later discussions of intimacy by Bagelman and presence by Darling in this volume.

Identity formation

A third aspect involves the transformation of political identities and subjectivities as well as re-imaging the city as a space of belonging. The literature on the sanctuary city in Canada, in particular, illustrates how expressions and practices of solidarity aim to facilitate the enactment of a collective urban community that brings together citizens and migrants, and inhabitants with and without status. Activist-scholar Harsha Walia (2014: n.p.) remarks that 'zones of sanctuary are actively constituted not by politicians but by us – as service providers, educators, healthcare professionals, and neighbours – on the basis of solidarity and mutual aid'. These grassroots practices of solidarity aim to create unity among activists, urban political and civic actors, as well as illegalised migrants and refugees.

Furthermore, concrete urban sanctuary policies, such as DADT policies, aim to enable all inhabitants to participate in the urban community as equal members – although Atak (this volume) highlights the challenges of achieving this aim in practice. When illegalised migrants are able to move about the city and participate in its everyday rhythms, they share the political stage of the city and present themselves as members of the urban community. In this way, refugees and illegalised migrants enact themselves as citizens and political subjects (Isin and Nielsen, 2008; Nyers, 2010), and exercise what Henri Lefebvre would call their 'right to the city' (Bauder, 2016; Purcell, 2002, 2013). Although there are practical limits on illegalised migrants' ability to enact citizenship and exercise their right to the city (American Immigration Council, 2015; Tramonte, 2011), sanctuary cities seek to rescript urban belonging.

This aspect is not lost on City of Sanctuary organisers in the UK. In particular, the idea that urban sanctuary practices alter the geographical imagination of the city (Darling, 2010) suggests that cities of sanctuary involve not only new forms of urban politics but also novel types of community membership. This aspect of the sanctuary city resonates with Jacques Derrida's (2001) idea of the 'city of refuge' which also entails new forms of urban politics beyond conventional modes of belonging and membership that frame urban politics today (Bauder, 2016).

Scale

An aspect that is common to sanctuary city policies and practices in the USA, the UK, and Canada involves rejecting or challenging national approaches to migration and refugee admission. In fact, urban sanctuary initiatives can be interpreted as an attempt to rescale migration and refugee policies and practices from national to urban scales. Sanctuary cities in the USA and Canada especially illustrate how urban communities do not see themselves as bound by federal migration and refugee laws that illegalise some of their inhabitants. Rather, these cities evoke the *domicile* rule of belonging, which suggests that de facto residents in a community should also be recognised as members of this community and correspondingly possess legal entitlements and receive municipal services and police protection (Varsanyi, 2007; Bauder, 2014a). By implementing this rule, sanctuary cities include all inhabitants in the local community, regardless of their national citizenship or status. Along similar lines, Squire and Bagelman observe in the context of the UK that the sanctuary city functions as a local political territory that operates 'according to a logic of open access rather than closed borders' (2012: 156), in which all inhabitants belong.

Through rescaling the policies and practices of migration and belonging, sanctuary cities assert a 'form of power and politics at the sub-national level' (Sassen, 2008: 314). In this way, urban sanctuary policies and practices challenge national sovereignty. This challenge to sovereignty is articulated through legal, discursive, and identity-formative aspects. The gravity of any *legal* threat to national sovereignty – for example through municipal DADT policies – is illustrated by the attempts by the US president and among US federal lawmakers to deny municipal governments funding for enacting local sanctuary policies. Issuing local identification cards or recognising cards issued by foreign governments also challenges national sovereignty and rearticulates who belongs in the community and who does not (Czajka, 2012). In respect to the *discursive* aspect, sanctuary discourses disrupt the nation-state's monopoly on defining who deserves to belong and who does not, shifting the scale of belonging from the national to the local. Regarding the *identity-formative* aspect, refugees and illegalised migrants are constituting themselves as political subjects in the space of sanctuary cities and thus deny the nation-state the authority to decide who is a legitimate member of the polity. Writing predominantly about Church-based sanctuary practices, Czajka (2012: 51) explains that acts of sanctuary

> can be interpreted as a challenge to the state's monopolization of deci-sions on the right of residence and citizenship … and thus the right to determine who has the right to have rights … The refugee, by refusing to be deported and enacting herself as belonging to the territory and political community in contradiction to the determination of the state, challenges not only state sovereignty, but also the state monopoly on the political.

Enacting sanctuary policies and practices at the urban scale is an even more serious threat to national sovereignty than Church sanctuary, because cities provide a territorial legal entity at a different scale at which sovereignty is articulated and because cities engage a far wider audience of citizens and urban inhabitants at an alternative scale of governance.

Discussion

Above, I examined the emergence of different urban sanctuary policies and practices in the USA, the UK, and Canada. A key finding is that there is no single set of policies or practices that define what a sanctuary city is. Rather, urban sanctuary policies and practices involve legal, discursive, identity-formative, and scalar aspects. Subsequent chapters will affirm the complex and multidimensional nature of urban sanctuary policies and practices. I therefore propose that the *combination* of various aspects and dimensions describe a coherent, yet flexible, approach to urban sanctuary. As I have shown, the various sanctuary city aspects assemble in variable and context-particular ways in different countries.

Local authorities in other countries, where the concept of 'sanctuary city' is not as prominently used as in the USA, the UK, and Canada, also try to accommodate illegalised migrants and refugees through legal, administrative, and discursive means that mirror aspects of sanctuary cities (Schech, 2013; Bauder and Gonzales, 2018). In Spain, Barcelona offers such a case. This city has demonstrated international leadership in advocating for a role for cities in accommodating illegalised migrants and refugees (Ayuntamiento de Barcelona, 2014). In 2010 Barcelona's city council launched the Anti-Rumour Strategy to shape migration discourse by challenging inaccurate information (Casademont et al., 2018). Five years later, the council officially declared Barcelona a 'Refuge City' (Ayuntamiento de Barcelona, Secretaría General, 2015). The city has been proactive in imagining itself as a space of co-belonging and has created a local infrastructure to provide services to inhabitants regardless of their national status. The Spanish constitution also grants municipal autonomy in policing matters, permitting the municipal police to be included in sanctuary-like urban policies.

In Chile, the municipality of Quilicura has initiated local programmes that address aspects of urban sanctuary (Thayer Correa
et al., 2014). This municipality actively engages in shaping public
discourse relating to migrants and refugees and creates opportunities for
fostering a sense of a unified urban community among all its inhabitants (Municipalidad de Quilicura, 2016). The Municipal Office for
Migrants and Refugees provides orientation, support, and information
about education and health services, and employment and training
opportunities to migrants and refugees (Leo et al., 2015). Chilean
municipalities, however, do not possess independent police forces
that could initiate similar sanctuary city policies to municipalities in
the USA.

In Germany, cities confront a similar situation as in Chile in that
they do not possess independent local police forces that could be
included in sanctuary city policies. In addition, national authorities
require stringent reporting from municipalities regarding the presence
and status of local residents (Buckel, 2008; Scherr and Hofmann,
2016). Nevertheless, civic society actors in cities such as Freiburg im
Breisgau are successfully mobilising local resources to counter national
discourses of undeserving refugees, to include illegalised migrants
and refugees in the urban community, and to offer medical, legal,
housing, and other services to illegalised inhabitants (Freiburger Forum
aktiv gegen Ausgrenzung, 2016). Cities in other countries, such as
Palermo in Italy or Zurich in Switzerland, also pursue initiatives that
resemble sanctuary city policies and practices.

These international comparisons illustrate how political actors
mobilise the various aspects of urban sanctuary in countries in which
national legal, political, and administrative systems, demographic
conditions, and geopolitical circumstances differ substantially from
each other. These comparisons highlights the importance of national
context. For example, municipal police forces in the USA have been
able to implement DADT policies relatively independently of federal
law enforcement policies and practices. Conversely, in countries such
as Chile and Germany, where independent municipal police are absent,
corresponding local DADT policies cannot be enacted (Scherr and
Hofmann, 2016).

There are also variations among sanctuary cities within countries.
Factors such as the size, proportion, growth, and origin of the migrant

and refugee population, as well as historical circumstances and political traditions, likely shape the possibility of implementing the various aspects of urban sanctuary. US-based research shows that similar factors influence whether local policies include or exclude illegalised migrants (Walker and Leitner, 2011). The level of education, diversity, and the political orientation of the urban population as well as economic and fiscal factors also shape a city's policies towards welcoming newcomers (Huang and Liu, 2018). Furthermore, the legal and administrative structures that enable sanctuary cities can be used to achieve opposing ends: in the USA, the complexity of the country's political and administrative systems has enabled municipalities to launch local policy responses to federal immigration laws (Wells, 2004) that result not only in sanctuary cities, but also in the further repression, exclusion, and banishment of unwanted migrants from the city (Strunk and Leitner, 2013; Varsanyi, 2010). Visser and Simpson (this volume) highlight such exclusionary policies and practices. Similar repressive municipal actions can be observed in European countries (Fauser, 2017). In this sense, the 'rescaling' of migration notable through sanctuary practices is often mirrored through the 'rescaling' of border control and enforcement measures to the urban level, such that cities are at the very forefront of contestations over migration and rights (see Darling and Bauder, this volume).

Despite national particularities, the idea of urban sanctuary for illegalised migrants and refugees is not contained within a particular national territory, but has travelled, like other urban policies (McCann, 2008; Peck and Theodore, 2010), across international borders. The mobility of the sanctuary city concept points towards the underlying structural forces of migrant and refugee exclusion that sanctuary policies and practices contest in different countries. Correspondingly, activists in cities across North America and Europe are travelling and networking internationally to exchange information and ideas, and help spread the idea of sanctuary cities and their experiences in implementing corresponding policies and practices. In the autumn of 2015, in the wake of Germany's 'long summer of migration' (Hess et al., 2017), I attended a presentation in Freiburg im Breisgau by a small delegation of sanctuary activists from Toronto who went on a lecture tour to several cities in Germany and Switzerland, where there were no cities labelled 'sanctuary' at the time. This lecture tour inspired local activists and informed them about the struggles and successes of Canadian activists on their path towards becoming a sanctuary city. In addition, sanctuary policies and practices are mobile between scales. Correspondingly, sanctuary policies and practices exist not only at the urban scale but also at scales of individual churches, mosques, and other places of worship, university campuses, and states and administrative regions.

The urban scale, however, has arguably been most prominent internationally when it comes to recent sanctuary policies and practices. What motivates urban activists and political authorities in different countries is a dissatisfaction with exclusionary national policies towards migrants and refugees, and the desire to elevate the local as the scale at which membership in the community and the polity is enacted. Policy innovations and activist strategies in different countries can draw on various sanctuary city aspects to craft local and contextualised responses that meet specific objectives and respond to particular national circumstances.

Urban sanctuary policies and practices have enlivened a range of scholarly debates: they relate to the growing literature on the right to the city (e.g. Lefebvre, 1996; Purcell, 2002), the local enactment of citizenship (e.g. Isin and Nielsen, 2008; Nyers, 2010), and sovereignty and migrant autonomy (e.g. Lippert, 2004, 2005; Mudu and Chattopadhyay, 2016). The optimistic outlook projected by local-scale inclusion and the prospect of human liberation, however, stands in dialectical tension with more pessimistic arguments that urban sanctuary policies and practices merely reinforce neoliberal urban governance by maintaining and even normalising the vulnerability of migrants and refugees, and in this way create an exploitable and politically excluded urban underclass (Bagelman, 2013; Scherr and Hofmann, 2016; Houston and Lawrence-Weilmann, 2016). The remaining chapters in this volume grapple with such contradictions and their manifestation at the local scale.

Acknowledgements

I thank Dayana Gonzales. This chapter draws on H. Bauder, 'Sanctuary cities: policies and practices in international perspective', *International Migration*, 55:2 (2017), 174–182.

References

American Immigration Council (2015) *'Sanctuary Cities,' Trust Acts, and Community Policing Explained*, www.immigrationpolicy.org/just-facts/sanctuary-cities-trust-acts-and-community-policing-explained (accessed 5 April 2016).

Ayuntamiento de Barcelona (2014) 'Call of Barcelona', www.bcn.cat/novaciutadania/pdf/ca/home/DeclaracioBcn.en.pdf (accessed 8 November 2018).

Ayuntamiento de Barcelona, Secretaría General (2015) 'Acuerdos adoptados por el Plenario del Consejo Municipal en la sesión ordinaria de 2 de octubre de 2015', http://ajuntament.barcelona.cat/sites/default/files/acords_021015_es_0.pdf (accessed 8 November 2018).

Bagelman, J. J. (2013) 'Sanctuary: a politics of ease?', *Alternatives: Global, Local, Political*, 38:1, 49–62.

Bagelman, J. J. (2016) *Sanctuary City: A Suspended State* (New York: Palgrave Macmillan).

Bau, I. (1994) 'Cities of refuge: no federal pre-emption of ordinances restricting local government cooperation with the INS', *Berkeley La Raza Law Journal*, 7:1, 50–71.

Bauder, H. (2011) *Immigration Dialectic: Imagining Community, Economy and Nation* (Toronto: University of Toronto Press).

Bauder, H. (2014a) 'Domicile citizenship, human mobility and territoriality', *Progress in Human Geography*, 38:1, 91–106.

Bauder, H. (2014b) 'Why we should use the term "illegalised" refugee or immigrant', *International Journal of Refugee Law*, 26:3, 327–332.

Bauder, H. (2016) *Migration Borders Freedom* (London: Routledge).

Bauder, H., and D. Gonzales (2018) 'Municipal responses to "illegality"', *Social Inclusion*, 6:1, 124–134.

Berinstein, C., J. McDonald, P. Nyers, C. Wright, and S. S. Zerehi (2006) '"Access not fear": non-status immigrants & city services', Centre of Excellence for Research on Immigration and Settlement (CERIS), https://we.riseup.net/assets/17034/Access%20Not%20Fear%20Report%20(Feb%202006).pdf (accessed 30 April 2013).

Buckel, S. (2008) 'Zwischen Repression und Integration: Wie gehen Kommunen mit dem Problem der Illegalität um?', in *Leben in der Illegalität: Ein Dossier* (Heinrich-Böll Stiftung), 35–39.

Caminero-Santangelo, M. (2012) 'The voice of the voiceless: religious rhetoric, undocumented immigrants, and the New Sanctuary Movement in the United States', in R. K. Lippert and S. Rehaag (eds), *Sanctuary Practices in International Perspectives: Migration, Citizenship and Social Movements* (Abingdon: Routledge), 92–105.

Casademont Falguera, X., P. Cortada Hortalà, and Ò. Prieto-Flores (2018) 'Citizenship and immigrant anti-rumour strategies: a critical outlook from the Barcelona case', *Citizenship Studies*, 22:1, 37–52.

CBS SF Bay Area (2015) 'Timeline: how San Francisco became a sanctuary city for undocumented immigrants', http://sanfrancisco.cbslocal.com/2015/07/08/timeline-how-san-francisco-became-a-sanctuary-city-for-undocumented-immigrants/ (accessed 2 June 2016).

Chishti, M., and F. Hipsman (2015) 'Sanctuary cities come under scrutiny, as does federal-local immigration relationship', *Migration Information Source – Policy Beat* (Migration Policy Institute), www.migrationpolicy.org/article/sanctuary-cities-come-under-scrutiny-does-federal-local-immigration-relationship (accessed 8 April 2016).

Cities of Migration (2009) 'Cities of sanctuary, communities of welcome', http://citiesofmigration.ca/good_idea/cities-of-sanctuary-communities-of-welcome/ (accessed 6 June 2016).

City and County of San Francisco (1989) 'San Francisco Administrative Code Chapter 12H: Immigration Status', http://sfgov.org/ccsfgsa/san-francisco-administrative-code-chapter-12h-immigration-status (accessed 2 June 2016).

City of Sanctuary (2016a) 'About City of Sanctuary', https://cityofsanctuary.org/about/ (accessed 1 June 2013).

City of Sanctuary (2016b) 'Annual Review 2015/16', https://cityofsanctuary.org/wp-content/uploads/2015/01/ANNUAL-REVIEW-2015-16-FINAL.pdf (accessed 16 September 2016).

Czajka, A. (2012) 'The potential of sanctuary: act of sanctuary through the lens of camp', in R. K. Lippert and S. Rehaag (eds), *Sanctuary Practices in International Perspectives: Migration, Citizenship and Social Movements* (Abingdon: Routledge), 43–56.

Darling, J. (2010) 'A city of sanctuary: the relational re-imagining of Sheffield's asylum politics', *Transactions of the Institute of British Geographers, NS* 35, 125–140.

Darling, J. (2013) 'Moral urbanism, asylum, and the politics of critique', *Environment and Planning A*, 45:8, 1785–1801, DOI: 10.1068/a45441.

Darling, J., and V. Squire (2012) 'Everyday enactments of sanctuary: the UK City of Sanctuary movement', in R. K. Lippert and S. Rehaag (eds), *Sanctuary Practices in International Perspectives: Migration, Citizenship and Social Movements* (Abingdon: Routledge), 191–204.

Derrida, J. (2001) *On Cosmopolitanism and Forgiveness*, trans. M. Dooley and M. Hughes (London: Routledge).

Fauser, M. (2017) 'The emergence of urban border spaces in Europe', *Journal of Borderlands Studies* (early view).

Freiburger Forum active gegen Ausgrenzung (2016) 'Freiburg – Eine Zufluchts-Stadt!', www.freiburger-forum.net/2016/10/freiburg-eine-zufluchts-stadt-die-alle-ihre-buergerinnen-schuetzt/ (accessed 8 November 2018).

Hannan, C.-A., and H. Bauder (2015) 'Towards a sanctuary province: policies, programs, and services for illegalised immigrants' equitable employment, social participation, and economic development', *RCIS Working Paper* 2015/3, www.ryerson.ca/content/dam/rcis/documents/RCIS_WP_Hannan_Bauder_No_2015_3.pdf (accessed 1 July 2016).

Harvey, D. (2012) *Rebel Cities: From the Right to the City to the Urban Revolution* (London: Verso).

Hess, S., B. Kasparek, S. Kron, M. Rodaz, M. Schwertl, and S. Sontowski (eds) (2017) *Der lange Sommer der Migration: Grenzregime III* (Berlin: Assoziation A).

Hier, S. P., and J. L. Greenberg (2002) 'Constructing a discursive crisis: risk problematization and illegal Chinese in Canada', *Ethnic and Racial Studies*, 25:3, 490–513.

Houston, S. D., and O. Lawrence-Weilmann (2016) 'The model migrant and multiculturalism: analyzing neoliberal logics in US sanctuary legislation', in H. Bauder and C. Matheis (eds), *Migration Policy and Practice: Interventions and Solutions* (New York: Palgrave Macmillan), 101–26.

Huang, X., and C. Y. Liu (2018) 'Welcoming cities: immigration policy at the local government level', *Urban Affairs Review*, 54:1, 3–32.

Hudson, G., I. Atak, M. Manocchi, and C.-A. Hannan (2017) '(No) Access T.O.: a pilot study on sanctuary city policy in Toronto, Canada', *RCIS Working Paper* 2017/1, www.ryerson.ca/content/dam/rcis/documents/RCIS%20Working%20Paper%20GHudson%20et%20al.%20finalV2.pdf (accessed 8 November 2018).

Isin, E. F., and G. M. Nielsen (eds) (2008) *Acts of Citizenship* (London: Zed Books).

Keung, N. (2015) 'Toronto policy urged to stop immigration "status checks"', *The Toronto Star*, 24 November 2015, www.thestar.com/news/investigations/2015/11/24/toronto-police-urged-to-stop-immigration-status-checks.html (accessed 1 July 2016).

Lefebvre, H. (1996) 'The right to the city', trans. E. Kofman and E. Lebas, in E. Kofman and E. Lebas (eds), *Writing on Cities* (Oxford: Blackwell), 147–159.

Leo, C. C., M. Morand, and J. C. Murillo (2015) *Building Communities of Practice for Urban Refugees – Americas Regional Workshop Report* (United Nations High Commissioner for Refugees), www.unhcr.org/5617bb709.pdf (accessed 8 November 2018).

Lippert, R. K. (2004) 'Sanctuary practices, rationalities and sovereignties', *Alternatives: Global, Local, Political*, 29:5, 535–555.

Lippert, R. K. (2005) *Sanctuary, Sovereignty, Sacrifice: Canadian Sanctuary Incidents, Power and Law* (Vancouver: UBC Press).

Lippert, R. K., and S. Rehaag (2012) 'Introduction: sanctuary across countries, institutions, and disciplines', in R. K. Lippert and S. Rehaag (eds), *Sanctuary Practices in International Perspectives: Migration, Citizenship and Social Movements* (Abingdon: Routledge), 1–12.

Loga, J., M. Pyykkönen, and H. Stenvaag (2012) 'Holy territories and hospitality: Nordic exceptionality and national differences of sanctuary incidents', in R. K. Lippert and S. Rehaag (eds), *Sanctuary Practices in International Perspectives: Migration, Citizenship and Social Movements* (Abingdon: Routledge), 121–134.

Malpass, A., P. Cloke, C. Barnett, and N. Clarke (2007) 'Fairtrade urbanism? The politics of place beyond place in the Bristol Fairtrade City campaign', *International Journal of Urban and Regional Research*, 31, 633–645.

Mancina, P. (2012) 'The birth of a sanctuary-city: a history of governmental sanctuary in San Francisco', in R. K. Lippert and S. Rehaag (eds), *Sanctuary Practices in International Perspectives: Migration, Citizenship and Social Movements* (Abingdon: Routledge), 205–218.

McCann, E. J. (2008) 'Expertise, truth, and urban policy mobilities: global circuit of knowledge in the development of Vancouver, Canada's "four Pillar" Drug Strategy', *Environment and Planning A: Economy and Space*, 40:4, 885–904.

McDonald, J. (2012) 'Building a sanctuary city: municipal migrant rights in the city of Toronto', in P. Nyers and K. Rygiel (eds), *Citizenship, Migrant Activism and the Politics of Movement* (London: Routledge), 129–145.

Millner, N. (2012) 'Sanctuary sans frontières: social movements and solidarity in post-war Northern France', in R. K. Lippert and S. Rehaag (eds), *Sanctuary Practices in International Perspectives: Migration, Citizenship and Social Movements* (Abingdon: Routledge), 57–70.

Mudu, P., and S. Chattopadhyay (2016) *Migrations, Squatting and Radical Autonomy* (London: Routledge).

Municipalidad de Quilicura (2016) *Migrafest 2016: Vecinos Disfrutan de una gran fiesta intercultural*, www.muniquilicura.cl/2016/12/12/migrafest-2016-vecinos-disfrutaron-de-una-gran-fiesta-intercultural/ (accessed 18 November 2018).

Nail, T., F. Kamal, and S. Hussan (2010) 'Building sanctuary city: NOII-Toronto on non-status migrant justice organizing', *Upping the Anti*, 11, http://uppingtheanti.org/journal/article/11-noii-sanctuary-city/ (accessed 12 April 2016).

Nguyen, M. T., and H. Gill (2016) 'Interior immigration enforcement: the impacts of expanding local law enforcement authority', *Urban Studies*, 53:2, 302–323.

Nyers, P. (2010) 'No One Is Illegal between city and nation', *Studies in Social Justice*, 4:2, 127–143.

Peck, J., and N. Theodore (2010) 'Mobilizing policy: models, methods, and mutations', *Geoforum*, 41:2, 169–174.

Purcell, M. (2002) 'Excavating Lefebvre: the right to the city and its urban politics of the inhabitant', *GeoJournal*, 58:2–3, 99–108.

Purcell, M. (2013) 'Possible worlds: Henri Lefebvre and the right to the city', *Journal of Urban Affairs*, 36:1, 141–154.

Riaño, Y., and D. Wastl-Walter (2006) 'Immigration policies, state discourses on foreigners, and the politics of identity in Switzerland', *Environment and Planning A*, 38, 1693–1713.

Ridgley, J. (2008) 'Cities of refuge: immigration enforcement, police, and the insurgent genealogies of citizenship in US sanctuary cities', *Urban Geography*, 29:1: 53–77, DOI: 10.2747/0272-3638.29.1.53.

Ridgley, J. (2012) 'The city as a sanctuary in the United States', in R. K. Lippert and S. Rehaag (eds), *Sanctuary Practices in International Perspectives: Migration, Citizenship and Social Movements* (Abingdon: Routledge), 219–231.

Robbins, L. (2017) '"Sanctuary city" mayors vow to defy Trump's immigration order', *New York Times*, 25 January 2017, www.nytimes.com/2017/01/25/nyregion/outraged-mayors-vow-to-defy-trumps-immigration-order.html (accessed 8 November 2018).

Robinson, M. (2016) 'City of Vancouver grants access without fear', *Vancouver Sun*, 6 April 2016, http://vancouversun.com/news/local-news/vancouver-considers-access-without-fear (accessed 17 September 2016).

Sassen, S. (2008) *Territory, Authority, Rights: From Medieval to Global Assemblages* (Princeton, NJ: Princeton University Press, rev. edn).

Schech, S. (2013) 'Rescaling sovereignty? Sub-state responses to irregular migrants', *Griffith Law Review*, 22:3, 785–802.

Scherr, A., and R. Hofmann (2016) 'Sanctuary cities: Eine Perspektive für deutsche Kommunalpolitik?', *Kritische Justiz*, 49:1, 86–97.

Schwarz, J. (2008) *Stadtluft macht frei: Leben in der mittelalterlichen Stadt* (Darmstadt: Primus Verlag).

Shoemaker, K. (2012) 'Sanctuary for crime in the early common law', in R. K. Lippert and S. Rehaag (eds), *Sanctuary Practices in International Perspectives: Migration, Citizenship and Social Movements* (Abingdon: Routledge), 15–27.

Solidarity City Network (2013a) *A Short History of How We Got There* (leaflet).

Solidarity City Network (2013b) *Towards a Sanctuary City: Assessment and Recommendations on Municipal Service Provision to Undocumented Residents in Toronto* (Toronto), http://solidaritycity.net/learn/report-towards-a-sanctuary-city/ (accessed 20 December 2013).

Squire, V., and J. Bagelman (2012) 'Taking not waiting: space, temporality and politics in the City of Sanctuary movement', in P. Nyers and K. Rygiel (eds), *Citizenship, Migrant Activism and the Politics of Movement* (London: Routledge), 146–164.

Strunk, C., and H. Leitner (2013) 'Resisting federal-local immigration enforcement partnerships: redefining "secure communities" and public safety', *Territory, Politics, Governance*, 1:1, 62–85.

Thayer Correa, L. E., S. Correa, and T. Novoa (2014) *Plan de Acogida y Reconocimiento de Migrantes y Refugiados de la Comuna de Quilicura (Municipalidad de Quilicura)*, www.minsal.cl/wp-content/uploads/2015/09/BP04Plan-acogida-y-reconocimiento-Quilicura-2014.pdf (accessed 4 December 2018).

Tramonte, L. (2011) *Debunking the Myth of 'Sanctuary Cities': Community Policing Policies Protect American Communities* (Immigration Policy Centre, 2011), www.immigrationpolicy.org/sites/default/files/docs/Community_Policing_Policies_Protect_American_042611_update.pdf (accessed 5 April 2016).

van Leeuwen, T., and R. Wodak (1999) 'Legitimizing immigration control: a discourse-historical analysis', *Discourse Studies*, 1:1, 83–118.

Varsanyi, M. W. (2007) 'Documenting undocumented migrants: the *Matrículas Consulares* as neoliberal local membership', *Geopolitics*, 12:2, 299–319.

Varsanyi, M. W. (ed.) (2010) *Taking Local Control: Immigration Policy Activism in U.S. Cities and States* (Stanford, CA: Stanford University Press).

Walia, H. (2014) 'Sanctuary city from below: dismantling the city of Vancouver', *The Mainlander*, http://themainlander.com/2014/06/02/sanctuary-city-from-below-dismantling-the-city-of-vancouver/ (accessed 12 April 2016).

Walker, K. E., and H. Leitner (2011) 'The variegated landscape of local immigration policies in the United States', *Urban Geography*, 32:3, 156–178.

Wells, M. J. (2004) 'The grassroots reconfiguration of US immigration policy', *International Migration Review*, 38:4, 1308–1347.

2

Uncovering sanctuary cities: between policy, practice, and politics

Janika Kuge

Throughout 2017 so-called sanctuary cities received intense interest from the international media. This popularity was largely triggered by the Trump administration announcing a crackdown on sanctuary cities, cutting them off from federal funds (Trump, 2016). In response, sanctuary city supporters went to court to prevent the federal government from taking such measures. In March 2017, at a meeting between members of the Department of Justice (DOJ) and mayors of sanctuary cities, the mayors asked 'a multimillion-dollar question: what's a sanctuary city?' (Gomez, 2017). The answer from the DOJ members remained vague, due, they argued, to the pending litigation. Yet their definition matters decisively, because it will play a role in decisions to grant or withhold funds from any city that implements such a policy. It also conveys the contested definition of what and who counts as the population of the country: de facto or only de jure residents? Indeed, what a sanctuary city is remains controversial, despite the fact that over 300 jurisdictions in the USA alone can be subsumed under this label (Gomez, 2017), and the first sanctuary city ordinance was implemented in the 1980s (Lippert, 2005: 382). Despite or maybe precisely because of the vagueness of the concept, the definition of sanctuary city has become highly significant, a question of definitional power. In this chapter, I will give an overview of why defining the term is as controversial as it is difficult. Instead of a set definition, I will introduce three distinct dimensions of sanctuary cities that help to illustrate the conflicting logics of governing tied to different rationales and political scales.

Sanctuary and the limits of definition

The sanctuary concept has a rich and long history; its story spans different countries with different legal traditions, social circumstances, and, most importantly, very different practical approaches to, and implementations of, the concept (see Bauder, this volume). Deriving originally from religious practices and a European medieval tradition, the idea of providing sanctuary to illegalised[1] persons was introduced in the 1970s in the USA and first put into practice in the 1980s. The sanctuary concept has taken on various different shapes since then; it not only varies through time but also through space, as do the aims, rationales, and practices associated with sanctuary. The essence of the idea, linking the different phenomena throughout the USA, Canada, the UK, central and southern Europe, and recently Chile (Bauder, 2017 and in this volume), can be summarised as follows: sanctuary city legislation tends to appear whenever a gap between the de facto and the de jure population becomes evident and where this gap challenges the municipal organisation of care and service (see Atak and Hudson in this volume). For immigrants with or without papers, short-term residents, and other non-citizens, eligibility for accessing services and exercising rights varies widely. For example, getting a work permit, applying for financial support, enrolling in educational services, or taking part in elections is widely restricted for non-citizens. Eligibilities are largely dependent on what status a person has, turning a multicultural city population into a multi-status population with differing entitlements. In the case of illegalised persons, even accessing basic services, such as healthcare, can lead to expulsion or deportation. This often results in a complete avoidance of any contact with official institutions by illegalised populations despite a real need for basic rights and services (for example the ability to demand fair wages, or access to education and healthcare). The lack of access to such services often means drastic disadvantages for the non-citizen population. On the other hand, for the city institutions, this means that a part of its population is not accessible; it remains invisible in the sense that it does not appear in official statistics. Hence little is known about the precise demography or the specific problems of this group, which makes it rather ungovernable. The larger the 'invisible' population, the more complicated governing processes become (Mancina, 2016).

But even though access to and exercising of rights are conditioned by national citizenship, thereby restricting the rights of non-citizens, services are often granted beyond formal entitlements. This situation has been referred to as sanctuary city practice.

A growing number of documented and undocumented non-citizens reside in cities, where everyday processes of production, reproduction, and organisation take place (Saunders and Roller, 2011; Bauder, 2014; Sassen, 2012). To meet and fulfil all the needs of the heterogeneous municipal population, local institutions have certain special duties, authorities, and capabilities, usually bestowed by federal law. Healthcare, education, and other functions of everyday organisation are, in contrast, often local responsibilities. Municipalities, by definition, have to organise service demands in an everyday context that changes frequently, and that often poses particular challenges and needs specific to individual municipalities. Gesemann and Roth explain that due to this context, municipalities often have the right to autonomously create and organise institutions to meet service needs (Gesemann and Roth, 2018). When parts of city communities cannot access these institutions, then the organisation of municipal service delivery can be disrupted, endangering public health, public safety, and economic resilience. The discrepancy between the de facto and the de jure population thus becomes a challenge for municipalities at the level of everyday organisation, since the local institutions lack information and access to a part of the municipality's residents. To draw on Foucault, these institutions do not have 'the right mandate and knowledge to govern their subjects' (Foucault, 2015: 171). But as Sassen argues, municipalities also possess the capacity to face these challenges that result from a multifaceted patchwork of city populations: 'Cities have increasingly begun to pass their own ordinances that contrast with state and national policy norms, designating their cities as sanctuaries for undocumented immigrants' (Sassen, 2012: 87). Urban capabilities thus mean that cities can retain the ability to react autonomously to special conditions on the municipal level, based on the challenges of the everyday organisation of the city as a space of migrant lives.

Alongside Sassen, Bauder too sees strong potential in the role of cities to address the challenges deriving from multi-status populations. Relating to the visions of urban capacities of David Harvey and Henri Lefebvre (Harvey, 2013), Bauder argues that sanctuary cities can be seen as creative and pioneering responses towards social justice (Bauder, 2016a). For instance, Wong's comparative study focusing on US sanctuary cities underlines the positive impact of sanctuary policies where they are implemented: sanctuary cities are more likely to have higher per capita income, a lower crime rate, fewer people relying on financial aid programmes, and an overall stronger economy than non-sanctuary cities (Wong, 2017). Wong argues that these effects can be explained through the ability of all inhabitants to access municipal services. Assuming that the effects of such policies are as positive as Wong suggests, the sanctuary city model could thus be an economically attractive one for municipalities to adopt.

The reasons for cities not to introduce such policies inter alia may be tied to legal challenges: sanctuary cities are said to subvert governmental tasks and circumvent federal law. In the US, President Donald Trump promised repeatedly to 'ban sanctuary cities' in his first 100 days in office by cutting them off from federal funding (Trump, 2016). Thus, federal and state government institutions criticise sanctuary cities, considering their local policies a breach of federal authority and prerogative over immigration. The rationale behind this is the enforcement of federal immigration law within the territory of the nation-state. By establishing a sanctuary jurisdiction, this enforcement is seen to crack. And in sanctuary cities' not differentiating between de facto and de jure populations, the federal state sees its monopoly on membership and belonging undermined (Varsanyi, 2008b: 880). The conflict between municipal and federal institutions is thus a question of how far the border can follow immigrants inside the nation-state territory (Varsanyi, 2008b: 880) and how much federal authorities can have a say over local policy making. Through the sanctuary city phenomenon, the differing rationales of government[2] at different scales become obvious. Contradictions and conflicts arise between the different scales, because each scale has a different definition of what the resident population is. Thus the political objectives deriving from that shift in scale and in population will also, necessarily, differ.

Decried as illegal liberal policy making on the one hand, further censure comes from critical scholars: sanctuary city policies have been suspected of not fulfilling their promised emancipatory potential and actually doing little to solve the challenges of mixed-status populations (Laman, 2015; Redazione Rossa e Nera, 2018; Scherr and Hofmann,

2016). On the contrary, these policies are criticised for normalising deportation and facilitating the exploitation of non-citizens, tensions that both Atak and Hudson reflect on in the case of Toronto in this volume. Indeed, as Laman (2015: 50) asserts 'Rather than fostering forms of local citizenship, it renders many undocumented migrants apolitical. First, through the maintenance of precarious status and secondly, through the further rendering of undocumented migrants invisible. Together, these reinforce a relationship of being dominated and oppressed by sub-national authorities.'

Drawing on these critiques, it becomes clear that sanctuary cities are not a one-dimensional phenomenon, but rather a focal point of dissent in current political debates around immigration and governing. Different actors, their interests, rationales, and incentives shape what a particular sanctuary policy can be (Leitner and Strunk, 2014), while the framework, for instance national politics and laws, determines the scope of any specific sanctuary city or policy (Bauder, 2017).

I argue that a set definition of the phenomenon is not expedient. Instead, I suggest a multidimensional approach that honours its richness and complexity along with its fault lines. These dimensions intertwine, overlap or contradict each other, but can offer a useful baseline for exploring the phenomenon. The first dimension is about human and citizenship rights. The sanctuary city concept began as a civic movement for 'insurgent citizenship' as a concept that permits traditional citizenship through alternative access to belonging (see Bauder, 2014, 2016b; Rygiel, 2010) and it is this vision that has remained at the heart of many organisations still aligned with sanctuary framings (see Bauder and Darling in this volume). The second dimension is about governing a municipality with a mixed-status population which turns the concept into a pragmatic governing rationale. The third dimension touches on state authority and the prerogative to regulate and control immigration. When sanctuary cities provide access to services and rights for illegalised persons, this challenges national immigration law, as noted above.

Between these three particular dimensions there are obvious conflicts, because each dimension draws on a different rationale. The rationale of the federal state authorities does not comply with the municipal rationale. Likewise the rationale of civic sanctuary movements is not congruent with the municipal one. The conflicts between these different dimensions derive from different interests in and perspectives on the concept of sanctuary city, but also from different concepts of governing. Still, these three dimensions, as in different spheres of rationality and logic, are crucial for the shape and character of the current sanctuary city phenomenon. While I will mostly focus in the remainder of this chapter on the US context, where the sanctuary phenomenon is so far most frequent and influential, in other national contexts, younger sanctuary movements and policies exist, too, but in less developed ways. By analytically separating but practically drawing on all of these three dimensions, we can analyse the sanctuary city as a relatively coherent phenomenon in its varied appearance. Through this, it will become clear how a definition of what determines a sanctuary city is a question of political dispute, and thus an essential question of perspective and power.

Sanctuary as movement

The first dimension is sanctuary as movement, describing grassroots organisations and their perspective on the sanctuary city. As noted above, the story of sanctuary is often narrated with respect to its long history. It is said to have roots in antiquity, in different religious practices in different parts of the world (Bauder, 2017; Houston and Lawrence-Weilmann, 2016; Kuge, 2017; Lippert, 2005). Then it had a revival in medieval city politics and Church sanctuary, where it became an element of good kingship (Shoemaker, 2012: 18–19), as well as a beacon of urban citizenship models ('Stadtluft macht frei'[3] was a slogan that promised freedom to those who had fled serfdom after living undetected in a city for more than a year and a day) that resemble current sanctuary city policies in practice (Bauder, 2017: 174).

In the US context, the contemporary movement is said to have had its beginnings in 'the early 1980s through the mid-1990s, [when] religious congregants as order members of a variety of faiths decided to take firm action' (Mancina, 2016: 205) to help refugees from Central and South America fleeing to the USA. Local civic movements battled the high rejection rate of asylum requests by organising local resettlement for families and individuals. By taking action overtly, the activists aimed to pressure the US government into ending its involvement in the civil wars in Central and South America and accepting more of the refugees who were fleeing these wars. In this context, insurgent urban citizenship was not only organised by civil and clerical activists but partly also by local governments (Lippert, 2005: 383; Mancina, 2016: 9). This is a powerful example of grassroots movements directly challenging national migration and citizenship policies and attempting to implement at a city scale what had before been limited to church premises. Furthermore, the struggle for urban inclusion can be substantially connected to civil rights movements and their seditious 'acts of citizenship' (Rygiel, 2010: 41) on behalf of other underprivileged groups in Western societies making claims for inclusion, such as Indigenous groups, women, and people of colour. On the one hand, the sanctuary movement is tapping into a long tradition of political struggle whereby 'the articulation of rights for various groups has been the most recurring theme of "Western" political history' (Isin and Turner, 2002: 1). On the other hand, attempts to rescale citizenship at a local scale by placing local communities and their everyday lives at the centre of interest in order to bypass national immigration laws has been an innovative feature.

In fact, the city-scale governance structures of social movements tactically lobbying members of the municipal government seems to be what makes the current sanctuary movement so prolific. These kinds of constellations appear in many countries: sanctuary city movements are not limited to the USA but can be found in several Western countries. An international sanctuary umbrella network does not exist, and although cases of cooperation occur (Leitner and Strunk, 2014), policies and practices vary in different regions. For example, the 'City of Sanctuary' movement has existed in the UK since 2005, and over 70 cities have passed council motions that aim to 'create a culture of welcome' and participation on a local basis (Bagelman, 2016: 47; Darling, 2010). Cities of sanctuary in this context mainly facilitate cultural activities to create a positive atmosphere between old and new populations. The initiatives are not directed at unauthorised populations but rather at asylum seekers and refugees specifically (Bagelman, 2016; Darling, 2010).

In Canada, the first city to call itself a sanctuary city was Toronto in 2013. Similar to the sanctuary concept prevalent in the US, Toronto grants municipal services to persons formerly ineligible to receive them. Furthermore, the policy aims to limit accessibility to information about residents' national status to immigration enforcement (Hudson et al., 2017; but see also Atak, this volume, on the lack of enforcement of sanctuary policies in Toronto). Other Canadian cities followed Toronto's lead, among them London, Ajax, and Hamilton (all Ontario), Montréal, and Vancouver. Common among these cities is a general aim to supply a mixed-status population with access to municipal services. However, concrete contextual histories, policies, and practices vary, particularly between the North American model and its European adaptations. They all share constellations of both civic movements and official institutions. They also share a very open concept of population that is neglectful of formal citizenship.

With this mix of actors, it can be hard to distinguish what was brought about by the grassroots movements in relation to the contribution of local government. But the social groups are dynamic, flexible, and are thus able to push the concept forward. Sanctuary city, in these terms, is a highly mobile and adaptable concept, because it focuses on the limited and concrete territory of everyday life, everyday struggle, and relative physical proximity that has been taken to define the city as a social and spatial form (Leitner and Strunk, 2014; Sassen, 2012). Scholars have highlighted the proximity of social relations within municipalities as an important factor in the implementation of sanctuary policies: as Mancina shows in the US, activists were approaching progressive members of city boards and were often voted into city council and board positions so as to shape debates and exercise influence. In some cities, they were able to form an alliance that 'had the power to pass resolutions that served as statements of political opinion, moral orientation and legal directives for practical government business' (Mancina, 2016: 207), directing power to sanctuary movements.

Whereas municipal institutions play a vital role in the establishment of sanctuary cities, grassroots movements and their political struggle for immigrant rights often precede municipal involvement. Leitner and Strunk show how migrant advocacy 'is creating new political spaces and advancing new values and rationalities beyond those generally associated with liberal democratic citizenship' (Leitner and Strunk, 2014: 351), and that such groups are active 'in many ways – as civic mobilizations, acts of resistance, constructions of a counter public to the dominant public realm, and citizenship practices' (Leitner and Strunk, 2014: 350). In other words, immigrant advocacy does not exhaust itself in engaging in formal political processes or lobbyism but is rather polyvalent. The organisation of civic movement groups can be highly localised (like city-based action groups) or embedded in wider-reaching networks and alliances. An example is how the sanctuary movement came to Germany and Switzerland in late 2016 and early 2017 through the mobility of Canadian sanctuary city activists. Canadian activists travelled to several German and Swiss cities, giving presentations about the Torontonian sanctuary model, and in doing so they caused a spin-off effect, nudging many local coalitions to take up the idea (see Jungfer, 2018). Although there is no official urban sanctuary legislation in Germany or Switzerland at the time of writing, a growing network exists, forming coalitions with existing immigrant advocacy groups and preparing to lobby city officials in the future, with the concept of sanctuary as a key framing device (Kuge, 2017).

Neither the social movement network for immigrant rights nor the choice of the local community as a frame for pro-immigrant activism (for example, the Charter of Palermo, 2015)[4] are necessarily new in Europe. For instance, 'right to the city' movements, drawing on Lefebvre's (1996) famous formulation of urban rights, have been popular in anti-gentrification protests (e.g. Krajewski, 2015) and the idea of a city-wide ID for all inhabitants regardless of status is currently being discussed within sanctuary city movement coalitions in Bern and Zurich (Landolt, 2017; 'Wir alle sind Bern', 2018).[5] What is new is the combination of these two elements and the explicit reference to the North American framing of sanctuary as a political concept.

In this way, sanctuary city movements make up fluid networks of practice, as Bagelman (2016) puts it. Furthermore, such movements 'do not simply involve particular places, of course, but connect them through extra-local relations and flows, in both material and cyberspace. Mobilities, essential to political struggles for a number of reasons, are a strategic tool to gain publicity, register discontent, and promote alternative imaginaries' (Leitner and Strunk, 2014: 353). Scholars and activists note the importance of the involvement of bottom-up activism in the evolution of sanctuary cities (e.g. Walia, 2014). Apart from creating an alternative public discourse about immigrant rights, which can lead to their codification in municipal law, grassroots initiatives can also make visible those who are formally and politically invisible and at the same time shelter and protect them from deportation

(Bagelman, 2016; Mancina, 2016; Solidarity City Network Toronto, 2014). Advocacy groups push the boundaries of national belonging and current citizenship models through insurgent acts of citizenship. Through these acts, they manage to manifest alternative models to belonging that exceed the status quo (Leitner and Strunk, 2014). At the same time, through focusing on the idea of urban citizenship, they rescale it to a local level.

To summarise, civic sanctuary movements are a mostly informal, rather fluent and versatile, but also absolutely indispensable part of sanctuary cities. The sanctuary movement started a trend in the 1980s for American cities to implement protective policies, after it strategically approached members of city boards and councils. In addition, the movement is responsible for the continuity, national and international dissemination, and development of the phenomenon. Its volatile character enables the movement to flexibly address, demand, and attain progressive practices of citizenship and inclusion without being necessarily tied to legal margins. On the contrary, the movement is able to point out possible future policies, and create discourses, forums, and spaces of deviant and progressive practices (Leitner and Strunk, 2014). It also enables the core idea of sanctuary to be conserved through changing legal, political, and social circumstances, making it available and applicable in different contexts. The social movement perspective thus plays an essential role in theory and practice concerning the sanctuary city. The social movement often precedes formal political changes and generates public interest and debate about immigrants' rights. In this sense, it can begin to influence the design and implementation of local ordinances. In the following section, I will elaborate further on this formal policy level.

Sanctuary as local policy

The second dimension is local sanctuary policy. In the following section, I focus on the municipal rationales behind the implementation of sanctuary jurisdiction. First, to locate cities under sanctuary jurisdiction is quite complicated. What sanctuary status means can be elusive, as a look into endeavours to create a listing of sanctuary cities shows. The only definitive lists have been created by opponents of sanctuary cities and they only exist for the US. Opponents of the concept, such as the Center for Immigration Studies (CIS), list cities' names to identify dissenters, record deviations, and affirm the national immigration regime (Salvi, 2006). But these lists are not coherent. The difference may owe mostly to inconsistencies in the criteria qualifying a sanctuary city as such. The only information indicated in the lists is whether a city has sanctuary status or not. Biases between different listings can stem from whether they focus on de facto or de jure implementation of sanctuary policy. This means that city administrations may sometimes not officially support sanctuary policies but still grant services unofficially – but systematically – to their illegalised population, making these cites hard to categorise. Conversely, there are also cities with sanctuary legislation that fail to enforce the policy (see Atak in this volume), so they may appear on the lists when their status is actually dubious.

Supporters of sanctuary cities, such as the Immigrant Legal Resource Center (ILRC), have compiled lists, too. By contrast, they indicate a continuum from 0 (most involvement) to 7 (least involvement), gradually marking the counties involvement with the federal immigration police agency, Immigration and Customs Enforcement (ICE) (ILRC, 2018: 13). Cities, as ILRC remarks, are not the focus of the analysis, so their list does not show sanctuary cities but gives an overview of policing methods, often constituting the basis for further sanctuary policy making (ILRC, 2018: 8).

Institutions practising sanctuary can be the police, but also city service bureaus or other service providers (Hudson et al., 2017). Practice, in this context, can consist of neglecting obligations such as collecting information on a person's legal status, or of providing services to persons who are not eligible to receive them. But neither the omissions nor the performance of services are random. Rather, they follow a distinct rationale that can be found in the very nature of the services provided and in the way they are justified by their positive social effects for the population as a whole (Wong, 2017). For example, comparative case studies have found that sanctuary is able to ameliorate the situation of vulnerable populations, decrease crime rates, improve public safety, and build a stronger social community (see e.g. State of California Senate Bill No. 54, Chapter 495, 2017; Civil Case 5:17 – 00404, 2017). Which public services are made available to all in sanctuary cities, as well as their potential ramifications, are indicated in the bill of indictment of a small Texan county on the US-Mexican border addressing the State of Texas. This lawsuit aimed to uphold sanctuary status against more rigorous federal immigration enforcement and states that:

> Plaintiffs are safer when all people, including undocumented immigrants, feel safe, when the local law enforcement officers can be trusted for reporting crimes […] Plaintiff's communities are healthier, when all residents, including undocumented immigrants, access public health programs […] And Plaintiff's communities are economically and socially stronger, when all children, including undocumented immigrants, attend school. (Civil Case 5:17 – 00404, 2017)

The argument made for sanctuary legislation is based on the anticipated positive effects of this legislation and implies that opposing the legislation could harm public health, safety, and the community's social and economic resilience. Instead of demanding human rights or decrying the inequality or vulnerability of undocumented immigrants, the argument focuses on the positive effects for the community as a whole. The bill of indictment does not demand the political recognition of illegal immigrants, as the civic movements might have done, but simply describes a technique of inclusive administration as a practice with good results for the city.

Scholars have uncovered parallels in historical sanctuary cases: throughout history, sanctuary has been performed not necessarily in times of weak statehood and 'relative disorder and violence', but also in periods of relative stability and strong governance' (Shoemaker, 2012: 18–19). In the case of San Francisco, Mancina shows that the apparatus of a sanctuary city was assembled in the first place to 'manage and improve the precarious situation of undocumented Central American refugees' (Mancina, 2016: 34). 'This effectively institution-alised sanctuary as a governmental strategy […] for governing a mixed-status city population' (Mancina, 2016: 34). The services granted aim to make a municipality safer, 'healthier', and 'economically and socially stronger', as indicated in the legal case from Texas. Sanctuary is thus not undermining government, but it is a strategy of it (Houston and Lawrence-Weilmann, 2016; Mancina, 2016: 34; Sajed, 2012: 23) that can be understood through the notion of governmentality as an economic logic of government (Dean, 2010; Foucault, 2015: 171).

Alongside these governmental dimensions, other scholars have emphasised that sanctuary ordinances can also have negative effects. For example, Houston and Lawrence-Weilmann point out how the emancipatory content of sanctuary ideas evolved to become a tool for neoliberal image politics without really combating social inequalities (see also Darling, this volume). They argue that 'the simultaneous reaction against and incorporation of neoliberal rationales and approaches mitigate the possibilities for sanctuary legislation to bear out the goal of affording safe and just spaces to migrants, authorised and unauthorised, and creating sustained social change' (Houston and Lawrence-Weilmann, 2016: 103–104). As a result, they suggest that sanctuary policies are not necessarily progressive or radical (Houston and Lawrence-Weilmann, 2016: 104). The administrative effort to uphold social support, healthcare, or education for mixed-status populations is not only intensive in working hours and bureaucratic procedures, but also costly and error-prone. The intention to eliminate these problems is primarily an administrative and pragmatic one. Instead of bestowing rights on populations previously excluded and disenfranchised, sanctuary policies and their implementation can be a governing strategy to cope with a diversifying population. If the city denies services to persons in need, it could be seen as cruel, so in response services are (theoretically) open to everyone. People living on the streets or lacking medical attention are not then the fault of the city, but of an individual failure to access city services when needed.

Implementing sanctuary legislation enables undocumented migrants and other non-citizens to obtain city services to ameliorate their situation (Lippert, 2005: 138), for example to access legal advice. Generally, this seems inclusive. But in this way, the mostly precarious living conditions of illegalised populations become depoliticised and framed as individual mistakes. Further, sanctuary policies have a pastoral element, because services are granted to non-citizens as an act of mercy, but are not guaranteed rights. Thus 'sanctuary entails the coupling of [...] pastoral rationality with a liberal rationality – that is, a marriage of governing through freedom and governing through need' (Sajed, 2012: 27).

Lawrence-Weilmann and Houston further argue that 'sanctuary legislation also frequently extols the benefits of diversity' and thus becomes 'a strategy for managing [...] the roles of productive neoliberal subjects and do[es] not challenge the systems and power relations that routinely contribute to the struggles and inequities experienced by low-income and frequently racialised communities' (Houston and Lawrence-Weilmann, 2016: 103). While some scholars see a chance of creating an immigration-friendly environment through promoting diversity, others say that this could lead to accepting discrepancies and inequalities as normality or even individual failure (e.g. Laman, 2015; Redazione Rossa e Nera, 2018).

A more positive outlook asserts that urban sanctuary 'can inspire innovative political and practical approaches towards migration and belonging' (Bauder, 2017: 175). I argue, in line with Bauder, that drawing from the status quo of 'structural exclusion that migrants and refugees experience' at the national scale (Bauder, 2017: 175), the social and economic vulnerability of illegalised persons *can* be mitigated at the local scale. But to be inclusive, a sanctuary policy not only has to be adopted; it also has to be enforced and to be regularly evaluated and audited – otherwise it is nothing but a label. Enforcement and evaluation needs to include the opportunity for everyone to demand services and submit complaints, and the effective and democratic monitoring of whether sanctuary legislation is functioning. Atak reviews in this volume the findings of the first audit of the effects of sanctuary legislation in Toronto. The audit showed that the policy was impaired by a failure to enforce it on the front line. In fact, this failure can endanger the very people the policy aims to protect: failure to enforce the policy, for instance in police work, could mean that a non-status person seeking protection from an abusive partner could end up being deported (Sullivan, 2009: 580). In short, a sanctuary policy that encourages an illegalised population to expose themselves to official institutions but that fails to be enforced on the front line can be counterproductive (Hudson, this volume). The study by Atak and her colleagues (Hudson et al., 2017: 7) thus recommends special comprehensive training for people working in front-line positions. Similarly, Sullivan notes that 'sanctuary policies are limited in practice by knowledge gaps and local confusion' (Sullivan, 2009: 577), making the promotion and training of city staff a vital element to the policy's success and efficacy.

The adoption of urban sanctuary policies is naturally not sufficient to permanently dissolve structural inequalities. Therefore, it is very important to scrutinise front-line work so as to use the commitments, ordinances, and policies as effective tools. As Ahmed argues of institutional cultures: 'Practitioners can use commitments because they fail to describe what is ongoing or going on within organizations. If organizations are saying what they are doing, then you can show they are not doing what they are saying' (Ahmed, 2012: 126–127). The passing of a sanctuary policy can be an important commitment, promising more equality, democratic influence, and social agency to disenfranchised populations. The implementation of the policy, however, is an ongoing process conditional on many factors (Walia, 2014). The success of the policy hinges on its enforcement and evaluation – as is the case with any other policy. However, in the case of sanctuary city policies, this is closely tied to the social emancipatory movement that exceeds and usually pre-dates the policy itself, and that often follows a different rationality. A reciprocal relation between these two elements, influencing and evaluating the goals and contents of what a sanctuary city can become, makes it a process rather than a status or a condition (Walia, 2014).

The efficacy of sanctuary cities is also tied to legal boundaries that are pre-set by laws at other spatial and legal scales. What practices institutions can facilitate is often shaped by national legal frameworks. In the following section, I will discuss the intricate relationship between sanctuary cities and the nation-state by taking up recent developments in the USA.

Sanctuary and the federal state

The third dimension is the federal state and its relation to sub-national sanctuary jurisdictions. This dimension shapes possibilities for and limitations to the concept (see Bauder, this volume). Conversely, sanctuary cities can have an impact on federal state politics, as currently shown in the US context. In the following, I outline the conflict in the US and thus debate the political effects of the current sanctuary movement.

One of the key issues in the current public debate is that sanctuary policies are circumventing or even deliberately breaking state or federal law. Indeed, some supporters of the concept claim that national immigration laws are unjust and therefore need to be circumvented.

For instance, Mayor Rivera from the sanctuary city of Lawrence, Massachusetts, states: 'I start every conversation about immigration by saying the federal government has abdicated its role in providing clear, well-funded immigration policy' (Rivera, 2018). Senate Bill 54, chapter 495 from California, which was passed in October 2017, encourages the state's institutions to actively withhold information from federal institutions and even to provide corresponding training:

> The bill would require the Attorney General to publish guidance, audit criteria, and training recommendations regarding state and local law enforcement databases, for purposes of limiting the availability of information for immigration enforcement. (State of California Senate Bill No. 54, 2017)

Sullivan calls this 'enforcing non-enforcement' (2009: 569). Here sanctuary policy is shielding the immigrant population from state or federal institutions and instates a more liberal immigration policy in lieu of the national one. In other words, sanctuary policy is claiming jurisdiction over federal tasks, forming a state within a state.

Generally, the federal US state grants widespread autonomies to sub-national governments. Whether this self-confident conduct of sub-national governments is unconstitutional is an open question. The US sanctuary movement has been debated in court in several cases in 2017 and is still an open point of legal argument at present. The public debate makes it seem as though the conflict was caused by the politics of the Trump administration. But the problem is much more complex. The biggest waves of local administrations declaring sanctuary status have resulted when international conflicts have caused an increase in migration rates (Sullivan, 2009: 572), or when domestic anti-migrant sentiment has acted as a force behind executive orders and appeals. Pham describes how this situation applied after 9/11 (Pham, 2006: 1375), and it may also apply to the time of President Trump's inauguration and the government's remittance of anti-migration decrees (e.g. the immigration ban on several countries with mostly Muslim populations and the termination of the DACA programme). Sullivan and Pham both argue that sanctuary policies represent a local response to the passage and enactment of stricter national or state-wide immigration laws and anti-immigrant ambience. Creating safe spaces for immigrants thus means countering illiberal federal and/

or state politics by setting a local counter-example. In this context, fighting the announced 'crackdown on sanctuary cities' (Trump, 2016) as unconstitutional in court is a step in seeking to uphold the principles of US statehood. The peaks of public interest in sanctuary cities and the activity of sanctuary coalitions are each correlated with illiberal turns in immigration politics. Emerging sanctuary policies were tied to the civil wars in Central America in the 1980s, the aftermath of 9/11, the migrant protests of 2006, and the latest wave of civil protest against the Trump administration (Bauder, 2017, 2016b; Blitzer, 2017; Laman, 2015; Leitner and Strunk, 2014; Lippert, 2005; Mancina, 2016; Varsanyi, 2010). Each wave of protest and social movement is closely tied to conservative lawmaking by the US federal government, implementing a more top-down style of governing immigration which clearly collides with the municipal sanctuary rationales of governance.

In 2009 Sullivan counted almost 70 jurisdictions with sanctuary policies (Sullivan, 2009: 573).[6] The ILRC, tracing the 'rise of sanctuary' by mapping local policies that restricted collaboration with ICE since 2013, notes an incremental prevalence of the phenomenon from 2013 (ILRC, 2018: 10–11). In early 2018 the number of administrations that have implemented sanctuary policies was said to surpass 300 (Griffith and Vaughan, 2017). Thus, the majority of sanctuary policies were passed during the period of a liberal US administration. The Obama administration oversaw a growth in deportations alongside the practical effects of the restrictive immigration laws that had been passed by preceding administrations. The continuous aggravation of immigration law thus affected the increase in sanctuary ordinances, long before the Trump administration took over. Prior to the surge since 2013, the sanctuary city movement is said to have remained 'largely dormant', with social and political unrest largely dissipating after specific high-profile incidents of sanctuary (Sullivan, 2009). Hence, the rise of sanctuary policies started before Trump's inauguration as president and therefore must be tethered to other processes as well.

Scholars of multi-level governance show that in the last decades, 'decision-making at various territorial levels is characterised by the increased participation of non-state actors' (Bache and Flinders, 2004: 2), and therefore horizontal power relations are often being challenged. However, 'in this changing context, the role of the state is being transformed as state actors develop new strategies of coordination, steering and networking that may protect and, in some cases, enhance state autonomy' (Bache and Flinders, 2004: 2). Indeed, the growing entanglement of sub-national governments with immigration law enforcement since the 1990s has led to a pervasive reworking of responsibilities.

Before the Illegal Immigration Reform and Immigrant Responsibility Act (IIRIRA) was passed in 1996, enforcing immigration control was solely the responsibility of federal immigration authorities. The IIRIRA aimed to coerce local police into cooperation with federal authorities. Scholars have additionally linked this development to an overall increase of migration and cut-backs to the welfare state, resulting in the devolution of national immigration law enforcement to sub-national governments, consigning more responsibilities and autonomy to cities. For example, Varsanyi (2008b: 879) argues:

> Devolution [of select immigration powers to local and state governments], combined with border militarization and lax internal enforcement, allows the federal government to appear tough on border enforcement [...] while leaving the messy and costly details of servicing and policing expanding non-citizen populations to state and local governments.

On the one hand, 'states and local governments [have] newfound and increasing powers to discriminate on the basis of alienage or non-citizen status' (Varsanyi, 2008b: 878), and here scholars have shown that sanctuary supporters see this shift as an unconstitutional interference with local autonomy, a means of meddling with local police work (e.g. Varsanyi, 2008a; Houston and Lawrence-Weilmann, 2016; Sullivan, 2009). On the other hand, there is a newfound potential for rescaling membership and belonging at a city level (Varsanyi, 2008b: 882), evoking notions of 'urban citizenship' (Bauder, 2016a, 2016b, 2014; Isin and Turner, 2002; Rodatz, 2014; Rygiel, 2010; Varsanyi, 2008b). Urban citizenship practices draw on the everyday experience of belonging at a local rather than a national scale. The practices, as realised, for instance, by a city ID card for all residents of New York City, circumvent the federal monopoly on membership. However, in contrast to how these practices are often framed, the city ID concept is not a rebellion organised by local governments to subvert federal law (Lebuhn, 2016: 115). Rather, as discussed above, it can be explained through municipal rationales of government. Sanctuary cities can result from problematic relationships between different levels of government that result from the 'overlapping mandates which national and sub-state tiers have for immigration controls' (Spencer, 2018: 2039). The shared responsibilities but differing objectives of immigration control have led to a 'decoupling' of some sub-national governments from these cooperative responsibilities with the federal state (Spencer, 2018: 2039). In this situation, cities assert their right to 'decide for [themselves] how to ensure public safety for all [their] residents' (Houston and Lawrence-Weilmann, 2016: 105).

However beneficial the effects of sanctuary jurisdictions may be, the current federal government deems these practices unlawful. In January 2018 the Trump administration threatened 23 designated sanctuary cities with subpoenas, which could lead to a revoking of public funds, if the cities did not abrogate their policies (Gerstein, 2018). Centre for American Progress sources indicate that several cities have subsequently revoked their status or broken their ordinances by cooperating with immigration enforcement institutions under this pressure (Frederick, 2017). ILRC sources, on the other hand, note an increase of local sanctuary ordinances (ILRC, 2018), illustrating the contested nature of claims around the precise status, significance, and reach of the sanctuary city model.

While the struggle between federal and local authorities continues, the future development of the sanctuary city concept remains a divisive question. On the one hand, the federal government could be successful in its battle against sanctuary cities and drive the phenomenon back to an existence as a social movement without official institutional support. In this case, the hierarchical order of the nation-state would be reaffirmed. On the other hand, an incremental number of cities implementing sanctuary policies could lead to a long-term up-scaling of the phenomenon to become a best practice for communal governing. For example, California has recently implemented sanctuary status as a state. In the future other states could follow California's example. This could lead to a widespread rescaling process, devolving more responsibilities to sub-national units. It could mean a rescaling of political power to cities, counties, and states, making way for an alternative politics of belonging (Darling, 2017). However, negative effects of this growing autonomy must also be anticipated, as there is a risk that such rescaling could lead to more repressive forms, with local states gaining greater powers to control the lives of migrants. For example, a growing number of 'rule of law' cities in the US have pushed through stricter handling of illegalised populations (Esbenshade et al., 2010; Visser and Simpson, this volume). As a result, while a political change towards 'urban citizenship' has been received mostly in a positive way in sanctuary city research (Bauder, 2016a, 2016b; Bauder and Matheis, 2016; Sassen, 2012), there are risks that such 'rescaling' may be mobilised towards less progressive political ends.

Conclusion: policy, practice, and politics

Sanctuary city is a contested term. Its definition is recalcitrant, as a result of topical political controversies. It cannot simply be defined through the sanctuary status that some cities have, and that others lack. To specify the phenomenon and the conflicts around it, I have described three different dimensions in which the incongruent political logics and rationales of governing are outlined. The first dimension is the civic movements that contest the social exclusion of illegalised populations (Isin and Turner, 2002; Varsanyi, 2008b) through protest and advocacy (Lippert, 2005; Leitner and Strunk, 2014), but also through strategic lobbying of local institutions. The second dimension is sanctuary city policy. It can appear on different levels of formality, sometimes as an ordinance, sometimes as policy, in other cases as an informal practice of city workers. In all cases, though, sanctuary city policies serve as a rational tool for governing a mixed-status population (Mancina, 2016). It is not necessarily a policy that ideologically aims to mitigate social injustice, though it can contribute to that (Bauder, 2017). At the same time, and because it is a pragmatic tool of government, it is criticised for depoliticising the social exclusion of illegalised persons and normalising deportations (Bagelman, 2016; Laman, 2015; Houston and Lawrence-Weilmann, 2016; Mancina, 2016). Still, the policy aims to benefit all of a city's population in terms of economic resilience, public health, and safety. While the beneficiary effects of sanctuary policies for city populations have been foregrounded in past studies (Wong, 2017; ILRC, 2018), the impact of the local policy is far wider. Sanctuary city policies challenge the traditional role of cities and sub-national governments, because, through these policies, municipal governments circumvent national immigration law (Houston and Lawrence-Weilmann, 2016; Sullivan, 2009). Thus in the US context, even though the policy might not originally have aimed to challenge federal authority, throughout 2017 the federal government has begun to crack down on sanctuary cities, trying to coerce them to drop the policy. This conflict points to the third dimension of the sanctuary city, which is the relation between federal government and sub-national jurisdictions.

Within each of these three dimensions, the question of what a sanctuary city is would provoke a different answer. The answer from the dimension of the social movement would be that the sanctuary city is a progressive alliance of immigrants' rights advocacy groups, who fight against the expulsion and disenfranchisement of illegalised populations (Walia, 2014). Here the city space is not the limit to the movement, but a current strategic form (Mancina, 2016). This movement aims to extend sanctuary to a wider context (Landolt, 2017; Leitner and Strunk, 2014).

The answer given from the dimension of city policy would be rather pragmatic and would draw on goals of municipal development. It is not a municipal prerogative to bestow rights on illegalised populations, but to invent tools that ensure public safety, and social and economic resilience within the city population (Houston and Lawrence-Weilmann, 2016). The sanctuary city here is a pragmatic governing tool tactically used to provide for the municipal population. The city space is conditional for the policy because sanctuary city policy specifically operates on municipal prerogatives and duties.

The third answer would be determined by city and federal state relations. Given the pending litigation, the answer will be inherently vague, but reflective of urban autonomy and federal hierarchies. The answer is tied to issues of scale, politics, and responsibilities within the force field of neoliberalism. As the current government of the USA has made clear, sanctuary cities overstretch their municipal rights and infringe upon federal immigration law. But court cases suggest that this claim may be invalid (ILRC, 2018: 21, 22).

Although sanctuary cities are a multidimensional phenomenon, they have a common underlying foundation: sanctuary cities are reacting to a perceived change in material circumstances and everyday living conditions. Wherever immigration increases within democratic states, the organisation of everyday life is affected (Nail, 2015). Populations with different legal statuses have different access to public services, whereby formal citizens enjoy the greatest privileges and illegalised migrants remain largely disenfranchised. In this context, sanctuary movements can be interpreted as a part of a struggle for political and social recognition, as 'new claims for inclusion and belonging'. Thus as Isin and Turner (2002: 1) assert:

> What has been happening in the past few decades then is neither revolutionary nor new but has been a recurrent, if not fundamental, aspect of democratic or democratizing polities. What are new are the economic, social and cultural conditions that make possible the articulation of new claims as citizenship rights.

Sanctuary city status is not only a state that can be achieved or lost. It is rather part of a negotiation process within debates of citizenship and belonging, an adaptation to migration on a sub-national level. As Walia and Bauder suggest, the procedural character and the involvement of many different aspects and dimensions are as important to the concept as its policy aspects, its social and political effects and practices (Walia, 2014; Bauder, 2017: 180–181). As a result, what a sanctuary city is, and what it may become, is highly controversial.

Notes

1 Although the term 'illegalised' is rarely used in this context, many scholars, among them Bauder (2013) and Goldring and Landolt (2013), use it to point out the precariousness of the status. This term is sensitive to legal and political processes and stresses such people's vulnerability in institutional treatment by the nation-state.

2 The notion of 'government' in this context refers to the Foucauldian concept: 'the entirety of institutions and practices, through which people are guided, from administration to education' (Foucault, 1996: 118–120).

3 'City air makes you free.'

4 The Charter of Palermo was introduced by Leoluca Orlando, the liberal mayor of Palermo, in 2015. The political impact is yet to be examined and discussed. However, the charter claims that the right to mobility must be an inalienable human right. It furthermore proposes to abolish the residence permit. All in all, the charter represents a very progressive commentary on the European 'refugee crisis'.

5 'We all are the city of Bern.'

6 Without explaining the system that was used to determine how the sanctuary cities were counted.

References

Ahmed, S. (2012) *On Being Included: Racism and Diversity in Institutional Life* (Durham, NC: Duke University Press).

Bache, I., and M. Flinders (2004) 'Themes and issues in multi-level governance', in I. Bache and M. Flinders (eds), *Multi-level Governance* (Oxford: Oxford University Press), 1–14.

Bagelman, J. J. (2016) *Sanctuary City: A Suspended State* (New York: Palgrave Macmillan).

Bauder, H. (2013) 'Nation, migration and critical practice', *Area*, 45:1, 56–63.

Bauder, H. (2014) 'Domicile citizenship, human mobility and territoriality', *Progress in Human Geography*, 38:1, 91–106.

Bauder, H. (2016a) *Migration Borders Freedom* (London: Routledge).

Bauder, H. (2016b) 'Possibilities of urban belonging', *Antipode*, 48:2, 252–271.

Bauder, H. (2017) 'Sanctuary cities: policies and practices in international perspective', *International Migration*, 55:2, 174–187.

Bauder, H., and C. Matheis (eds) (2016) *Migration Policy and Practice: Interventions and Solutions* (New York: Palgrave Macmillan).

Blitzer, J. (2017) 'The Trump era tests the true power of sanctuary cities', *The New Yorker*, 18 April 2017.

Center for Immigration Studies (2017), https://cis.org/ (accessed 8 November 2018).

Charter of Palermo (2015), www.iom.int/sites/default/files/our_work/ICP/IDM/2015_CMC/Session-IIIb/Orlando/PDF-CARTA-DI-PALERMO-Statement.pdf (accessed 8 November 2018).

City of Boston, Boston Trust Act (2014), https://cliniclegal.org/sites/default/files/boston_ma_0.pdf (accessed 8 November 2018).

Civil Case 5:17 – 00404 (2017) 'Complaint for declaratory judgment and injunctive relief', https://static.texastribune.org/media/documents/El_Cenizo_Maverick_County_lawsuit.pdf?_ga=2.3443632.1248728145.151499933 8-1821699501.1514999338 (accessed 8 November 2018).

Darling, J. (2010) 'A city of sanctuary: the relational re-imagining of Sheffield's asylum politics', *Transactions of the Institute of British Geographers, NS* 35, 125–140.

Darling, J. (2017) 'Forced migration and the city: irregularity, informality, and the politics of presence', *Progress in Human Geography*, 41:2, 178–198.

Dean, M. (2010) *Governmentality. Power and Rule in Modern Society* (London: Sage).

Esbenshade, J., B. Wright, P. Cortopassi, A. Reed, and J. Flores (2010) 'The "law and order" foundation of local ordinances. A four-locale study on

Hazleton, PA, Escondido, CA, Farmers Branch, TX and Prince William County, WA', in M. W. Varsanyi (ed.), *Taking Local Control: Immigration Policy Activism in U.S. Cities and States* (Stanford, CA: Stanford University Press), 255–274.

Foucault, M. (1996) *Der Mensch ist ein Erfahrungstier. Gespräch mit Ducio Trombadori* (Frankfurt am Main: Suhrkamp).

Foucault, M. (2015) *Analytik der Macht* (Frankfurt am Main: Suhrkamp).

Frederick, R. (2017) '3 communities that would be devastated by Trump's threat against sanctuary cities', *Center for American Progress*, 25 April 2017, www.americanprogress.org/issues/poverty/news/2017/04/25/431152/ 3-communities-devastated-trumps-threats-sanctuary-cities/ (accessed 8 November 2018).

Gerstein, J. (2018) 'Justice threatens subpoenas in sanctuary cities funding fight', *Politico*, 24 January 2018, www.politico.com/story/2018/01/24/ sanctuary-cities-justice-department-subpoenas-365465 (accessed 8 November 2018).

Gesemann, F., and R. Roth (eds) (2018) *Handbuch lokale Integrationspolitik* (Wiesbaden: Springer Verlag).

Goldring, L., and P. Landolt (eds) (2013) *Producing and Negotiating Noncitizenship: Precarious Legal Status in Canada* (Toronto: University of Toronto Press).

Gomez, A. (2017) 'A multimillion-dollar question: what's a sanctuary city?', *USA Today*, 27 April 2017, https://eu.usatoday.com/story/news/world/2017/04/26/ multi-million-dollar-question-whats-sanctuary-city/100947440/ (accessed 8 November 2018).

Griffith, B., and J. M. Vaughan (2017, updated 2018) 'Maps: sanctuary cities, counties and states', *Center for Immigration Studies (CIS)*, https://cis.org/ Map-Sanctuary-Cities-Counties-and-States (accessed 27 November 2018).

Harvey, D. (2013) *Rebel Cities: From the Right to the City to the Urban Revolution* (London: Verso).

Heuser, H. (2017a) 'Sanctuary cities in der BRD. Widerstand gegen die Abschiebepolitik der Bundesregierung' (*Netzwerk Flüchtlingsforschung*), http://fluechtlingsforschung.net/sanctuary-cities-in-der-brd/ (accessed 8 November 2018).

Heuser, H. (2017b) 'Sanctuary cities sind in Deutschland nicht utopisch. Gespräch über kommunale Spielräume für eine Politik des Willkommens', *Luxemburg. Zeitschrift für Gesellschaftsanalyse und linke Praxis*: 1.

Houston, S., and O. Lawrence-Weilmann (2016) 'The model migrant and multiculturalism: analyzing neoliberal logics in US sanctuary legislation', in H. Bauder and C. Matheis (eds), *Migration Policy and Practice: Interventions and Solutions* (New York: Palgrave Macmillan), 101–126.

Hudson, G., I. Atak, M. Manocchi, and C.-A. Hannan (2017) '(No) Access T.O.: a pilot study on sanctuary city policy in Toronto, Canada', *RCIS Working Paper* 2017/1, www.ryerson.ca/content/dam/rcis/documents/RCIS%20 Working%20Paper%20GHudson%20et%20al.%20finalV2.pdf (accessed 8 November 2018).

ILRC (Immigrant Legal Resource Center) (2018) 'The rise of sanctuary. Getting local officers out of the business of deportations in the Trump era', www.ilrc.org/sites/default/files/resources/rise_of_sanctuary-lg-20180201.pdf (accessed 8 November 2018).

Isin, E., and B. Turner (2002) 'Citizenship studies: an introduction', in E. Isin and B. Turner (eds), *Handbook of Citizenship Studies* (Los Angeles: Sage), 1–10.

Jungfer, E. (2018) 'Selbstverständnis', *Solidarity City*, https://solidarity-city.eu/ de/selbstverstaendnis/ (accessed 8 November 2018).

Krajewski, C. (2015) 'Arm, sexy und immer teurer. Wohnungsmarktentwicklung und gentrification in Berlin', *Standort*, 39:1–2, 77–85.

Kuge, J. (2017) 'Wenn Städte rebellieren. Das Konzept der sanctuary und solidarity cities', *IZ3W*, 362, 12–13.

Laman, J. (2015) 'Revisiting the sanctuary city: citizenship or abjection? Spotlighting the case of Toronto', http://cerlac.info.yorku.ca/files/2016/06/ John-Laman.pdf (accessed 8 November 2018).

Landolt, N. (2017) 'Illegalisiert und trotzdem sicher', *Augustin*, 429:2, 14–17.

Lebuhn, H. (2016) 'Ich bin New York. Bilanz des des kommunalen Personalausweises in New York City', *Luxemburg. Einstürzende Überbauten*, 3, 114–119.

Leitner, H., and C. Strunk (2014) 'Spaces of immigrant advocacy and liberal democratic citizenship', *Annals of the Association of American Geographers*, 104:2, 348–356.

Lippert, R. (2005) 'Rethinking sanctuary: the Canadian context, 1983–2003', *International Migration Review*, 39:2, 381–406.

Mancina, P. (2016) 'In the Spirit of Sanctuary: Sanctuary-City Policy Advocacy and the Production of Sanctuary-Power in San Francisco, California', PhD thesis, Vanderbilt University, https://etd.library.vanderbilt.edu/available/ etd-07112016-193322/unrestricted/Mancina.pdf (accessed 18 November 2018).

Nail, T. (2015) *The Figure of the Migrant* (Stanford, CA: Stanford University Press).

Pham, H. (2006) 'The constitutional right not to cooperate? Local sovereignty and the federal immigration power', *University of Cincinnati Law Review*, 74, 1374–1418.

Redazione Rossa e Nera (2018) 'Urban citizenship mit neoliberalem Nachgeschmack', *AntidotInclu*, 28, 6–7.

Rivera, D. (2018) 'How we are building real trust in Lawrence. Statement by Lawrence Mayor Dan Rivera', *Valley Patriot*, http://valleypatriot.com/lawrence-mayor-rivera-opposes-sanctuary-cities-but-will-not-veto-councils-decision/ (accessed 8 November 2018).

Rodatz, M. (2014) 'Migration ist in dieser Stadt eine Tatsache. Urban politics of citizenship in der neoliberalen Stadt', *sub/urban. Zeitschrift für kritische Stadtforschung*, 2:3, 35–58.

Rygiel, K. (2010) *Globalizing Citizenship* (Vancouver: UBC Press).

Sajed, A. (2012) 'Securitized migrants and postcolonial (in) difference: the politics of activisms among North African migrants in France', in P. Nyers and K. Rygiel (eds), *Citizenship, Migrant Activism and the Politics of Movement* (London: Routledge), 20–29.

Salvi, S. (2006) 'The original list of sanctuary cities, USA', *Ohio Jobs and Justice PAC*, www.ojjpac.org/sanctuary.asp (accessed 8 November 2018).

Sassen, S. (2012) 'Urban capabilities: an essay on our challenges and differences', *Journal of International Affairs*, 56:2, 85–95.

Saunders, D., and W. Roller (2011) *Arrival City. Über alle Grenzen hinweg ziehen Millionen Menschen vom Land in die Städte, von ihnen hängt unsere Zukunft ab* (Munich: Blessing).

Scherr, A., and R. Hofmann (2016) 'Sanctuary cities: Eine Perspektive für deutsche Kommunalpolitik?', *Kritische Justiz*, 49:1, 86–97.

Shoemaker, K. (2012) 'Sanctuary for crime in the early common law', in R. K. Lippert and S. Rehaag (eds), *Sanctuary Practices in International Perspectives: Migration, Citizenship and Social Movements* (Abingdon: Routledge), 15–28.

Solidarity City Network Toronto (2014) http://toronto.nooneisillegal.org/thecityisasweatshop (accessed 8 November 2018).

Spencer, S. (2018) 'Multi-level governance of an intractable policy problem: migrants with irregular status in Europe', *Journal of Ethnic and Migration Studies*, 44:12, 2034–2052, DOI: 10.1080/1369183X.2017.1341708.

State of California Senate Bill No. 54, Chapter 495 (2017), https://leginfo.legislature.ca.gov/faces/billNavClient.xhtml?bill_id=201720180SB54 (accessed 8 November 2018).

Sullivan, L. (2009) 'Enforcing the non-enforcement: countering the threat posed to sanctuary laws by the inclusion of immigration records in the national Crime Information Center database', *California Law Review*, 96, 567–600.

Trump, D. (2016) 'Donald Trump's contract with the American voter', https://assets.donaldjtrump.com/_landings/contract/O-TRU-10231 6-Contractv02.pdf (accessed 8 November 2018).

Varsanyi, M. W. (2008a) 'Immigration policing through the backdoor: city ordinances, the "right to the city," and the exclusion of undocumented day laborers', *Urban Geography*, 29:1, 29–52.

Varsanyi, M. W. (2008b) 'Rescaling the "alien," rescaling personhood: neoliberalism, immigration and the state', *Annals of the Association of American
   Geographers*, 98:4, 877–896.

Varsanyi, M. W. (ed.) (2010) *Taking Local Control: Immigration Policy Activism
   in U.S. Cities and States* (Stanford, CA: Stanford University Press).

Walia, H. (2014) 'Sanctuary city from below: dismantling the city of Vancouver', *Mainlander*, 2 June 2014, http://themainlander.com/2014/06/02/
   sanctuary-city-from-below-dismantling-the-city-of-vancouver/ (accessed
   8 November 2018).

Wir alle sind Bern', *Manifest*, https://wirallesindbern.ch/manifest/ (accessed
   8 November 2018).

Wong, T. K. (2017) 'The effects of sanctuary policies on crime and the economy',
   Center for American Progress, 26 January 2017, https://americanprogress.org/
   issues/immigration/reports/2017/01/26/297366/the-effects-of-sanctuary-
   policies-on-crime-and-the-economy/ (accessed 8 November 2018).

3

City of hope, city of fear: sanctuary and security in Toronto, Canada

Graham Hudson

Canadian cities have joined what seems to be a global sanctuary city movement (Bauder, 2017; Caminero-Santangelo, 2012; Loga et al., 2012; Millner, 2012). Toronto was the first city to do so in February 2013, followed shortly thereafter by Hamilton (2014), Vancouver (2016), Montreal (2017), London (2017), and the town of Ajax (2017). Distinct in many ways, each city shares with their American counterparts faith in the transformative potential of formal policies, procedures, and directives – what I shall hereafter refer to loosely as 'law' (Houston and Lawrence-Weilmann, 2016; de Graauw, 2014; Walker and Leitner, 2011; Varsanyi, 2010; Ridgley, 2008). Among the hallmarks of legal approaches are directives to city staff and volunteers not to 1) inquire into immigration status when providing a selection of services, 2) deny non-status residents access to services to which they are entitled, and 3) share personal or identifying information with federal authorities, unless required to do so by federal or provincial law.

But the constitutive function of a meaningful sanctuary city movement is not to change the practices of city officials – it is to unsettle conventional understandings of citizenship, rights, and belonging. At the very least, sanctuary city policies raise questions about the authority of municipal governments to pass laws that conflict with and, indeed, purposefully impede federal laws. But sanctuary can (and should) mean more than how municipal governments administer services. Using a geographical lens, Harald Bauder suggests that sanctuary cities offer a 'scale of formal belonging' which can 'supersede regional and national scales', so that relations that occur in a bounded social and physical space eventually produce new sociopolitical identities (Bauder, 2016). Most radically, sanctuary cities can support wholly non- or even anti-state programmes that urge us to reject the concepts and assumptions underpinning the state system and/or centralised government (Squire and Bagelman, 2012; Nail et al., 2010; Villazor, 2010; Isin, 2007; Varsanyi, 2006).

Praising the relative virtues of the city, scholars have not always appreciated how questions about the governance of migration are inextricably bound up with questions about the governance of security; nor do they fully appreciate that the tendency of cities to govern through broad discretionary powers provides fertile ground for the projection of exclusionary power, regardless of what formal laws may state. As a wave of sanctuary city policies moves across Canada, there is mounting evidence that local authorities frequently participate in the enforcement of immigration laws in the contexts of policing, education, employment, shelters, and hospitals (Hudson et al., 2017; NOII, 2015, P. Villegas, 2015; F. Villegas, 2013). These practices draw from broader ideological and political discourses related to the securitisation and criminalisation of migration that cast non-status migrants as risks to the national and economic security of the state (Hudson, 2018; Atak et al., 2018). The vibrancy of urban securitisation (Valverde, 2015, 2008; Lippert and Walby, 2013) suggests the presence of a diffuse field of security that cuts across scales, undermining even the most modest objectives of sanctuary.

The purpose of this chapter is to appraise the philosophy and practice of Access T.O. ('Access to City Services for Undocumented Toronto-nians', Toronto's city sanctuary policy established in 2013) within the context of the securitisation of migration in Canada, while reflecting on the utility of the concept of scale towards that end. In this way, this chapter complements the chapter by Idil Atak in this volume, while suggesting that the interplay of sanctuary and security is a common dynamic in cities across the world. I argue that security has undermined sanctuary in two ways. First, local police and other law enforcement agencies are integrated in a field of security professionals, which provides federal authorities with expanding influence at the local level; and second, the underlying assumptions and programmes built into security logic have negatively influenced conceptions of deservingness among front-line city staff. One way of interpreting this uneven dynamic is to say that certain qualities of local governance, including the existence of broad discretion and minimal rule-of-law constraints, make cities especially hospitable to the securitisation of migration.

The chapter begins with an overview of Access T.O., in which I define formalist approaches to sanctuary and explore their inherent limits. Next, I outline the role of scale in conceptualising the possibilities of sanctuary. While a valuable heuristic device, I argue that the concept of scale should be used cautiously and with an eye to how various forms of power inimical to sanctuary city values 'shift' across scales rather easily. Next, I exemplify this through the securitisation of migration in Canada, highlighting the existence of a field of security professionals that transcends formal institutional and jurisdictional boundaries. Finally, I use the case of Toronto to reflect on the possible role that sanctuary city policies can have in countering the local influence of security professionals and logics more generally.

Access T.O.: an overview

There are many varieties of sanctuary across different jurisdictions and historical contexts. Although each city is different, all sanctuary cities in North America have adopted a formalist model, whereby city councils oblige city staff to comply with prescribed policies, procedures, and practices (Bauder, 2017). Insofar as these rules are applicable in concrete factual scenarios, are officially binding, and are sourced in the statutory (or constitutional) authority of the city council, I refer to them as law. Access T.O. is a good example, consisting of a body of directives that oblige city staff and volunteers to provide access to most municipal services without regard to immigration status. City staff are also not to collect information relating to status and, if such information is collected for a legitimate purpose, they are not to share it with federal authorities unless required to do so by federal law or policy (City of Toronto, 2013). The council has also mandated compulsory training and education of relevant staff and volunteers, and has directed relevant city divisions, agencies, and corporations (including directors, managers, and policy personnel) to both comply with and implement Access T.O. While the substance of these laws is laudable, the sheer number of city staff and volunteers (approximately

60,000), the geographical size of the city (632 sq km), and the number of applicable service areas (21) render them weaker the further out one goes. Among the 21 divisions, agencies, and corporations responsible for implementing Access T.O. are Toronto Public Health, Shelters, Support and Housing, Toronto Public Libraries, Children's Services, emergency response teams, and Employment and Social Services. Each provides unique services across all of the administrative sectors of the city. There is only one person responsible for assessing the implementation of Access T.O. within each service area, and this role is only a fraction of that person's overall responsibilities. Once a year, representatives from each service area meet for a few hours to share updates, best practices, and innovations (Hudson et al., 2017). Otherwise, personnel do not interact across service areas, even if they work in the same neighbourhood (Hudson et al., 2017).

In 2017 a research team of which I am part published the results of a pilot socio-legal study on the implementation of Access T.O. (Hudson et al., 2017; see also Atak in this volume). The project explored whether formal sanctuary laws have been internalised and implemented within the city's varied institutions. We found that requisite divisions or agencies have not absorbed formal norms, which is to say that there was little evidence that the internal operations of service areas have been changed, much less consciously so. This complemented previous findings that city staff were not consistently complying with Access T.O. (FCJ Refugee Centre, 2015). These failings are attributable to a combination of factors, including the absence of funding for implementation, insufficient training of staff and volunteers, and the lack of coordination and communication across service areas.

For the purposes of this chapter, I will focus on arguably the largest factor: discretionary power. The whole point of formalist models of sanctuary is to remove discretion over the provision of services to non-status migrants, or at least ensure that discretion is exercised consistently with the principles and purposes of sanctuary norms. Audits of city staff indicate that discretion is typically exercised to exclude non-status migrants on the basis of negative and unfair conceptions of deservingness (FCJ Refugee Centre, 2015). The misuse of discretion has been observed (and theorised) in other areas, including public education, where exclusion is rationalised by reference to narratives of risk, danger, and undeservingness (F. Villegas, 2013;

Landolt and Goldring, 2015). Underlying these narratives are logics
related to security and neoliberalism, which together construct irregular
migrants as disentitled from accessing social services and even rights
(Atak et al., 2017; Düvell, 2011).

Sanctuary and scale

There are many ways of theorising sanctuary. For some, the sanctuary
city movement is primarily concerned with facilitating access to
municipal services and in this way is delimited by jurisdictional
technicalities and constitutional constraints. Higher ambitions related
to progressive change in federal law or an expanding role for the city
in the governance of migration are laudable, but sanctuary is practically
limited to the provision of 'local bureaucratic membership' (de Graauw,
2014). For others, sanctuary cities are sites within which established
conceptions of political membership and rights can be shifted, enabling
local authorities (state and non-state) to play a role in the governance
of migration, quite aside from what formal constitutional laws say.
Using the geographical concept of scale, Bauder argues that the city
can be viewed as a 'scale of formal belonging' which can 'supersede
regional and national scales', in part by virtue of the fact of inhabitance
and in part by virtue of how (self-awareness of) subsequent social
interactions can produce influential sociopolitical identities capable
of shifting political structures and conceptual frameworks (Bauder,
2016). It is not immediately clear what the relative role of the municipal
government is in such a view, to what extent sanctuary is a local rather
than an interconnected transnational or global phenomenon, or how
global cities negotiate the incompatible pressures exerted by local,
national, and global authorities.

For others still, the sanctuary city movement is less about the
municipal government than about the autonomy of non-state political
and normative communities that seek greater authority vis-à-vis the
state in all of its guises (Squire and Darling, 2013; Squire and Bagelman,
2012; Squire, 2011; Nail et al., 2010; Isin, 2007; Varsanyi, 2006). And
then there are those who caution against the illusion that one can
analyse sovereignty and law as concerned with 'the relationship between
state and society', as though the two can be disentangled (Bigo, 2002:
68). Documenting the sanctuary city movement in Ontario well before

Toronto adopted Access T.O., Randy K. Lippert showed that churches and other non-state actors deployed a host of governmental logics in exercising sovereign power over migrants, describing this practice as 'sovereignty from below' (Lippert, 2006).

Different as they are, all of these perspectives see the city as a dynamic social space within which a plurality of normative orders coexist and compete with each other (McDonald, 1997). The sheer scale and scope of this legal or normative pluralism requires one to simplify the field of study and to use caution in developing a theory of what sanctuary *is*. The concept of scale is a useful tool in this respect since it allows us to focus on a sub-set of events, people, and relationships as they exist within a spatial context, and to (momentarily) ignore that which occurs beyond. Scalar thought also allows us to slow down the dynamics of normative interaction within a given field, in the way that maps present still-images of terrain that tend not to represent the passage of time, that is, change (Valverde, 2015).

But scale has well-documented theoretical and political limitations. Because legal maps are static representations with outer limits, they do not present a full picture of how various forms of power expand, contract, enter, and depart jurisdictional borders. In his pioneering work on legal maps, Boaventura de Sousa Santos showed that scales and maps are inherently political and ideological artefacts. States use maps to smooth out competition between normative communities, creating and granting legal sub-systems exclusive authority to govern on one scale, for example local, provincial, national (Santos, 1987). But these maps predetermine critical questions about the nature and source of authority by distorting or altogether omitting reference to alternative arrangements that conflict with the unrepresented interests and identities of the cartographer.

Because there are various, contesting authorities within any given scale, it follows that there can be multiple maps within a given scale, each of which privileges certain views of rightful authority. Valverde extends this insight, arguing that scale is deficient insofar as it is static, omitting reference to time and, therefore, the dynamics of power relations – how these grow and change (Valverde, 2015, 2009, 2008). The concept of 'scale shifting' helps remedy this problem, guiding the analysis of how fields of practices, understandings, relations, and institutions (or we might call these assemblages) operate across scales (Landolt and Goldring, 2015, 2013; Valverde, 2009; Isin, 2007). I would add, and will later argue, that scale is also not especially apt at uncovering the ways in which power moves across jurisdictional boundaries that exist within the confines of, say, the local scale. For the moment, the value of scale-shifting is that it highlights that the movement of various kinds of power is not only subtle (if not invisible) – it can be purposeful. Using a broad conception of security, Valverde argues that the governing logics and practices of local governments differ in kind from those of the nation-state along the parameter of discretionary power exercised in the service of public welfare (among others) (Valverde, 2015, 2009). That is to say that municipalities are not simply localised instantiations of the nation-state, but employ distinctive modalities of political and legal authority. This can be most useful to federal authorities, which can conscript local government to perform actions that would be relatively difficult to perform at the national scale.

The relative absence of constitutional rights and the rule of law at the local scale is of interest in this regard. Cities deploy broad discretionary powers regarding the finest details of life in relative autonomy from judicial or constitutional review, so much so that urban regulation may be regarded to be 'antithetical to rights claims' (Blomley, 2013: 10) and, I would add, the rule of law. However, as scholars of migration, we are well placed to note that constitutional rights and the rule of law are not a reliable marker of the differences between the local and national scales when non-citizens are concerned, and nor for that matter is discretion. Courts in Canada have a long history of minimising if not ignoring the human rights consequences of detention and deportation. The Supreme Court of Canada has steadily ruled that the Charter of Rights and Freedoms does not apply to immigration proceedings, unless they are 'analogous to criminal proceedings' or otherwise lead to an 'irreparable' harm, such as torture, death, or cruel and inhumane punishment (*Dehghani* v. *Canada*, 1993; *Suresh* v. *Canada*, 2002; *B010* v. *Canada*, 2015). Courts in the United States similarly withhold rights to due process unless an immigration measure, practice, or consequences is criminal in nature (Stumpf, 2013; *Padilla* v. *Kentucky*, 2010).

With broad discretion being the norm in matters of migration and security, national governments have practical incentives to shift scales.

The most apparent benefit is that local authorities are geographically and administratively better positioned to collect information regarding non-status migrants. It is no surprise then to see formal information-sharing among national, provincial/state, and municipal authorities (West Coast LEAF, 2015; Hannan and Bauder, 2015; Hudson, 2011; Moens, 2011). Many of these connections inhere among law enforcement agencies, evidencing what Didier Bigo calls a 'field of the security professionals' – a transnational social space that stretches across jurisdictional and institutional boundaries and hosts interactions among professionals with shared identities, understandings, and roles in the 'management of fear and unease' (Bigo, 2002: 65, 74–75). But it is not just security professionals we have to worry about. Local actors in schools, hospitals, shelters, and other institutions participate in security work, drawing on common ideological and normative sources that support illusory boundaries between internal/external, us/them, and illegal/deserving (F. Villegas, 2013; Marsden, 2012; Bloch and Chimienti, 2011). Similar dynamics have been documented in the United States (Mancina, 2016, 2012; Gardner II, 2014).

All of this is to say that scale is a useful heuristic device, but it obscures the ways in which political authority expands, contracts, and moves across jurisdictional and institutional boundaries. One cannot speak of sanctuary cities as a scale of belonging without also speaking of securitised cities as a scale of exclusion. These two dynamics coexist and compete within and across scales, suggesting that faith in cities as an antidote to the obstinacy of national governments should be tempered with a dose of scepticism.

Security and scale-shifting

As elsewhere, sanctuary city policies in Canada have emerged in the context of the harsh national and international treatment of migrants, and asylum seekers in particular (Atak et al., 2018; Dauvergne, 2008, 2016; Squire and Bagelman, 2012). Between 2010 and 2013 the Canadian federal government passed three laws that gutted the Refugee Status Determination (RSD) system and made it easier to strip permanent resident status from persons involved in even relatively minor criminal offences. The government linked the amendments to the

2009 and 2010 arrival of two boats carrying Tamil asylum seekers off the west coast of Canada. It alleged that at least one-third of the passengers aboard were 'suspected human smugglers and terrorists' working to reconstitute the Liberation Tigers of Tamil Eelam's 'base of operations overseas in order to renew resistance to the Government of Sri Lanka' (The Canadian Record, 2010). All of the passengers were detained, and concerted efforts were made to exclude them from claiming refugee status, including by intervening in RSD hearings (Hudson, 2018).

Links between security and irregular migration have been a constant theme in Canada (Robinson, 1983), but the period between 2010 and 2013 was especially toxic (Krishnamurti, 2013; Kaushal and Dauvergne, 2011). Irregular migrants were cast as 1) dangerous, deceitful, threatening, and underserving, and 2) an economic drain – a combination that supports the imposition of laws that allow for the social and legal exclusion of persons who can then be subject to economic exploitation (Huysmans and Squire, 2015; Huysmans, 2000; Bigo and Tsoukala, 2008). After at first sounding the alarm of terrorism, politicians quickly shifted discourses, describing the passengers en masse as 'bogus refugees' and 'queue jumpers' seeking to exploit the generosity of the Canadian RSD system (Canada, 2010). In presenting the 2012 refugee reform for parliamentary debate, the then immigration minister argued that Canada's asylum system was 'broken', inefficient, costly, and subject to 'abuse', and that the proposed amendments

> would make Canada's refugee determination process faster and fairer and would result in faster protection for those who legitimately need refugee protection. It would also, and this is the important aspect of it, ensure faster removal of those whose claims are withdrawn, those claims that are bogus and those claims that have been rejected. (Dykstra, 2012)

The reforms sharply reduced and in some cases extinguished basic procedural rights. Measures included broadened criteria of inadmissibility, the denial of the right to appeal against certain classes of inadmissibility determinations, expedited refugee claim hearings (when one was entitled to them), and restricted access to pre-removal risk assessments designed to guard against deportation to persecution as well as torture or similar abuses. Legislation also introduced a host of obstacles to the acquisition of permanent residency, including unreasonably broad criteria of exclusion on grounds of security and criminality and the denial to such persons of access to humanitarian and compassionate considerations (Atak et al., 2018). In short, pathways to status were narrowed and rights to procedural fairness were dismantled.

These illiberal exclusionary practices contrast with parallel efforts to increase economically beneficial temporary foreign work. In 2011 parliament enacted the 'cumulative duration' or 'four-and-four' rule, which was aimed at limiting the access of temporary foreign workers to permanent resident status. The rule limited temporary foreign workers to four-year contracts. Once the contract expired, workers had to leave Canada for four years or apply for student or visitor status (Nakache and Dixon-Perera, 2015).

These laws have had a number of direct consequences on sanctuary cities. First, it is reasonable to suppose that encouraging temporary migration while denying (fair) access to status has increased the numbers of non-status and precarious status migrants (Nakache and Dixon-Perera, 2015). While there is little data on the numbers or demographics of non-status migrants in Canada (Hudson et al., 2017), a recent study found that the use of emergency healthcare by uninsured persons who are highly likely to be non-status migrants was largest in areas with high concentrations of temporary foreign workers (Hynie et al., 2016). Second, non-status and precarious status migrants have few incentives to apply for permanent residency in the current system, given its palpable unfairness. Recent empirical research shows that they are also committed to finding ways of securing permanent residency – even at great personal cost (Nakache and Dixon-Perera, 2015). The most reliable pathway to status is to wait for the opportune moment to file a humanitarian and compassionate (H&C) grounds application, where the Minister of Immigration, Refugees and Citizenship Canada (IRCC) may issue a discretionary decision to grant status (Atak et al., 2017). Length of residency in Canada, family, and community ties all increase the chances of securing a favourable H&C decision, suggesting a clear incentive to live and work without status for extended periods of time.

These consequences exemplify the 'legal construction' of irregularity, where selectively enforced exclusionary laws combine with a mixture of social, economic, and political 'draw' factors to create conditions of foreseeable precariousness, subjecting migrants to exploitation and abuse (Düvell, 2011; Dauvergne, 2008). In this context, the federal government absolves itself of responsibility through avoidance and denial mechanisms, failing to produce a single official policy or statement on the rights of non-status residents in Canada. At the same time, security agencies have escalated their operations. The Canada Border Services Agency (CBSA) is chiefly responsible for border control, assuming a wide range of criminal law enforcement powers. Created in 2005, the CBSA reports, not to the Minister of IRCC, but to the Minister of Public Safety Canada (PSC), who oversees most of Canada's criminal and national security operations. This includes the Royal Canadian Mounted Police (RCMP), Corrections Canada, and the Canadian Security Intelligence Service (CSIS).

As a law enforcement agency, the CBSA employs technologies and practices similar to those used by police services through its Criminal Investigations Division (CBSA, 2009). Turning its gaze inward, the CBSA partners with the RCMP, provincial police, and local police through 'joint force operations' which run through local settings, such as cities and townships. Cooperation is mandated in Canada's official national security policy, which is premised on the ideal of an 'integrated security system' (Canada, 2004). The passage of Bills C-44 and C-51 in 2015 also mandated the sharing of security-based information among federal institutions, with special focus on those operating out of PSC (Forcese and Roach, 2015). Finally, the CBSA has authority to partner with international agencies, which it uses to gather information, facilitate deportations, and physically obstruct access to Canadian territory (CBSA, 2005). It works regularly with the United States in this respect (Moens, 2011). Bigo's concept of a field of security professionals is apt here, especially when placed in the context of legislative and policy structures for an integrated security system replete with cross-institutional and inter-jurisdictional information sharing. Being placed in PSC has deepened shared identities and interests between the CBSA, the RCMP and, to a lesser extent, CSIS. The CBSA is subject to similar political influences and policy priorities, and has a corresponding measure of influence over policy priorities and the legislative process. Shared functions and competition for resources among PSC agencies provides incentives for the CBSA to aggressively expand and justify its operations.

One formal, institutional manifestation of the field of security professionals are Integrated National Security Enforcement Teams (INSETs), which are composed of national agencies (e.g. CBSA, CSIS, RCMP) as well as provincial and local police. There are INSET offices in all major Canadian cities, including the sanctuary cities of Toronto, Montreal, and Vancouver. One of the objectives of INSETs is to enhance enforcement capacities, including criminal laws, immigration laws, and the gamut of security legislation. Operationally, it turns out that INSETs are concerned with a relatively small number of high-level targets or risks, the collection, analysis and dissemination of security intelligence, and preventing/investigating terrorist activities. These operations are more attuned to counter-terrorism and conventional national security risks than securing the border or the enforcement of immigration and refugee law. Still, they are one of the ways in which local police forces and the CBSA have adopted shared identities and interests, and the belief among local police is that they have a role in the management of (global) risks to the state. A disproportionate focus on racialised and migrant communities in Canadian national security has likely solidified a broader sense of authority to collect and share information on the non-status community when the opportunity arises (Dhamoon and Abu-Laban, 2009).

Another formal channel of cooperation is the Canadian Police Information Centre (CPIC), which is a central database that contains information 'about crimes and criminals' (CPIC, 2018). Managed by the RCMP, it is apparently 'the only national information-sharing system that links criminal justice and law enforcement partners across Canada and internationally' (CPIC, 2018). Since the CPIC must concern criminals, the CBSA's involvement is notionally limited by its interest in non-citizens engaged in criminal activity or who are subject to a federal arrest warrant. Simply being non-status is not a valid condition for personal data to be stored here.

A less formal channel of cooperation is the CBSA's Warrant Response Centre, where a law enforcement officer can check whether a particular person has a warrant issued against them. According to an Access to Information request filed by No One Is Illegal – Toronto, 4,392 out of 10,700 calls made between 4 November 2014 and 28 June 2015 were made from the Greater Toronto Area (NOII, 2015: 21). The Toronto Police Service (TPS) made 75 per cent (3,278) of those calls, which is more than the RCMP (1,197), and greater 'than the police services of Montreal, Quebec City, Ottawa, Calgary, Edmonton, and Vancouver combined (2,729)' (NOII, 2015: 21). What is more, 'status checks' were the most common reasons for calls – 83.35 per cent in the case of the TPS as against a national average of 72 per cent (NOII, 2015: 22). To be clear, CBSA call centre procedures define status check as, among other things, when 'law enforcement officers [...] call to verify the immigration status of a subject because they have a suspicion a subject may not have legal status in Canada and therefore may be of interest to CBSA' or when they call 'to confirm the status of a subject they have in custody' (NOII, 2015: 22).

There is no statutory basis for this practice. The Police Services Act and regulations allow for, but do not require, the sharing of information with federal authorities if this is necessary to facilitate an investigation. The existence of a federal arrest warrant would fall into that category, but that is what the CPIC is for. The TPS use the Warrant Response Centre to check status, and so obviously do not have any basis for suspecting that a person they have encountered has an outstanding warrant issued against them. It is probable that race, ethnicity, or language are associated with non-citizenship and that racial profiling is common (NOII, 2015). Even if there is a warrant issued, officers have discretion whether or not to share information. The protection of victims and witnesses, and the relatively more important role of investigating crime rather than immigration violations, should weigh against (systematic) sharing of information.

The TPS has also contravened its own policies. In 2006 the TPS adopted an 'Access Without Fear' or a 'don't ask' policy. According to this policy, any person may request and will receive police response and police services without being asked about their immigration status. Police officers are trained not to ask victims and witnesses of crime for their immigration status, unless there are '*bona fide*' reasons to do so (City of Toronto, 2015). In 2007 a new TPS policy, entitled 'Victims and Witnesses without Legal Status', clarified the concept of '*bona fide* reasons', allowing investigations where the circumstances make it clear that it is essential to public or officer safety and security to ascertain the immigration status of a victim or witness (Standards of Conduct, Section 1.35). This policy states that police training also takes into account the many dynamics that impact a domestic situation, such as the immigration/legal status of the parties involved, the vulnerabilities of complainants, and the mechanisms of control and influence.

One cannot understand the relationship between the TPS and the CBSA without considering the role of 'crimmigration': a process in which the functions of criminal law and immigration law blur even while they retain their distinct forms (Stumpf, 2006; Hudson, 2018). Immigration law and criminal law are matters within the exclusive constitutional jurisdiction of the federal government. Provinces and cities have no constitutional role whatsoever in the enforcement of immigration law. However, they do have authority over the enforcement of criminal law, including the organisation and operation of local/provincial policing. Provinces also administer criminal courts and correctional institutions for those convicted of summary offences (less serious crimes). Conceiving of irregular migration as quasi-criminal – or of policing as preventive rather than responsive (Zedner, 2005; McCulloch and Pickering, 2009) – provides the institutional, ideological, and jurisdictional basis for cooperation between the CBSA and police forces in contexts that are formally outside the purview of criminal law. Put another way, formal differences between criminal law and immigration law matter less than the fact that the TPS and the CBSA share a common identity as law enforcement agencies responsible for protecting the state and its citizen against perceived dangers. This common identity and the practices it produces blur the functions of criminal law and immigration law at least as much as political discourses and legislative provisions.

Returning to the concept of scale, one could conceive of this dynamic using the spatial metaphor of a top-down projection of federal power; however, this would miss an important nuance: power is also moving side-to-side (criminal-to-immigration) and from below, as it were. We have already surveyed the ways in which security and neoliberal logics combine to inform conceptions of deservingness among city staff and volunteers. These logics follow trajectories that spiral around and through formal state agencies and the field of security professionals, but also throughout society. It is not as though city staff are security professionals, but they are able to draw from the same ideological and normative sources and participate in security work. I hasten to add that so too do non-state actors. Beyond the scope of this chapter, it should at least be noted that employers leverage fear of deportation to maintain relations of exploitation (Hannan and Bauder, 2015). Fear of being reported also helps explain why non-status women and children remain in abusive homes (P. Villegas, 2015; West Coast LEAF, 2015).

Revisiting Access T.O.: what role for sanctuary?

The above discussion raises the question: what can we reasonably expect from sanctuary city policies? The answer to this question depends on what we take the goals of the policy to be. The most obvious goal is to ensure that non-status and precarious status migrants have access to municipal services without fear of being identified, detained, and deported by federal authorities. As Els de Graauw (2014) terms it, sanctuary policies are concerned only with 'local bureaucratic membership' and do not seek to push against the constitutional and material constraints faced by cities.

This conception may be pragmatic, but it is normatively unsatisfying; it invites us to accept the status quo, and relegate the city to passively offering access to purely municipal services rather than finding ways of breaking through jurisdictional constraints. Among the most serious limitations of a purely bureaucratic conception of sanctuary is that it is concerned with only the most rudimentary of social services to which non-status migrants should have access. In Canada, provinces and not cities determine eligibility for the most significant social services, including social assistance, housing, many labour rights, healthcare, and education. Of these services, only education is formally accessible to non-status migrants under provincial law, with the exception of post-secondary education.

A more pluralist and progressive conception of sanctuary envisions a role for cities in challenging broader provincial/federal regulatory frameworks and, wherever possible, pushing the boundaries of its jurisdiction to envelop a greater range of legal and political relationships. This requires sustained dialogue with regional and federal governments about the policy and human rights consequences of living without status. To its credit, Toronto has called on the provincial and federal government to 'review' and 'reconsider' policies relating to non-status migrants, to provide additional funding for the implementation of Access T.O., and to enter dialogue with the city. In January 2017

Mayor John Tory motioned the city council to urge a newly elected federal government to 'continue an immigration and refugee policy based on the values of inclusion, acceptance and non-discrimination, and that the position of Council be forwarded as a letter to the Government of Canada and Federal Opposition parties to that end' (City of Toronto, 2017c). In April 2017 the city reaffirmed its commitment to non-status migrants and requested the provincial and federal governments to provide more funding to alleviate 'the increased pressure on the shelter system, the Toronto Newcomer Office and social programming systems from refugee and refugee claimants' (City of Toronto, 2017b).

As of the time of writing, there has been no meaningful dialogue with the government about the rights of non-status migrants, and little indication that the city has pressed the issue. However, recent changes to the Access T.O. implementation strategy suggest an opportunity for change. In 2017 primary responsibility for implementing Access T.O. was placed in the Toronto Newcomer Office (TNO). The TNO is a unique agency, being the only one in the country that works in partnership with the IRCC. In fact, until recently the TNO was fully funded by the federal government, which co-implements the 2013 Toronto Newcomer Strategy. The objective of the strategy is to ensure that 'all newcomers reach their full potential to thrive and contribute to their local neighbourhood, community and city' (City of Toronto, 2016). The TNO has earned a reputation for developing socially responsive policies and establishing strong community networks. Since assuming leadership over Access T.O., the TNO has urged the city council to 'continue to advocate' for reform at the federal and provincial levels and to 'come to a clear understanding of … how these incongruent policies will be handled at the municipal level in the interim' (City of Toronto, 2017d).

While cooperation with the IRCC is desirable in many ways, security is another matter. The bifurcation of immigration law into policy/administration (IRCC) and enforcement (CBSA) requires two very distinct strategies regarding the city's relationship to the federal government. The creeping influence of the CBSA at the local scale is inimical to sanctuary city values. In this context, a good dose of conflict over jurisdiction may be just what is called for. Given limitations of space, I will consider one area where greater resistance would be welcome:

laws and policies governing the sharing of information between the city and the CBSA.

As noted, Access T.O. expressly directs city staff and volunteers not to share information concerning non-status migrants with federal authorities. It also directs staff and volunteers to not inquire about status, but there are times when this is necessary. For example, the Toronto District School Board (TDSB) is required to keep records for all its students, which includes information about citizenship or status. The city does not seem to consider this problematic, as information is protected. All forms containing information about non-status students are coded 'status pending', and placed along with records of students who are in the process of acquiring status (Hudson et al., 2017). There is no evidence to suggest that the TDSB has shared personal information with the CBSA.

The collection of data is a recurring issue in the context of healthcare, where access to demographic data (age, gender, country of origin, sexual orientation, length of residence without status) could be used to sharpen our understanding the social determinants of health (Access Alliance, 2017; Hudson et al., 2017). Data would also be useful for assessing what services non-status persons need/use, what barriers they face, and how this differs across demographic sub-groups. Until now, public and academic research has omitted non-status migrants as a category of persons with distinct experiences and needs. Finally, the issue of data collection arises in discussions about the use of municipal ID cards, which are issued in New York, New Haven, San Francisco, and elsewhere (de Graauw, 2014). The city of Toronto has flatly rejected the use of such cards in part because of concerns that it could not control personal information (City of Toronto, 2014b).

These concerns are warranted. The city council included within Access T.O. the caveat that the city may share information if 'specifically required by either Provincial or Federal legislation, policies or agreements' (City of Toronto, 2014a). While the adverb 'specifically' suggests that the federal or provincial government must clearly and expressly declare intentions that are incompatible with Access T.O., reference to 'policy' is too broad and can by definition include directives and mandates that emanate from the executive branch and not Parliament. Even a cursory reading of border enforcement manuals and policies highlights a fundamental incompatibility between Access T.O. and the policies and practices of the CBSA. We have already seen that the TPS has used precisely this reasoning in justifying its recalcitrance. A clearer sense of when conflicts between Access T.O. and federal law require the sharing of information would be welcome, which is not to settle on the contentious issue of whether collecting data is necessary.

Legal doctrine would play an important role in strengthening municipal control over information. Under section 32 of the province's Municipal Freedom of Information and Protection of Privacy Act (MFIPPA), the city cannot disclose personal information to any authority except under limited circumstances. Two of these are directly relevant to the enforcement of the immigration law:

1   If disclosure is to an institution or a law enforcement agency in Canada, to aid an investigation undertaken with a view to a law enforcement proceeding or from which a law enforcement proceeding is likely to result;
2   For the purpose of complying with an Act of the Legislature or an Act of Parliament, an agreement or arrangement under such an Act or a treaty.

With respect to law enforcement cooperation, city staff must not disclose information without a formal written request from a law enforcement body that has first been vetted by Corporate Information Management Services. When information exchanges are formal, they will occur pursuant to an internal process with oversight, and not at the discretion of front-line staff. With respect to the second, statutory requirement, the city must disclose personal information to a government agency where the law in question requires disclosure, upon a written request from that agency. Examples include Canada Revenue Agency for tax audit purposes, and the Ministry of Labour for health and safety purposes (City of Toronto, 2014b). This law could be clarified to expressly indicate that compliance with immigration law is not a statutory condition of information sharing, but that law enforcement cooperation could be if in the context of an ongoing investigation concerning a specified individual (e.g., a federal arrest warrant).

More research is required into how section 32 of the MFIPPA is to be interpreted and applied in the context of Access T.O., including informal routes that bypass the oversight mechanisms already in place.

The foregoing suggests that information collected by the city may not be legally shared with federal immigration authorities unless there is an active investigation against a specified individual. The CBSA cannot access information kept by the city so that it can embark on a 'fishing expedition' for non-status Torontonians; it would have to already have an individual's name and some evidentiary basis for supposing that he or she is a resident in Toronto.

The city itself has done virtually nothing to press these legal issues, which is surprising given its adoption of a formalist model of sanctuary; the result has been unworkable uncertainty concerning the scope of its control over identifying information or more broadly its jurisdiction to even pursue a sanctuary city mandate. Advocates have taken up some of this slack. In a 2008 report, the Immigration Legal Committee (ILC) examined the juridical relationship between local police and the CBSA. It related these relationships to empirical research documenting how unprompted status checks disproportionately affect racialised minorities and women, whose fear of arrest prevents them from calling the police when they are the targets of crime, including domestic violence, sexual assault, and human trafficking. The ILC concluded that the police lack a statutory and common law authority to collect and share information, that this practice undermines the core goals of policing (e.g. investigating, helping victims and witnesses) and that there are good reasons to think that over-policing of non-status migrants violates constitutional rights. The former two conclusions bear directly to the question of the rule of law, insofar as it accurately portrays police enforcement of the IRPA in the absence of a *bona fide* criminal law connection as arbitrary, that is, inconsistent with the terms, principles, and purposes of the Police Services Act.

Rights and rule of law arguments could reduce formal links between local authorities and the CBSA, but it is also possible that courts will prioritise the interests of security, concretising their practices. Even if the rights of non-status migrants are formally recognised in law, we return to the same problem as before, which is consistent, informal information-sharing. Still, the fact that formal law cannot guarantee improvements in the well-being of non-status migrants or dissolve security logics is not a good argument for abandoning carefully designed legal strategies. The city can, should, and has promised to establish the normative conditions under which the values of the sanctuary city are most likely to be internalised. This has to include obstructing the local influence of security professionals, putting up roadblocks wherever it can.

Conclusion

The sanctuary city movement is a response to the causes and consequences of exclusionary national and international laws, where rights-based strategies of resistance at these scales have proven to be largely ineffective. Despite the failings of 'high' law, North American sanctuary cities have adopted formalist models, believing that local law will build relations of trust and enhance access to municipal services. But the experience of Toronto highlights the limits of this model. Formal laws exist in a complex environment marked by extreme normative and bureaucratic complexity, where discretion continues to be informed by disparate and incompatible conceptions of deservingness. Underfunding and the nascence of Access T.O. surely contribute to this dynamic, but much relates to the fact that discretionary power and the relative weakness of rights and the rule of law are defining features of local governance.

The city is a social space within which many political and legal authorities coexist and compete with each other. Scale is a useful means of momentarily simplifying the messiness of this reality, but it does so by bracketing a sub-set of interactions within one frame while rendering their dynamics static. Even within a given scale, there are a multiplicity of legal maps that represent, construct, reinforce, and exclude competing claims to authority. Added to this are the ways in which power shifts, spills, and undulates across multiple scales and in all directions. The case of Toronto documents two contrasting realities, where formal sanctuary law has failed to rise above incompatible norms that shape discretionary decision-making at the local scale, while security logics have speedily traversed legislative, jurisdictional, and constitutional boundaries. This is most evident in the local influence of the CBSA, which is projected through its membership in a semi-autonomous field of security professionals who conflate migration, security, and criminality. However, the work of security is also done by city staff and even non-state actors, who draw on a common pool of ideological and normative resources that link non-status and illegality with perceived risks to security, including economic security. There is no evidence of a comparable 'field of sanctuary' in Toronto.

One lesson that may be drawn from this is that asking the question 'who governs migration (better)?' can obscure the ways in which the political – the constructed and not the objective – concept of immigration is inextricably linked to the equally political concept of security. As Bigo notes, the two actively work to forge the central illusion of power as a body, through homogeneity, sovereignty, and law, which prevents an understanding of the global social transformations concerning the movement of people and identity politics (Bigo, 2002: 68).

The antidote to this problem is far from evident. I suggest that the concept of scale, while useful in many ways, must be supplemented with a more supple resource. Following Valverde, I suggest that future research would be well served by drawing distinctions between scale and jurisdiction, where the latter describes both technical doctrine governing the distribution of formal authority and a set of normative practices oriented to the resolution of conflicts about governance and authority (Valverde, 2008, 2009). One of the qualities that distinguish jurisdiction from scale is attentiveness to time and change, which we find in accreted but fluctuating doctrine, customs, and constitutional conventions. Another is that it is capable of exploring authority as dispersed among different actors and institutions within one scale (e.g. immigration law, criminal law, tax law) and how/why these arrangements persist or do not. Finally, it helps us analyse and contest the operation of assemblages across scales. Consequently, jurisdiction can attune us to the tensions that arise, but are often obscured, when power shifts across horizontal (within a scale) and vertical (scale-shifting) boundaries. All of these dynamics are visible in the case of Toronto, with the criminalisation of migration at the national scale over time shifting downwards, helping police link crime and irregular migration in ways required by constitutional structures and statutory provisions.

Jurisdiction also suggests a possible response. The rule of law is an especially enticing notion, being concerned with sourcing discretionary power in the principles and purposes of enabling law (Ellermann, 2014). It is evident in how advocates challenge crimmigration at the national scale by arguing that expanding, coercive powers require greater procedural protections and other constraints on discretionary power. Advocates are also challenging securitisation at the local scale by reinforcing the statutory limits of police powers. There are risks to this strategy, to be sure, but if formal sanctuary policies are to work, municipalities and advocates cannot afford to be conservative; they must assertively obstruct the local expansion of federal power while expanding the scope of municipal jurisdiction beyond its traditional boundaries.

References

Access Alliance (2017) 'Non-insured walk-in clinic (NIWIC) annual report: April 2016–March 2017', http://accessalliance.ca/wp-content/uploads/2017/12/NIWIC-Annual-Report-2016-2017.pdf (accessed 5 December 2018).

Atak, I., G. Hudson, and D. Nakache (2017) 'Making Canada's refugee system faster and fairer: reviewing the stated goals and unintended consequences of the 2012 reform', *Canadian Association for Refugee and Forced Migration Studies (CARFMS) Working Paper Series* 2017/3.

Atak, I., G. Hudson, and D. Nakache (2018) 'The securitisation of Canada's refugee system: reviewing the unintended consequences of the 2012 reform', *Refugee Survey Quarterly*, 37:1, 1–24, doi.org/10.1093/rsq/hdx019.

B010 v. Canada (Citizenship and Immigration) (2015) 3 S.C.R. 704.

Bauder, H. (2016) 'Possibilities of urban belonging', *Antipode*, 48:2, 252–271.

Bauder, H. (2017) 'Sanctuary cities: policies and practices in international perspective', *International Migration*, 55:2, 174–187.

Bigo, D. (2002) 'Security and immigration: toward a critique of the governmentality of unease', *Alternatives*, 27:1, 63–92.

Bigo, D., and A. Tsoukala (eds) (2008) *Terror, Insecurity and Liberty: Illiberal Practices of Liberal Regimes after 9/11* (London: Routledge).

Bloch, A., and M. Chimienti (2011) 'Irregular migration in a globalizing world', *Ethnic and Racial Studies*, 34:8, 1271–1285.

Blomley, N. (2013) 'What kind of legal space is a city?', in B. Andre (ed.), *Urban Interstices: The Aesthetics and Politics of Spatial In-betweens* (London: Routledge).

Caminero-Santangelo, M. (2012) 'The voice of the voiceless: religious rhetoric, undocumented immigrants, and the New Sanctuary Movement in the United States', in R. K. Lippert and S. Rehaag (eds), *Sanctuary Practices in International Perspectives: Migration, Citizenship and Social Movements* (Abingdon: Routledge), 92–105.

Canada (2004) *The Government of Canada. Securing an Open Society: Canada's National Security Policy* (Ottawa: Queens Printer).

Canada (2010) 'Office of the Prime Minister, Minister of Immigration, Refugees and Citizenship Mandate Letter', https://pm.gc.ca/eng/mandate-letters (accessed 9 November 2018).

The Canadian Record (2010) 'Terrorists or civilians? MV *Sun Sea* passengers face scrutiny in days ahead', 13 August 2010, www.therecord.com/sports-story/2565119-terrorists-or-civilians-mv-sun-sea-passengers-face-scrutiny-in-days-ahead/ (accessed 9 November 2018).

CBSA (Canada Border Services Agency) (2005) *Canada Border Services Agency Act*, SC 2005, c 38.

CBSA (Canada Border Services Agency) (2009) *CBSA Enforcement Manual Part 1, Chapter 1 – Introduction to CBSA Enforcement* (30 April), 2–6, http://vancouverlaw.ca/resources/Customs-Enforcement-Manual-1-of-3.pdf (accessed 5 December 2018).

City of Toronto (2013) 'Undocumented workers in Toronto', City Council Resolution, ref. no. CD18.5.

City of Toronto (2014a) 'Access to city services for undocumented Torontonians', City Council Resolution, ref. no. CD29.11.

City of Toronto (2014b) 'Access to city services for undocumented Torontonians', City Council Resolution, Staff Report, ref. no. CD29.11.

City of Toronto (2015) 'Toronto Police Service: service governance pertaining to the access to police services for undocumented Torontonians', City Council Resolution, ref. no. CD4.2.

City of Toronto (2016) 'Toronto Newcomer Strategy – progress report', Staff Report, ref. no. CD15.5.

City of Toronto (2017a) 'Managing refugee flows', Staff Report, ref. no. CD23.12.

City of Toronto (2017b) 'Refugees, refugee claimants and undocumented Torontonians – recent trends and issues', City Council Resolution, ref. no. CD19.9.

City of Toronto (2017c) 'Toronto for all – united as an inclusive sanctuary city – by Mayor John Tory, seconded by Councillor Joe Cressy and Councillor Joe Mihevc', Member Motions, ref. no. MM 24.23.

City of Toronto (2017d) 'Refugees, refugee claimants and undocumented Torontonians – recent trends and issues', Staff Action Report, ref. no. CD19.9.

CPIC (Canadian Police Information Centre) (2018), http://www.cpic-cipc.ca/index-eng.htm (accessed 5 December 2018).

Dauvergne, C. (2008) *Making People Illegal: What Globalization Means for Migration and Law* (Cambridge: Cambridge University Press).

Dauvergne, C. (2016) *The New Politics of Immigration and the End of Settler Societies* (Cambridge: Cambridge University Press).

de Graauw, E. (2014) 'Municipal ID cards for undocumented immigrants: local bureaucratic membership in a federal system', *Politics & Society*, 42:3, 309–330.

Dehghani v. Canada (Minister of Employment and Immigration) (1993), 1 S.C.R. 1053.

Dhamoon, R., and Y. Abu-Laban (2009) 'Dangerous (internal) foreigners and nation-building: the case of Canada', *International Political Science Review*, 30:2, 163–183.

Düvell, F. (2011) 'Paths into irregularity: the legal and political construction of irregular migration', *European Journal of Migration and Law*, 13:3, 275–295.

Dykstra, R. (2012) 'Parliamentary Secretary to the Minister of Citizenship and Immigration, CPC', House of Commons: Bill C-31, 2nd Reading (8 June 2012).

Ellermann, A. (2014) 'The rule of law and the right to stay: the moral claims of undocumented migrants', *Politics & Society*, 42:3, 293–308.

FCJ Refugee Centre (2015) 'Audit report Access T.O. initiative', www. fcjrefugeecentre.org/wp-content/uploads/2016/02/AUDIT-REPORT-ACCESS-T.O.-INITIATIVE.pdf (accessed 9 November 2018).

Forcese, C., and K. Roach (2015) *False Security: The Radicalization of Canadian Anti-Terrorism* (Toronto: Irwin Law).

Gardner II, T. G. (2014) 'The safest place: immigrant sanctuary in the Homeland Security era', PhD dissertation, University of California, Berkeley.

Hannan, C.-A., and H. Bauder (2015) 'Towards a sanctuary province: policies, programs, and services for illegalised immigrants' equitable employment, social participation, and economic development', *RCIS Working Paper* 2015/3, www.ryerson.ca/content/dam/rcis/documents/ RCIS_WP_Hannan_Bauder_No_2015_3.pdf (accessed 9 November 2018).

Houston, S. D., and O. Lawrence-Weilmann (2016) 'The model migrant and multiculturalism: analyzing neoliberal logics in US sanctuary legislation', in H. Bauder and C. Matheis (eds), *Migration Policy and Practice: Interventions and Solutions* (New York: Palgrave Macmillan), 101–126.

Hudson, G. (2011) 'Transnational human rights advocacy and the judicial review of global intelligence agency cooperation in Canada', in C. Forcese and F. Crépeau (eds), *Terrorism, Law and Democracy: Ten Years after 9/11* (Montreal: Canadian Institute for the Administration of Justice), 173–235.

Hudson, G. (2018) 'The (mis-)uses of analogy: constructing and challenging crimmigration in Canada', in I. Atak and J. Simeon (eds), *The Criminalization of Migration: Contexts and Consequences* (Montreal: McGill-Queens University Press).

Hudson, G., I. Atak, M. Manocchi, and C.-A. Hannan (2017) '(No) Access T.O.: a pilot study on sanctuary city policy in Toronto, Canada', *RCIS Working Paper* 2017/1, www.ryerson.ca/content/dam/rcis/documents/RCIS%20 Working%20Paper%20GHudson%20et%20al.%20finalV2.pdf (accessed 8 November 2018).

Huysmans, J. (2000) 'The European Union and the securitization of migration', *Journal of Common Market Studies*, 38:5, 751–777.

Huysmans, J., and V. Squire (2015) 'Migration and security', in T. Balzaqc, M. Dunn Cavelty, and V. Mauer (eds), *The Routledge Handbook of Security Studies* (Abingdon: Routledge), 161–171.

Hynie, M., C. I. Ardern, and A. Robertson (2016) 'Emergency room visits by uninsured child and adult residents in Ontario, Canada: what diagnoses, severity and visit disposition reveal about the impact of being uninsured', *Journal of Immigrant and Minority Health*, 18:5, 948–56, DOI: 10.1007/ s10903-016-0351-0

Immigration Legal Committee (2008) 'Police services: safe access for all. Legal arguments for a complete "Don't Ask, Don't Tell" policy', a report by the Immigration Legal Committee, presented to the Toronto Police Services Board (November 2008).

Isin, E. F. (2007) 'City.State: critique of scalar thought', *Citizenship Studies*, 11:2, 211–228.

Kaushal, A., and C. Dauvergne (2011) 'The growing culture of exclusion: trends in Canadian refugee exclusions', *International Journal of Refugee Law*, 23:1, 54–92.

Krishnamurti, S. (2013) 'Queue-jumpers, terrorists, breeders: representations of Tamil migrants in Canadian popular media', *South Asian Diaspora*, 5:1, 139–157.

Landolt, P., and L. Goldring (2013) 'The social production of non-citizenship: the consequences of intersecting trajectories of precarious legal status and precarious work', in L. Goldring and P. Landolt (eds), *Producing and Negotiating Non-citizenship: Precarious Legal Status in Canada* (Toronto: University of Toronto Press), 154–174.

Landolt, P., and L. Goldring (2015) 'Assembling noncitizenship through the work of conditionality', *Citizenship Studies*, 19:8, 853–869, special issue: 'Theorising Noncitizenship'.

Lippert, R. (2006) *Sanctuary, Sovereignty, Sacrifice: Canadian Sanctuary Incidents, Power, and Law* (Vancouver: University of British Columbia Press).

Lippert, R., and K. Walby (2013) *Policing Cities: Urban Securitization and Regulation in a 21st Century World* (Abingdon: Routledge).

Loga, J., M. Pyykkönen, and H. Stenvaag (2012) 'Holy territories and hospitality: Nordic exceptionality and national differences of sanctuary incidents', in R. K. Lippert and S. Rehaag (eds), *Sanctuary Practices in International Perspectives: Migration, Citizenship and Social Movements* (Abingdon: Routledge), 121–134.

Mancina, P. (2012) 'The birth of a sanctuary city: a history of governmental sanctuary in San Francisco', in R. K. Lippert and S. Rehaag (eds), *Sanctuary*

Practices in International Perspectives: Migration, Citizenship and Social Movements (Abingdon: Routledge), 205–218.

Mancina, P. (2016) 'In the Spirit of Sanctuary: Sanctuary-City Policy Advocacy and the Production of Sanctuary-Power in San Francisco, California', PhD thesis, Vanderbilt University, https://etd.library.vanderbilt.edu/available/etd-07112016-193322/unrestricted/Mancina.pdf (accessed 18 November 2018).

Marsden, S. (2012) 'The new precariousness: temporary migrants and the law in Canada', *Canadian Journal of Law and Society*, 27:2, 209–229.

McCulloch, J., and S. Pickering (2009) 'Pre-crime and counter-terrorism: imagining future crime in the "War on Terror"', *British Journal of Criminology*, 49, 628–645

McDonald, R. (1997) 'What is a critical legal pluralism?', *Canadian Journal of Law and Society*, 12:2, 25–46.

Millner, N. (2012) 'Sanctuary sans frontières: social movements and solidarity in post-war northern France', in R. K. Lippert and S. Rehaag (eds), *Sanctuary Practices in International Perspectives: Migration, Citizenship and Social Movements* (Abingdon: Routledge), 57–70.

Moens, A. (2011) 'The challenging parameters of the Border Action Plan in perimeter security and the beyond the border dialogue', special report, Border Policy Research Institute (Western Washington University), 15–21.

Nail, T., F. Kamal, and S. Hussan (2010) 'Building sanctuary city: NOII-Toronto on non-status migrant justice organizing', *Upping the Anti*, 11, http://uppingtheanti.org/journal/article/11-noii-sanctuary-city/ (accessed 9 November 2018).

Nakache, D., and L. Dixon-Perera (2015) 'Temporary or transitional? Migrant workers' experiences with permanent residence in Canada', *IRPP Study*, 55, 1–55, http://irpp.org/wp-content/uploads/2015/10/study-no55.pdf (accessed 5 December 2018).

NOII (No One Is Illegal) (2015) 'Often asking, always telling: the Toronto Police Service and the sanctuary city policy', http://rabble.ca/sites/rabble/files/often_asking_always_telling_-_kedits_dec_1.pdf (accessed 9 November 2018).

Padilla v. *Kentucky* (2010) 559 *U.S.* 356, 08–651.

Ridgley, J. (2008) 'Cities of refuge: immigration enforcement, police, and the insurgent genealogies of citizenship in US sanctuary cities', *Urban Geography*, 29:1, 53–77, DOI: 10.2747/0272-3638.29.1.53.

Robinson, W. G. (1983) *Report to the Honourable Lloyd Axworthy, Minister of Employment and Immigration, on Illegal migrants in Canada* (Ottawa: Public Affairs Division, Employment and Immigration Canada).

Royal Canadian Mounted Police (2005) 'Canadian Police Information Centre privacy impact assessment – 2005', www.rcmp-grc.gc.ca/en/privacy-impact-assessment-canadian-police-information-centre (accessed 9 November 2018).

Santos, B. de Sousa (1987) 'Law: a map of misreading. Toward a postmodern conception of law', *Journal of Law and Society*, 14:3, 279–302.

Squire, V. (2011) 'From community cohesion to mobile solidarities: the city of sanctuary network and the strangers into citizens campaign', *Political Studies*, 59:2, 290–307.

Squire, V., and J. Bagelman (2012) 'Taking not waiting: space, temporality and politics in the City of Sanctuary movement', in P. Nyers and K. Rygiel (eds), *Citizenship, Migrant Activism and the Politics of Movement* (Abingdon: Routledge), 146–164.

Squire, V., and J. Darling (2013) 'The "minor" politics of rightful presence: justice and relationality in City of Sanctuary', *International Political Sociology*, 7:1, 59–74.

Stumpf, J. (2006) 'The crimmigration crisis: immigrants, crime, and sovereign power', *American University Law Review*, 56:2, 367–419.

Stumpf, J. (2013) 'The process is the punishment in crimmigration law', in M. Bosworth and K. Aas (eds), *The Borders of Punishment: Criminal Justice, Citizenship and Social Exclusion* (Oxford: Oxford University Press).

Suresh v. Canada (Minister of Citizenship and Immigration) (2002) 1 S.C.R. 3.

Valverde, M. (2008) 'Analyzing the governance of security: jurisdiction and scale', *Behemoth: A Journal on Civilisation*, 1:1, 3–15, https://ojs.ub.uni-freiburg.de/behemoth/article/view/748 (accessed 8 November 2018).

Valverde, M. (2009) 'Jurisdiction and scale: legal "technicalities" as resources for theory', *Social and Legal Studies*, 18:2, 139–158.

Valverde, M. (2011) 'Questions of security: a framework for research', *Theoretical Criminology*, 15:1, 3–22.

Valverde, M. (2015) *Chronotopes of Law: Jurisdiction, Scale and Governance* (London: Routledge).

Varsanyi, M. W. (2006) 'Interrogating "urban citizenship" vis-à-vis undocumented migration', *Citizenship Studies*, 10:2, 229–249.

Varsanyi, M. W. (ed.) (2010) *Taking Local Control: Immigration Policy Activism in U.S. Cities and States* (Stanford, CA: Stanford University Press).

Villazor, R. C. (2010) 'Sanctuary cities: and local citizenship', *Fordham Urban Law Journal*, 37:2, 574–598.

Villegas, F. J. (2013) 'Getting to don't ask don't tell at the Toronto district school board: mapping the competing discourses of rights and membership of stakeholders', in L. Goldring and P. Landolt (eds), *Producing and Negotiating Precarious Legal Status in Canada* (Toronto: University of Toronto Press).

Villegas, P. E. (2015) 'Fishing for precarious status migrants: surveillant assemblages of migrant illegalization in Toronto, Canada', *Journal of Law and Society*, 42:2, 230–252.

Walker, K. E., and H. Leitner (2011) 'The variegated landscape of local immigration policies in the United States', *Urban Geography*, 32:3, 156–178.

West Coast LEAF (2015) 'Position paper: sanctuary city policy', www. westcoastleaf.org/wp-content/uploads/2015/01/WCL-Position-Paper-Sanctuary-City.pdf (accessed 8 November 2018).

Zedner, L. (2005) 'Securing liberty in the face of terror: reflections from criminal justice', *Journal of Law and Society*, 32, 507–533.

4

Toronto's sanctuary city policy: rationale and barriers

Idil Atak

With a population of 2.73 million people, Toronto is Canada's largest city and a major national economic driver. Immigrants make up 47 per cent of Toronto's population, which is the highest proportion of any major urban centre in the country (City of Toronto, 2017a). Although there are no official statistics, the majority of Canada's undocumented migrants[1] are believed to reside in Toronto (Magalhaes et al., 2010). Research shows that this population faces several barriers to accessing basic services, such as healthcare and social assistance. Undocumented migrants are exposed to a heightened risk of marginalisation, exploitation, and abuse (Magalhaes et al., 2010; McDonald, 2009; Hudson et al., 2017). They also live in constant fear of being turned over to border enforcement officers for detention and removal from Canada.

These concerns were acknowledged on 21 February 2013 when the city council passed a motion declaring Toronto the first 'sanctuary city' of Canada (City of Toronto, 2013a). The policy entitled 'Access to City Services for Undocumented Torontonians' (Access T.O.) directs city officials not to inquire into immigration status when providing select services or to deny undocumented migrants access to services for which they are eligible.[2] Accordingly, the following services are available to Torontonians, that is, individuals resident in the city, regardless of immigration status: acquiring licences and permits, by-law enforcement, children's programmes, emergency services (911), emergency shelter and housing support, employment help, library services, public health services, public transportation, and recreation programmes. These services are either provided by the city or by agencies and corporations that receive funding from the city to deliver services to Torontonians. In addition, the city cannot disclose personal information to the federal or provincial government, except in very limited circumstances (City of Toronto, 2013a).

Since 2013 measures taken to implement the policy have mainly consisted of education and awareness raising about Access T.O. FCJ Refugee Centre, a Toronto-based non-profit organisation, trained 133 front-line city staff and 42 community agency staff. The city also organised a public education campaign and developed awareness materials to publicise Access T.O. and to clarify which city services were accessible to undocumented Torontonians. These materials were posted to city divisions and their public locations, inside city workplaces, and in public transit shelters across Toronto. They were distributed to the city's community partners to share with their clients and at city events (City of Toronto, 2017b: 7).

Moreover, the city council has shown its commitment to Access T.O. by reaffirming, in 2014, 2015, and 2017, Toronto's status as 'a Sanctuary City where all residents have full rights to access City services without fear, regardless of their immigration status' (City of Toronto, 2017c: 3). Most notably, in the wake of the US President Donald Trump's executive orders temporarily to ban passport holders from seven primarily Muslim countries from entering the US and to halt the resettlement of refugees from Syria, the city council adopted the motion 'Toronto for all – United as an Inclusive Sanctuary City' on 31 January 2017. The motion called on city divisions, agencies, and corporations to review their policies and procedures and those of their grant recipients to ensure consistency with council's commitment as a sanctuary city (para. 2). Referring to the recent US policies, Toronto's Mayor John Tory noted that the city council is 'here to recommit our city as a place of inclusion and acceptance, where people are welcomed and valued and where their fundamental rights are respected and enshrined' (Fox, 2017). The motion was also prompted by the sudden increase in illegal border crossings to Canada following the US presidential elections. Indeed 2,145 individuals crossed the land border *via* the US to claim asylum in Canada in the first two months of 2017 (Government of Canada, n.d.; Woods, 2017). The majority of these individuals arrived in Toronto and in other Canadian urban centres, triggering an emergency response from many municipal authorities (Maire de Montréal, 2017).

This chapter examines Toronto's sanctuary city policy, the rationale behind the policy, and its implementation. In doing so, I argue that Access T.O. represents a political discourse about the inclusive nature of municipal policies. In a global context where anti-immigrant narratives and policies are on the rise, this human rights-centred policy[3] illustrates the growing involvement of municipalities in the governance of migration (see Darling and Bauder, this volume). In Canada, the power of any city is constrained by federal and provincial law. Thus, Toronto has been a pioneer in its attempt to push the boundaries of the municipal jurisdiction in order to protect the fundamental rights of its undocumented residents. However, the city has not been successful in translating the positive narrative into concrete action. An audit undertaken in October 2015 on behalf of the city revealed that Access T.O. is not consistently applied by city divisions and agencies, and that service providers experience difficulties, including an unfamiliarity with the needs of undocumented migrants. The audit found that undocumented migrants continue to be denied access to some services (FCJ Refugee Centre, 2015). In this context, and drawing on the results of primary field research, this chapter discusses some of the barriers to the realisation of the policy to argue that in looking beyond the rhetoric of sanctuary and towards its implementation, we might gain an insight into the complex ways in which municipalities are negotiating the challenge of practising sanctuary in a context of growing anti-immigrant sentiment at a global level. The chapter contributes to the literature on sanctuary cities by highlighting the challenges faced by a city as diverse and complex as Toronto in embedding the sanctuary policy and practice across a range of service areas, including health, housing, and policing.

The field research on which this chapter is based was conducted from November 2015 to April 2016. It involved 22 semi-structured interviews with 24 stakeholders, including the legal and medical professions; community service, immigrant serving, and non-profit organisations; city staff and officials: Toronto Public Health; Toronto Public Libraries; Employment and Social Services; Parks, Forestry and Recreation; Emergency Shelter & Housing Supports; Toronto District School Board; the Toronto Police Service Board; the city council; and the undocumented migrant community.[4] Each interview was audio-recorded and transcribed. The data collected was treated according to Ryerson University's Research Ethics Board guidelines. The data analysis involved open coding and identification of emerging concepts that are in need of further examination (Hudson et al., 2017: 11). The use of grounded theory allowed the identification, development, and integration of concepts. 'It is concepts that drive the analysis and each case contributes to the development of the concepts therefore the resulting theory is an accumulation and representation of all the cases' (Corbin, 2017: 301). An initial report was published that is drawn upon here (see Hudson et al., 2017).

In the first two parts of this chapter, I discuss Access T.O.'s origins, policy rationale, and objectives. The chapter goes on to examine the current situation of undocumented migrants in Toronto to highlight the socio-economic marginalisation faced by this population. The last part offers a critical analysis of the barriers and difficulties experienced in the implementation of Access T.O. Ultimately this chapter aims to enrich the debate on issues around membership and access to rights in sanctuary cities.

The principle of inhabitance and access to city services

Across much of the world migrants settle in urban centres (IOM, 2018). Although central governments have the right to control the entry and residence of non-nationals, municipalities have increasingly taken a central role in managing the daily realities of immigrants. They play a key part in how immigrants settle and integrate into society (Provine and Varsanyi, 2012: 105), and thus municipal policies have a considerable impact on both migrants' well-being and on how other municipal residents engage with, and respond to, new arrivals.

In Canada, a federal state, the city lacks autonomous constitutional authority. As part of the province, its authority is circumscribed by provincial law and the constitutional division of powers. Immigration and refugee protection are matters of shared jurisdiction between the federal government and the provinces. The former possesses exclusive jurisdiction over 'naturalization and aliens', the authority to establish immigration selection criteria and to enforce the border (Constitution Act 1867, s. 91(25)). At the same time, matters pertaining to the settlement and integration of migrants are part of the provincial jurisdiction. These include education, most labour and economic relationships, policing, housing, and social assistance (Constitution Act 1867, s. 92). In this model, provinces delegate some of the power to govern these matters to cities.

In the case examined in this chapter, political authority has been delegated by the province of Ontario to the city of Toronto. The City of Toronto Act (COTA) states that the city may 'provide any service or thing that the City considers necessary or desirable for the public' (s. 8(1), 2006). Hence Toronto can pass by-laws ranging from health and safety to the city's economic, social, and environmental well-being (s. 8(2)). Moreover, COTA s. 3(1) defines 'municipality' as a geographic area whose inhabitants are incorporated, hence, as a municipal corporation, Toronto consists of *all* people living in the city, and municipal services are provided to 'inhabitants' of the city (City of Toronto, 2014a: 4).

Against this backdrop, Access T.O. aims to ensure the accessibility of select services to undocumented migrants. It advances the principle that the mere fact of residing in a city entitles inhabitants to certain rights and services. Leading scholars in the field of sanctuary policies in North America and Europe have highlighted how these policies promote the idea that membership of a community is based on physical presence in, and engagement with, that community, rather than on legal status alone (Varsanyi, 2006; Purcell, 2003; Bauder, 2016; Hudson, this volume). Varsanyi argues that such local membership policies have been formulated in response to the realities of the expanding presence of undocumented residents (2006: 240). Similarly, Purcell refers to the 'right to the city' which stems from the everyday experience of inhabiting the city (Purcell, 2003). According to Bauder, the 'domicile principle' of belonging entails that all residents belong to a territorial polity and should be recognised as citizen-subjects (Bauder, 2014). Similarly, Cuison Villazor has explored how some cities and states in the US use their discretionary administrative powers to develop programmes that enable undocumented migrants to participate in key aspects of city life (2013: 35). Moreover, Squire and Darling describe 'an analytics of rightful presence that aims to focus on a political dimension in which rightfulness is claimed, demanded, or assumed through presence' (2013: 69). Hence, sanctuary city movements have increasingly been seen as contributing to a shift in ideas around community and belonging. As such, they are geared towards facilitating transformation of current practices of sociopolitical inclusion and exclusion based on legal status (Bauder, 2016: 10; see also Bauder, this volume).

This line of reasoning based on the principle of inhabitance or physical presence is consistent with the human rights case-law pertaining to a state's obligations towards individuals under its jurisdiction. Although as a matter of well-established international law, states have the right to control the entry, residence, and expulsion of non-citizens (*Abdulaziz et al.* v. *UK*, 1985), sovereignty also involves a duty to protect everyone under the state's jurisdiction (*Island of Palmas*, 1928). Accordingly, the term 'jurisdiction' extends to *all* those who are physically present on a state's territory, regardless of their immigration status. In its landmark Singh decision, the Supreme Court of Canada ruled that the term 'everyone' in Section 7 of the Canadian Charter of Rights and Freedoms[5] includes 'every person physically present in Canada and by virtue of such presence amenable to Canadian law' (*Singh* v. *Minister of Employment and Immigration*, 1985: para. 35). As noted by Chetail (2013), the legal protection of migrants has evolved from the notion of a minimum standard based on state responsibility to fundamental rights consecrated in human rights law and, as such, available to every individual. Today, there is a wealth of domestic and international case-law confirming that the ground of legal status should not bar access to fundamental human rights, such as education, access to adequate food, shelter, and healthcare. These rights apply to everyone regardless of legal status and documentation (UN Committee on Economic, Social and Cultural Rights, 2009: para. 30; *Conference of European Churches (CEC)* v. *the Netherlands*, 2014).

The sanctuary city policy is also in step with the evolving interpretation of 'citizenship'. Supranational courts and other adjudication bodies increasingly question exclusionary decisions taken by nation-states against migrants who have spent a considerable amount of time in those states. Take the case of Jama Warsame, a Somali national permanently resident in Canada since the age of four who received an order of deportation from Canada for 'serious criminality'. The United Nations Human Rights Committee decided that Warsame should not be deported since Canada was his 'own country' within the meaning of Article 12, paragraph 4, of the International Covenant on Civil and Political Rights.[6] In its decision, the committee took into consideration the strong ties connecting Warsame to Canada, the presence of his family in Canada, the language he speaks, the duration of his stay in the country, and the lack of any ties other than at best formal nationality with Somalia (*Jama Warsame* v. *Canada*, 2011). In this emerging human rights case-law, the principle of inhabitance and engagement with community become key factors of membership of that community. In line with this case-law, the literature on 'human rights cities' across Europe and the US draws attention to the increasing use of the human rights discourse and policies in local government when states are seen to violate these rights (Grigolo, 2010; Smith, 2018). Grigolo notes that 'human rights certainly offer a space of recognition, agency, and eventually inclusion for marginal communities' in these cities (Grigolo, 2017: 96). Access T.O. reflects the political and legal interpretations that challenge the denial or limitation of fundamental rights of undocumented migrants. It is also motivated by the duty to resist unfair treatment of these individuals and to show solidarity with migrants experiencing socio-economic marginalisation. As discussed below, Toronto's sanctuary city policy embodies a wider sense of social justice and efforts to challenge poverty, inequality, and other forms of exclusion in the city.

Access T.O. as a politics of justice

Sanctuary policies have historically emerged as a grassroots approach aimed at creating a culture of justice and hospitality at a local level (Friese, 2010). As in many US states and cities, sanctuary practices in Canada involved churches and communities harbouring in a physical shelter migrants at risk of detention and deportation (Lippert, 2004: 536). A participant explained that the defence of the wrongfully rejected asylum seekers in the early 1990s marked the beginning of the sanctuary movement in Toronto:

> The Sanctuary Coalition began as a broad kind of group ... we decided that something had to be done with reference to refugees claimants who had been rejected, where we thought the grounds of the rejection

were not valid ... We held a press conference, in the early nineties, at the Church of the Holy Trinity ... at that point, we made quite a large group of people in, mostly Toronto, but Hamilton, other parts of southern Ontario, London, came together and said we would not abandon these people. (P-21, 2016)

These early sanctuary practices denounced federal decisions deemed unfair to precarious migrants. They were adopted in a context where local anti-poverty advocates identified immigration status barriers as a rising concern in addressing poverty in Toronto (Solidarity City Network, 2013). McDonald (2009: 67) explains how, from 1994 to 1998, these movements led the government to regularise several thousand failed refugee claimants from moratorium countries, such as China, Iran, and Algeria, who were generally stuck in limbo. However, despite these early successes, there have not been any such regularisation programmes since 2004. Taken together, these practices do, however, point to the grassroots origin of Access T.O. Bauder notes that the campaign to become a sanctuary city was spearheaded by the Solidarity City Network, which included a range of community organisations and advocacy groups (2017: 103; Nyers, 2010).

Importantly, the policy was driven by strong leadership. As discussed below, in the early 2000s grassroots movements were supported by individuals who were in key positions, such as the mayor of Toronto, influential city councillors, and the chief of police. Advocacy and activism in solidarity with undocumented migrants unfolded in a context of harsh immigration measures and enhanced policing at the local level (Hannan and Bauder, 2015). For example, in 2006 coordinated raids were conducted by the Toronto Police Service (TPS) and the Canada Border Services Agency (CBSA), in which many undocumented migrants from the Portuguese and Latin American communities were arrested and later deported (Berinstein et al., 2006: 22–23). As a city councillor recalled: 'Federal immigration officials would come to schools, would go to subway stops, and pick people out of lines. We heard stories like that' (P-16, 2016). A former member of the TPS Board (TPSB) – the police oversight body – remarked that a complaint was filed against TPS officers who were asking people for their immigration status in the city and reporting undocumented migrants to the federal government. When the TPS dismissed the complaint, the TPSB was asked to conduct a review of the decision (P-20, 2016). On 18

May 2006 the TPSB adopted a motion entitled 'Access without Fear', which has become a milestone in Access T.O. (TPSB, 2015a):

> From the policing side, the argument that helped us was that one prevention of victimization ... is a core police service by law. Our priorities included prevention of domestic violence, violence against women. So one argument was if there is any fear that coming forward might jeopardize the family's status here, then people who are subject of violence will not come forward. Second, it was also a time when there's a very high concern in the community with violent crime ... in order to solve crimes, you need witnesses ... But if there are people without 'legal documentation', and they are witness to crime ... they're not going to come forward and cooperate with the police, for fear that the police will put them in jeopardy. (P-20, 2016)

It is noteworthy that the 'Access without Fear' motion was passed at the same time as a motion to counter human trafficking. The policy was therefore adopted as part of a coordinated effort to make the city safer while preventing the victimisation of vulnerable populations. Accordingly, a routine order by the chief of police was issued that 'any person, whether resident or visitor to Toronto, may request and will receive police response and police services without being asked about their immigration status. Police officers were trained not to ask victims and witnesses of crime for their immigration status, unless there are *bona fide* reasons to do so' (TPSB, 2015b), thereby echoing many of the 'Don't Ask, Don't Tell' policies adopted by local police in US sanctuary cities (see Bauder, this volume).

In addition to these developments, a study published in 2011 served as an important trigger for Access T.O. The study revealed that undocumented workers suffered from high levels of anxiety, depression, chronic stress, and stress-related physical illnesses and faced many barriers in accessing care in Toronto (Toronto Public Health and Access Alliance Multicultural Health and Community Services, 2011: 109, 117). This work was referred to the city manager who, in October 2012, confirmed that undocumented workers in Toronto face a variety of challenges, including the inability to access programmes and services available for legal residents and a limited ability to deal with employment-related issues (City of Toronto, 2012).

Of note, the province of Ontario has enacted laws that protect undocumented migrants. Take Section 49.1 of the Education Act, which states: 'A person who is otherwise entitled to be admitted to a school and who is less than eighteen years of age shall not be refused admission because the person or the person's parent or guardian is unlawfully in Canada' (R.S.O. 1990, c.E.2). In 2004 the Ontario Ministry of Education reiterated this principle; so did the Toronto District School Board (TDSB) in 2007 after the CBSA arrested two undocumented students on a high school property. Similarly, under the provincial policy, public health services are delivered based on geographic residence. Thus anyone who lives in the city is eligible to receive these services. Arguably, this approach promotes public health through, for instance, the control of contagious diseases. Cost effectiveness is another reason, as preventative care helps reduce the need for and the cost of emergency care (City of Toronto, 2013b).

In sum, Toronto's sanctuary policy articulates the idea that, as a matter of justice and for the greater good of the city, all residents should have access to fundamental rights and services, regardless of their immigration status (Ridgley, 2008: 56). Ultimately, Access T.O. challenges the criminalisation of migration, a trend that has prevailed in Canada over recent decades. Indeed migrants' rights have been seriously impeded by the proliferation of security-related measures and restrictive migration policies by the federal government (Macklin, 2005; Crépeau and Nakache, 2006). In particular, the Conservative government of Stephen Harper (2006–15) introduced exceptionally harsh measures against asylum seekers arriving irregularly in Canada (Atak et al., 2018). Although this context has considerably constrained the achievement of the Access T.O. objectives (see below), the sanctuary city policy nevertheless entails a 'politics of justice' (Cuison Villazor, 2008) and a powerful statement against the exclusion of undocumented migrants from fundamental rights, such as housing, healthcare, education, and social assistance. As a city councillor put it:

> This is who we are as a city … as a state actor, our interests are not the same as the federal government. They have an interest in controlling the borders and entry and so on. It does us no good as a city, for our community, 'the way' we represent the community, to help the federal state determine who is documented and who is not documented. (P-16, 2016)

This political stance is clearly visible in Mayor Tory's above-mentioned statement which reiterated the city council's commitment that Toronto is a place of inclusion where individuals' fundamental rights are respected. Another telling example is found in Toronto becoming the first non-European city to sign the Integrating Cities Charter in 2014. This non-binding instrument compels the municipal government to provide equal opportunities for all residents (City of Toronto, 2016: 5). The Toronto Integrating Cities Action Plan 2016–2020 adopted as a follow-up includes a commitment to work with the provincial and federal governments to ensure equal access and non-discrimination across all city policies, and to increase access to services for undocumented Torontonians (City of Toronto, 2016: Appendix 2). In these policy positions, the city of Toronto has therefore shown a genuine will to make municipal services accessible.

Undocumented migrants in Toronto today

More than five years into Access T.O. and twelve years since the adoption of the 'Access without Fear' motion, undocumented migrants still experience marginalisation and difficulty in accessing services. In the absence of any reliable data, the precise socio-demographic characteristics of this population are unknown. However, several participants agreed that Toronto's undocumented migrants are diverse. Some immigrant-serving organisations pointed out that in the last couple of decades they have seen an increase in migrants from Africa, South Asia, and Latin America. As well, some participants remarked that the drastic changes in refugee policy and temporary workers' schemes under the previous Conservative government have had the effect of increasing the undocumented population (see also Marsden, 2012; Atak et al., 2018). Concern has also been expressed about the growth of this population in Toronto after the election of President Trump. FCJ Refugee Centre stated, for instance, that their services to refugees, refugee claimants, and undocumented persons have increased by at least 30 per cent (City of Toronto, 2017b: 6).

Some participants from legal clinics and non-profit organisations mentioned the high percentage of single women in the population they serve, as well as families with small children. In a similar vein, they drew attention to the increasing numbers of youths without status in Toronto and to the unique challenges they face. For instance, a participant from a non-profit organisation pointed out that after graduating from high school, these youths cannot access higher education. 'Their only option is precarious work' (P-1, 2015; see also Keung, 2016). In 2018 York University started a pilot allowing the enrolment of a small number of undocumented students into its programmes (CBC Listen Metro Morning, 2018). Such laudable initiatives remain, however, exceptional (Gonzales Mateus, 2017).

Elderly people are another group of undocumented Torontonians whose specific vulnerability remains mostly ignored. An immigrant-serving organisation representative stated that this population

> can't access pensions, old age pensions, even if they have worked and paid into the system. They have no access to housing, so we have senior folks who spent most of their lives here in Canada without any sort of immigration status who are living in rooms and barely getting by, other than through the food-banks ... or, through the goodness of friends. (P-9, 2015)

Similarly a Shelter, Support and Housing Administration representative noted, 'seniors ... maybe they were brought here as kids. Nobody did the paperwork. They've been in Canada, fifty, sixty, seventy years, however long, and we have them in shelter' (P-6, 2016). This participant said that many undocumented old people in communal shelters are in need of long-term care; they cannot, however, benefit from such care as they lack legal status. This finding, which contradicts the assumption that undocumented migrants are usually younger individuals, is worrisome. The many issues that people face in old age are indeed aggravated by lack of legal status. Undocumented elderly people are more likely to experience economic hardship, social isolation, health issues, and loss of independence than citizens.

Moreover, as a result of their lack of legal status, undocumented migrants tend to occupy precarious and difficult jobs. A participant described Toronto as 'the capital of precarious work of Canada' (P-1, 2015). These migrants are frequently paid less than the minimum wage, and often experience irregularities with regard to pay, such as non-payment or excessive delays in the payment of wages. They often receive their salaries in cash, which makes it difficult to prove when they have not been paid, or when unjustified deductions have been made from their salaries (Hannan et al., 2016; OHCHR, 2014). The enforcement of legal rights is often acutely difficult for migrant workers. Research shows that they may, in practice, lack the ability to raise concerns about their working and living conditions (ILO, 2006: para. 461; Magalhaes et al., 2010).

Being undocumented has dire consequences. Several research participants emphasised how negatively the lack of legal status affects migrants' health. As a family doctor remarked:

> Living as an undocumented person, in itself, is a huge source of stress. Whatever physical health issue that brought them in the door … there's always an underlying, ongoing stress, and many people have had traumatic experiences that have led them to come here in the first place, so there's often underlying trauma, and then this kind of chronic exposure to stress. (P-19, 2016)

Despite Access T.O., this population continues to experience barriers for reasons related to both the failure of the policy itself and the size of the issue faced by the city. Migrants are usually not aware of the public health services available to them. The fear of being turned over to the police may also explain their reluctance to reach out. Moreover, as explained below, the city cannot properly tackle issues such as access to healthcare without the support of the province. This situation has therefore serious effects on public health. A representative from Toronto Public Health noted that,

> with about 250 active cases, Toronto has one of the largest incidences of tuberculosis in the country. Toronto Public Health do the surveillance to identify people who are at risk, make sure they're tested. However the actual treatment of people who are identified with active disease is done by the healthcare system, by doctors in hospitals. And not all undocumented migrants do have access to healthcare in hospitals. (P-14, 2016)

The Community Health Centres (CHCs) were designated to receive a pot of funding from the province in order to provide primary care for marginalised individuals, such as undocumented migrants. However, this system has several limitations (City of Toronto, 2013b). As a family doctor put it:

> the problem is that CHC can't see everybody, a lot of times, they're closed to new patients, or they are closed to uninsured patients … funding only allows them to provide primary care (such as) basic blood-work and imaging, but then really anything beyond that, if they're

hospitalized, they need surgery, if they need chemo or radiation ...
there's no funds for that. (P-19, 2016)

Finally, a young migrant who had experienced being undocumented
after Access T.O. came into force summarised the hardship she went
through after a deportation order was issued against her family:

> we had to go into hiding. This meant leaving the places we were living
> at, leaving work. And basically, stopping all the connections we had,
> and the support we had. So, for a few months, we stayed underground,
> and those months were like, the times we couldn't support ourselves.
> And trying to find help as an undocumented, it's a really long process
> and really exhausting emotionally. Because, you start seeing how many
> doors are closed, once you lose status ... And that's where we found
> out that the shelter system is not as easy as people make it look to be.
> And, that's when I also started finding out all the stigma about the
> barriers the shelter system in Toronto has, against undocumented people.
> (P-23, 2016)

This quote highlights the social isolation and economic marginalisation
experienced daily by undocumented migrants and the barriers that
exist to accessing municipal services. The question then becomes:
why does Access T.O. fail to achieve its policy objectives?

Barriers to the implementation of Access T.O.

The first major impediment is the lack of appropriate municipal
resources. The province of Ontario's commitment is key for the success
of Access T.O., since many of the services delivered by the municipality
are formally the responsibility of the province. For example, the province
does not permit the city to use provincial funding to support healthcare,
community housing, and some other social services for the benefit
of undocumented migrants (Hannan and Bauder, 2018). Unsurprisingly
the original motion in 2013 invited the provincial government to
review its policies for provincially funded services for undocumented
residents with a view to ensuring access to healthcare, emergency
services, community housing, and support for such residents within
a social determinants of health framework. Since then, the city council
has called upon the federal and provincial governments to strengthen
intergovernmental partnerships and requested repeatedly that the

provincial government review its policies for provincially funded services for undocumented residents (City of Toronto, 2013a).

Linked to this, Access T.O. does not have a proper budget or dedicated personnel. Hence it lacks vital resources to promote and implement the policy through such activities as staff training, awareness raising, coordination, and oversight. As mentioned previously, the policy has recently been placed under the responsibility of a small team within a city division that is also in charge of other topical issues including the integration of newcomers. Several city staff and officials emphasised that Access T.O. is not the only task on their portfolio. In light of its unique nature and the specific needs of the target population, proper human and administrative resources should be allocated to the policy's implementation and its coordination with relevant city divisions as well as with community partners. Such a strategy that takes into account the diverse demographics and contexts of Toronto's undocumented migrant population is critical for the success of Access T.O.

The absence of demographic data on undocumented migrants is another problem hindering the design of effective municipal strategies. Under the Municipal Freedom of Information and Protection of Privacy Act, the city cannot collect personal information unless it is legally authorised to do so by statute or by-law. Of note, the 2013 city council report refers specifically to 'undocumented *workers*', thereby showing a lack of understanding of this population's diverse nature. Some city staff and community service organisation representatives stressed the need for accurate data. Take shelter services, where a city staff member stressed the importance of collecting information about immigration status in order to determine a case plan and work with migrants on an exit strategy from the shelter system (P-6, 2016). Similarly, a participant from Ontario Works remarked that collecting personal information is important from a case management perspective, notably in terms of assessing an individual's prospects in the labour market (P-7, 2015). A spokesperson for a settlement agency commented: 'we have to ask, we can't say don't ask-don't tell, if you don't ask, you don't have evidence to make a case ... for anything, for regularization, for services, like housing, and childcare' (P-10, 2016). A Toronto Public Health representative also supported demographic data collection for the purposes of programme evaluation: 'You need to know who you're serving and who you're not serving. Otherwise, it's very difficult to measure the success of the policy' (P-14, 2016). Without accurate data on the population being served via Access T.O. it is impossible to know the numbers involved and thus to make a viable case for further future funding to sustain the policy.

A third major obstacle to the implementation of Access T.O. is the Toronto Police Service's lack of compliance with the policy. The city council has recently acknowledged that undocumented Torontonians seeking emergency services from Toronto police may be at risk of being reported to the CBSA should their status be determined during service provision (City of Toronto, 2015: 7; 2017b: 6). In fact, research conducted by No One Is Illegal, a grassroots movement, based on an access to information request, showed that the TPS investigated people's immigration status during routine traffic stops, and reported 3,278 people to the CBSA between November 2014 and June 2015. Less than 7.1 per cent of those reported had outstanding immigration warrants (NOII, 2015). The TPS's non-compliance may stem from a lack of awareness of the policy among TPS officers recruited since the adoption of the 'Access without Fear' motion in 2006. A former TPSB member drew attention to the need to reactualise the policy through a regular routine order by the chief of police as well as in-service training of police officers (P-20, 2016). The criminalisation of undocumented migrants under the previous Conservative government is another reason why the TPS may be reluctant to implement Access T.O. (Atak et al., 2018). In fact, as stated previously, drastic legislative changes were made over the past decade to deter undocumented migrants and asylum seekers. The legislation was accompanied by a political discourse portraying these populations as security threats and as people taking advantage of Canada's generosity (Neylon, 2015; Kronick and Rousseau, 2015). The CBSA's power has been enhanced to track and deport undocumented migrants. Several participants noted how these policies have changed the public attitude towards migrants and reinforced unsubstantiated associations between undocumented migration, fraud and crime. As a participant noted: 'the challenge is to actually reframe that argument so that people who don't have status aren't viewed as the kind of freeloaders. Like the bogus (refugee) claimants, people who are coming in to take advantage of our goodwill' (P-18, 2016).

The criminalising narrative and tougher sanctions have exacerbated undocumented migrants' fears of being turned over to the police and created confusion as to the accessibility of city services, including 911 emergency calls. Additionally, the previous federal government's funding cuts to immigrant-serving agencies and advocacy work mostly impacted services for undocumented migrants. A representative from a major agency said: 'we have 230 member agencies, across the province and I would say that less than 5% provide services to those who are not permanent residents' (P-9, 2015). Another participant stressed the reluctance of these agencies to serve undocumented migrants for fear of losing their funding (P-2, 2015). In this context, outreach to undocumented migrants in the city has become even more challenging. As a participant stated: 'there's all the challenges of reaching out to a diverse community, in terms of language and cultural competency with reaching people and having the message received and acted on' (P-14, 2016).

The criminalisation process also aimed to deter those who act in solidarity with undocumented migrants. This has affected the consistent implementation of Access T.O. across city divisions and municipal services. A participant remarked: 'we are talking about a population that most people, including healthcare providers, social service providers are just not familiar with ... In the medical community there are a lot of people who in general may be uneasy with the idea of serving undocumented migrants because of the discourses around legality and criminality' (P-19, 2016).

Generally, the inconsistent and inaccurate implementation of Access T.O. has been identified as a major problem (City of Toronto, 2015: 1). The above-mentioned service audit conducted by FCJ Refugee Centre in October 2015 revealed that many front-line staff are inadequately informed and may provide erroneous information that can result in undocumented Torontonians being denied services for which they are eligible (City of Toronto, 2015: 6). Some participants agreed that undocumented migrants can be refused access depending on the front-line staff serving them. A city official said that 'the training or the awareness that's happened at the staff level has been quite broad and generic ... one of the mechanisms for making the policy more effective is very tailored training' (P-3, 2015).

Given the lack of resources, the implementation of an effective training programme seems challenging, even more so in view of the fact that, excluding its agencies and corporations, the city of Toronto has approximately 33,500 employees. To date, some 133 employees from the following services have received training in Access T.O.: Shelter, Support and Housing Administration, Toronto Public Health, and Toronto Public Library.

FCJ Refugee Centre recommended that the city should prioritise sensitivity training, in particular a focus on awareness and responsiveness to the specific vulnerabilities and needs of undocumented migrants. As underlined by a city official:

> If we're sending a public health nurse to provide you breastfeeding support, we need to know your name and your address and so forth. But that can be a huge deterrent in finishing that communication. So there could be a lot of hang ups, and another challenge for us is that providing a nuanced message to our intake staff, that you need to not only ask for, if you're trying to invite somebody in or enrol them in our program or service, we need to be clear about what information we need to collect versus what information they need to prove. (P-3, 2015)

Sensitivity training needs to be offered also to community agency staff who provide services funded by the city. Several participants noted that in some of these agencies, front-line staff lack knowledge about Access T.O., which in turn impacts the way services are accessed and delivered.

The situation is further complicated by the limited flow of information about the policy within particular programmes and service areas. Consistent implementation of Access T.O. requires clear guidelines about the policy and effective communication of information to front-line staff, including volunteer staff and seasonal employees, up to managers and directors within service areas. A city official acknowledged that in the absence of systematic training in Access T.O. for city staff, the promotion of the initiative depends on the efforts of a few dedicated staff members. Some service areas have a 'good solid champion there, that person will make sure to convey the message to our colleagues and to the directors and to the managers, and she makes sure it gets channeled down to the health officers, for all the different health centres across Toronto' (P-4, 2015). However, not all city divisions and service areas have these 'champions' who work relentlessly to promote the policy. This is yet another illustration of the inconsistent and discretionary nature of sanctuary practices within and across the city.

Some participants pointed to the need for greater integration across programmes and services in the city. As highlighted by a representative of Toronto Public Health, given the variety of programmes and their diversity across the city:

> creating a tailored response to people who are at either end of the continuum is really difficult ... The way that I would message this out and try to implement it at Public Health is fundamentally different than for libraries or for [Toronto Transit Commission] or for [Parks, Forestry and Recreation] or any of the other divisions that are on the organizational chart. And then, even within that, the roles we have are so different. With Public Health, we have direct service providers; we have policy people; we have administrative staff. And so the messaging that I need to convey [is different for] the person answering the phone, versus the person that's providing the service, versus the person that's providing the data, versus the person that's collecting the data, versus the senior management team, versus our division head, right? (P-3, 2015)

A Parks, Forestry and Recreations official explained the importance of both training front-line staff and enhancing coordination across programmes and services:

> It's really about organizing the front-line. Because there's a lot of front-line, but a lot of them operate within silos. So, the four of us literally could be working in the same neighbourhood, and we would never know. So, it's changing the model of practice on how do we take all four divisions here, represented, who work in the exact same dot on that map ... and how do I share information about your services to the people that I meet in this capacity? (P-17, 2016)

As an official from Ontario Works remarked, the city is expected to move to a more integrated, human services model where different divisions and service areas effectively coordinate their services to clients and collaborate with local communities (P-8, 2015). Such a model would be a step in the right direction towards improving the implementation of Access T.O. Finally, some participants identified the lack of political will and leadership as a main impediment. Representatives of an immigrant-serving agency said that the progressive public servants have been replaced by 'very by-the-book, career-focused folks who are making decisions in the government's bureaucracy, at all levels, but particularly at the federal level' (P-9 and P-10, 2016). Similarly, a participant from a community service organisation complained about 'the City Council that is not the most progressive council' (P-2, 2015). Yet another participant said, 'our current chief of police is much more sensitive about security issues that the previous one. The leadership shift also involves a shift in what areas of policing are being focused on' (P-20, 2016). A strong political commitment in favour of the policy is essential for Access T.O. The experience of Toronto as Canada's largest city illustrates the challenges of implementing a urban-scale sanctuary policy. Indeed, the sheer size of the city as a bureaucratic entity with a complex structure of governance requires a systematic approach with adequate funding and political commitment to the policy (Hudson et al., 2017: 25).

Conclusion

Undocumented migrants in Toronto are, in principle, eligible to access and use select municipal services. Access T.O. is in line with progressive international and domestic case-law that ties in the enjoyment of basic human rights to residence, rather than to legal status. In addition to the promotion of the general welfare and safety of all residents as well as social justice in the city, Toronto's sanctuary policy conveys a powerful political message about the city's inclusive nature. In a global context of the criminalisation of migrants, such positive narratives are important as they express the city's political will to protect the human rights of all migrants. Access T.O. thus illustrates the increasing involvement of municipalities in the governance of migration. This chapter contributes to the existing literature by its distinct focus on Toronto's sanctuary experience, which exemplifies the challenges large cities in a federal system of government may face as sanctuary cities. Although Toronto's policy has the potential to improve the condition of a considerable number of undocumented migrants, the city's size, diversity, and complex governance structure constitute important constraints to the effective implementation of Access T.O. across and within the city's service areas, as well as to communication between the city and local communities and service providers. Today, undocumented migrants in Toronto still experience significant barriers in accessing municipal services for which they are eligible. Access T.O. is notably underfunded and relies heavily on the hard work of a small group of dedicated City of Toronto staff. Migrants, most city staff, and agencies are not well informed about the policy. The lack of clear guidelines impedes the consistent delivery of the policy as well as its independent systematic overview and accountability. These issues are exacerbated by the unwillingness of the provincial government and the Toronto police to cooperate with the city on sanctuary measures. The lingering effects of criminalising policies against undocumented migrants are perhaps the main reason why the positive municipal discourse does not translate into effective implementation.

Notes

1 The term undocumented migrant is not defined in Canadian law. The Immigration and Refugee Protection Act (IRPA) defines the categories of individuals with an immigration status, such as permanent resident (s. 21(1)), protected person (s. 21(2)), and temporary resident (s. 22(1)), who are entitled to reside, study, or work in Canada. Non-citizens without immigration status are considered to be undocumented migrants.

2 The policy is driven by the City of Toronto's Social Development, Finance and Administration (SDFA) which, in the aftermath of the 2013 motion, convened the Access to City Services for Undocumented Torontonians Working Group (the 'Access T.O. Working Group'). This inter-divisional city staff team is composed of policy personnel from 21 city divisions, agencies, and corporations that assist the SDFA to implement Access T.O (City of Toronto, 2014a: 5). While previously under the aegis of the Social Policy team of the Social Policy, Analysis & Research Unit (SPARU) of SDFA, in 2017 Access T.O. was placed within the portfolio of the City of Toronto Newcomer Office, also embedded in the SPARU team of SDFA.

3 See, for instance, the report for action of the SDFA's executive director that highlights how the policy will ensure that undocumented Torontonians 'are able to access programs and services and improve their quality of life in Toronto' (City of Toronto, 2017b, 2).

4 Respondents are designated P-1, P-2, etc. in the text.

5 S. 7 guarantees 'everyone … the right to life, liberty and security of the person and the right not to be deprived thereof except in accordance with the principles of fundamental justice'.

6 Art. 12.4. No one shall be arbitrarily deprived of the right to enter his own country.

References

Abdulaziz, Cabales and Balkandali v. UK (1985) Series A, no. 94, European Court of Human Rights.

Atak, I., G. Hudson, and D. Nakache (2018) 'The securitisation of Canada's refugee system: reviewing the unintended consequences of the 2012 reform', *Refugee Survey Quarterly*, 37:1, 1–24, doi.org/10.1093/rsq/hdx019.

Bauder, H. (2014) 'Domicile citizenship, human mobility and territoriality', *Progress in Human Geography*, 38:1, 91–106.

Bauder, H. (2016) 'Possibilities of urban belonging', *Antipode*, 48:2, 252–271.

Bauder, H. (2017) *Migration Borders Freedom* (New York: Routledge).

Berinstein, C., J. McDonald, P. Nyers, C. Wright, and S. S. Zerehi (2006) '"Access not fear": non-status immigrants & city services', Centre of Excellence for Research on Immigration and Settlement (CERIS), https://we.riseup.net/assets/17034/Access%20Not%20Fear%20Report%20(Feb%202006).pdf (accessed 13 November 2018).

CBC Listen Metro Morning (2018) 'Canadian "dreamers" find home at York University', 2 January 2018, www.cbc.ca/listen/shows/metro-morning/episode/15386490 (accessed 9 November 2018).

Chetail, V. (2013) 'The human rights of migrants in general international law: from minimum standards to fundamental rights', *Georgetown Immigration Law Journal*, 28:1, 225–255.

City of Toronto (2012) 'Undocumented workers in Toronto', Executive Director, Social Development, Finance and Administration (SDFA), Staff Report, 15467 (22 October), 1–8.

City of Toronto (2013a) 'Undocumented workers in Toronto', City Council Decision, CD18.5 (20 February).

City of Toronto (2013b) 'Medically uninsured residents in Toronto', Medical Officer of Health, Staff Report (15 April), 1–22.

City of Toronto (2014a) 'Access to city services for undocumented Torontonians', Executive Director, SDFA, Staff Report, 18943 (7 May).

City of Toronto (2014b) 'Access to city services for undocumented Torontonians', City Council Decision, CD29.11 (10 June).

City of Toronto (2015) 'Access to city services for undocumented Torontonians: progress of the Access T.O. initiative', Executive Director, SDFA, Staff Report, 20866 (10 November), 1–9.

City of Toronto (2016) 'Toronto Newcomer Strategy – progress report', Executive Director, SDFA, Staff Report, CD15.5 (5 October), 1–24.

City of Toronto (2017a) '2016 Census: housing, immigration and ethnocultural diversity, aboriginal peoples', *Backgrounder* (26 October), 1–29.

City of Toronto (2017b) 'Refugees, refugee claimants and undocumented Torontonians. Recent trends and issues', Executive Director, SDFA, Staff Report, CD19.9 (30 March), 1–13.

City of Toronto (2017c) 'Toronto for all – united as an inclusive sanctuary city', City Council Decision, MM24.23 (31 January).

Conference of European Churches (CEC) v. *the Netherlands* (2014) Complaint No. 90/2013, European Committee of Social Rights.

Corbin, J. (2017) 'Grounded theory', *The Journal of Positive Psychology*, 12:3, 301–302.

Crépeau, F., and D. Nakache (2006) 'Controlling irregular migration in Canada. Reconciling security concerns with human rights protection', *IRPP Study*, 12:1, 42.

Cuison Villazor, R. (2008) 'What is a sanctuary?', *Southern Methodist University Law Review*, 61, 133–156.

Cuison Villazor, R. (2013) 'The undocumented closet', *North Carolina Law Review*, 92:1, 2–74.

FCJ Refugee Centre (2015) 'Audit report Access T.O. initiative', www. fcjrefugeecentre.org/wp-content/uploads/2016/02/AUDIT-REPORT-ACCESS-T.O.-INITIATIVE.pdf (accessed 8 November 2018).

Fox, C. (2017) 'Council to reaffirm Toronto's status as sanctuary city', CP24.com, 31 January 2017, www.cp24.com/news/council-to-reaffirm-toronto-s-status-as-sanctuary-city-1.3265171 (accessed 18 November 2018).

Friese, H. (2010) 'The limits of hospitality: political philosophy, undocumented migration and the local arena', *European Journal of Social Theory*, 13:3, 323–341.

Gonzales Mateus, D. (2017) 'Expanding access to post-secondary education for youth with precarious legal status: a Ryerson University case study', major research paper, Immigration and Settlement Studies, Ryerson University, https://digital.library.ryerson.ca/islandora/object/RULA%3A6987 (accessed 18 November 2018).

Government of Canada (n.d.) 'Asylum claims', www.cic.gc.ca/english/refugees/asylum-claims-made-in-canada.asp (accessed 9 November 2018).

Grigolo, M. (2010) 'Human rights and cities: the Barcelona Office for Non-Discrimination and its work for migrants', *International Journal of Human Rights*, 14:6, 896–914.

Grigolo, M. (2017) 'Local governments and human rights: some critical reflections', *Columbia Human Rights Law Review*, 49:1, 67–98.

Hannan, C.-A., and H. Bauder (2015) 'Towards a sanctuary province: policies, programs and services for illegalized immigrants' equitable employment, social participation and economic development', *RCIS Working Paper 2015/3*, https://www.ryerson.ca/content/dam/rcis/documents/RCIS_WP_Hannan_Bauder_No_2015_3.pdf (accessed 24 November 2018).

Hannan, C.-A., and H. Bauder (2018) 'Towards a sanctuary province', in I. Atak and J. C. Simeon (eds), *The Criminalization of Migration: Context and Consequences* (Montreal: McGill-Queen's University Press).

Hannan, C.-A., H. Bauder, and J. Shields (2016) 'Illegalised migrant workers and the struggle for a living wage', *Alternate Routes*, 27, 109–136.

Hudson, G., I. Atak, M. Manocchi, and C.-A. Hannan (2017) '(No) Access T.O.: a pilot study on sanctuary city policy in Toronto, Canada', *RCIS Working Paper* 2017/1, www.ryerson.ca/content/dam/rcis/documents/RCIS%20Working%20Paper%20GHudson%20et%20al.%20finalV2.pdf (accessed 8 November 2018).

ILO (International Labour Organization) (2006) *ILO Multilateral Framework on Labour Migration: Non-binding Principles and Guidelines for a Rights-based Approach* (Geneva: International Labour Organization).

IOM (International Organization for Migration) (2018) *World Migration Report 2018* (Geneva: International Organization for Migration).

Island of Palmas (U.S. v. Neth.) (1928) Hague Ct. Rep. 2d (Scott) 83, Permanent Court of Arbitration.

Jama Warsame v. *Canada* (2011) CCPR/C/102/D/1959/2010, UN Human Rights Committee (1 September 2011).

Keung, N. (2016) 'Undocumented migrants in Toronto describe life in the "shadows"', *Toronto Star*, 21 December 2016.

Kronick, R., and C. Rousseau (2015) 'Rights, compassion and invisible children: a critical discourse analysis of the parliamentary debates on the mandatory detention of migrant children in Canada', *Journal of Refugee Studies*, 28:4, 544–569.

Lippert, R. (2004) 'Sanctuary practices, rationalities, and sovereignties', *Alternatives: Global, Local, Political*, 29:5, 535–555.

Macklin, A. (2005) 'Disappearing refugees: reflections on the Canada–U.S. Safe Third Country Agreement', *Columbia Human Rights Law Review*, 36:2, 101–161.

Magalhaes, L., C. Carrasco, and D. Gastaldo (2010) 'Undocumented migrants in Canada: a scope literature review on health, access to services, and working conditions', *Journal of Immigrant and Minority Health*, 12, 132–151.

Maire de Montréal (2017) 'Montréal, ville sanctuaire', déclaration adoptée à l'unanimité par le conseil municipal, 20 February, https://observatoirevivreensemble.org/sites/observatoirevivreensemble.org/files/declaration_designant_montreal_ville_sanctuaire.pdf (accessed 18 November 2018).

Marsden, S. (2012) 'The new precariousness: temporary migrants and the law in Canada', *Canadian Journal of Law and Society*, 27:2, 209–229.

McDonald, J. (2009) 'Migrant illegality, nation-building, and the politics of regularization in Canada', *Refuge*, 26:2, 65–77.

Neylon, A. (2015) 'Ensuring precariousness: the status of Designated Foreign National under the Protecting Canada's Immigration System Act 2012', *International Journal of Refugee Law*, 27:2, 297–326.

NOII (No One Is Illegal) (2015) 'Often asking, always telling: the Toronto Police Service and the sanctuary city policy', http://rabble.ca/sites/rabble/files/often_asking_always_telling_-_kedits_dec_1.pdf (accessed 9 November 2018).

Nyers, P. (2010) 'No One Is Illegal between city and nation', *Studies in Social Justice*, 4:2, 127–143.

OHCHR (Office of the United Nations High Commissioner for Human Rights) (2014) *The Economic, Social and Cultural Rights of Migrants in an Irregular Situation* (New York and Geneva: United Nations).

Provine, D. M., and M. W. Varsanyi (2012) 'Scaled down: perspectives on state and local creation and enforcement of immigration law', *Law & Policy*, 34:2, 105–112.

Purcell, M. (2003) 'Citizenship and the right to the global city: reimagining the capitalist world order', *International Journal of Urban and International Research*, 27:3, 564–590.

Ridgley, J. (2008) 'Cities of refuge: immigration enforcement, police, and the insurgent genealogies of citizenship in US sanctuary cities', *Urban Geography*, 29:1, 53–77, DOI: 10.2747/0272-3638.29.1.53.

Singh v. *Minister of Employment and Immigration* [1985] 1 S.C.R. 177.

Smith, J. (2018) 'Responding to globalization and urban conflict: human rights city initiatives', *Studies in Social Justice*, 11:2, 347–368.

Solidarity City Network (2013) *Towards a Sanctuary City: Assessment and Recommendations on Municipal Service Provision to Undocumented Residents in Toronto*, http://solidaritycity.net/learn/report-towards-a-sanctuary-city/ (accessed 20 December 2013).

Squire, V., and J. Darling (2013) 'The "minor" politics of rightful presence: justice and relationality in city of sanctuary', *International Political Sociology*, 7:1, 59–74.

TDSB (Toronto District School Board) (2007) 'Students without legal immigration status', Board Policy P.061.

TPSB (Toronto Police Service Board) (2015a) 'Toronto Police Service: service governance pertaining to the access to police services for undocumented Torontonians' (12 March), https://www.toronto.ca/legdocs/mmis/2015/cd/bgrd/backgroundfile-79357.pdf (accessed 18 November 2018).

TPSB (Toronto Police Service Board) (2015b) 'Access to police services for undocumented Torontonians', extract from the Minutes of the Public Meeting of the Toronto Police Services Board, #P234 (17 September), www.toronto.ca/legdocs/mmis/2015/cd/bgrd/backgroundfile-85521.pdf (accessed 18 November 2018).

Toronto Public Health and Access Alliance Multicultural Health and Community Services (2011) 'The global city: newcomer health in Toronto', www.toronto.ca/legdocs/mmis/2011/hl/bgrd/backgroundfile-42361.pdf (accessed 18 November 2018).

UN Committee on Economic, Social and Cultural Rights (2009) *General Comment No. 20: Non-discrimination in economic, social and cultural rights (art. 2, para. 2)*, E/C.12/GC/20, 2 July 2009, www.refworld.org/docid/4a60961f2.html (accessed 18 November 2018).

Varsanyi, M. W. (2006) 'Interrogating "urban citizenship" vis-à-vis undocumented migration', *Citizenship Studies*, 10:2, 229–249.

Woods, A. (2017) 'Canada not ready for second-wave of asylum seekers, union head warns', *The Star*, 19 September 2017.

5

Sanctuary artivism: expanding geopolitical imaginations

Jen Bagelman

Today we are certainly witnessing the intensification of violent border regimes; however, we are also witnessing a vibrant range of politics that are generative of a more welcoming approach. In the last decade, 'sanctuary' has emerged as a particularly powerful expression of hospitality, garnering widespread attention within academic and activist circles. As a working definition, this chapter approaches 'sanctuary' as a movement that seeks to ensure that all people – regardless of citizenship – have safe access to the places in which they reside (be that an urban or non-urban dwelling).[1] Here, sanctuary is understood as a complex set of practices that consists of formal policies and ordinances and a myriad of creative expressions. These practices, it will be argued, belie simplistic normative frames. Rather, sanctuary enacts both generative openings that 'do not automatically replicate the closures of policies devised by national governments keen to absolve themselves of responsibility for the displaced' (Darling, 2010) and yet, in particular contexts, also entrenches exclusionary politics (Bagelman, 2016).

In light of these burgeoning sanctuary movements we have seen a proliferation of sanctuary scholarship. This literature has effectively explored sanctuary initiatives and policies in various geographical contexts (Bauder, 2017; Lippert, 2004; Mancina, 2012). This diverse literature has carefully mapped out the history and contemporary manifestation of sanctuary ordinances such as 'Don't Ask, Don't Tell' and 'Access without Fear' policies, and a host of other initiatives. Within this literature it has been widely argued that a deepened understanding of these policy fields (how they vary and travel) is vital, for it is partly through concrete policy change that we see our localities becoming more welcoming places. The argument rightly made by many sanctuary scholars is that, without evaluating these material policies, sanctuary may become hollowed out as a banal slogan or a dangerously misleading empty gesture.

While attending to these policy domains remains important, this chapter shifts the focus. I aim to foreground art. I draw on and expand upon work by scholars who have gestured towards artful expressions in sanctuary movements (Darling, 2010; Carney et al., 2017) while seeking to further concretise and theorise its role in reshaping our geopolitical landscapes. The guiding question animating this chapter is: how does art feature in sanctuary movements today? In particular I am interested in exploring how artful practice might advance the aspiration to make localities more welcoming places for all residents regardless of citizenship status.

To address this question, I reflect upon on a variety of artful practices. These empirical examples are gleaned from my own grounded engagement with and participation in sanctuary movements on Coast Salish territories (Vancouver Island, Canada) and in parts of the United Kingdom. Reflecting on these intimate experiences with activist networks in these contexts, this chapter identifies five main forms of artful practice and demonstrates how these enact an affective role in sanctuary struggles today. First, I explore how sanctuary *crafty maps* challenge abstract statist cartographies through situated place remaking. Second, I examine how sanctuary art in the form of *détournement* reroutes repetitive and exclusionary securitisation rituals. Third, I illustrate how sanctuary *zines* are mobilised as a resource to visually communicate and insist upon all having a 'right to have rights' (Arendt, 1973a). Fourth, I explore how *sanctuary music* performs an affective role in forging intersectional and unexpected solidarities. Finally, I show how sanctuary art in the form of *poetry* plays an intimate role in holding a space for testimony and challenging delimited representations of 'the' refugee.

Collectively, I suggest, these practices might be understood and theorised as diverse forms of 'sanctuary artivism'. Drawing on writings by Hannah Arendt, bell hooks, Audrey Lorde and M. K. Asante, I argue that although this artivism may speak to, influence, and shape sanctuary initiatives and government policies, it is a form of politics that – importantly – exceeds these fields.

In this chapter I am particularly concerned with the political affect of these forms of sanctuary artivism. When I refer to affect here I refer to a mood, atmosphere, or embodied feeling that is not quite reducible to a rational or conscious decision (Closs Stephens, 2016; Amin and Thrift, 2013: 161; Anderson, 2006; Massumi, 2015). This notion helps us understand how a 'structure of feeling' (Williams, 1977) or 'moody force field' (Amin and Thrift, 2013: 161) shapes the way we make sense of and act in our worlds. As various scholars have argued, these affective resonances play a key role in shaping, for instance, a sense of belonging (Closs Stephens, 2016). Vitally, affect is also more than just emotions or feelings (Massumi, 2015). It is more expansive than this, and also more erratic (Ahmed, 2004; Berlant, 2011). Affect can be a fleeting or lingering embodied sense of being moved by forces that elude clear description, like a sudden blush of the skin.

In drawing on these debates, I argue that sanctuary artivism plays a key role in stirring up an affective field, and particularly a 'scene of emotional contestation' (Berlant, 2000: 47) that compels us to think, and feel, differently about our forms of political attachment. Moreover, I illustrate how sanctuary artivism, which exceeds the conventional places of deliberative democracy, has a special power to illuminate the ways in which we are intimately connected beyond statist imaginaries. I suggest that these affective politics are intriguing, in part, because of their pre-figurative potential: they foreshadow more expansive forms of political belonging which cut across borders (of the city/nation/state) and imply complex forms of solidarities between human and more-than-human beings (Braun, 2005). I go on to argue that although such affective politics hold potential, they are not somehow completely emancipatory. Rather, I argue that sanctuary artivism is an agonistic field, or struggle, constituted by exclusionary modes of governance and (yet always) possibilities for living otherwise.

Crafty maps: place (re)making

How do we understand sanctuary? Though there is hardly a consensus around the normative appeal of sanctuary, in debates regarding sanctuary's merit, historical development, and contemporary expression you can almost always expect to see one thing: a map.

In mainstream media, academic texts, and activist literatures the map serves as an anchoring point to determine the limits and possibilities of sanctuary. More than simply identifying 'where' sanctuary exists, the map is used to shape how sanctuary is being perceived and how it might be practised. Figure 5.1 is one cartographic representation that has circulated widely in dominant print and online media, produced by the Center for Immigration Studies.

As geographers have argued, maps are not neutral representations (Massey, 2005; de Certeau and Mayol, 1998). Rather, they render visible certain realities while eclipsing others, and in so doing inform how we might act in and upon our worlds. As such, maps are perhaps best understood as a 'technology of power' (Massey, 2005: 106). Like the visual from the Center for Immigration Studies featured here, maps have a role in narrating political movements such as sanctuary. Here we see how sanctuary is framed in a way that reifies conventional statist geopolitical imaginaries. Colonial borders dividing Canada/ the US/Mexico remain firmly in place and are taken as given. A map recently published by the *Houston Chronicle* (available here: http:// patterico.com/wp/wp-content/images/sanctuary-cities.gif) depicts sanctuary through a similarly statist frame and adds the tagline 'currently, these cities and communities do not require law enforcement officers to report illegal immigrants to federal officials'. In the *Houston Chronicle* map sanctuary is framed as an 'illegal' movement while, on the other hand, statist laws and modes of governance – which criminalise and irregularise certain forms of mobility – are taken as given.

We have seen a proliferation of other kinds of cartographic representations, which challenge this discursive framing of the migrant and sanctuary movement as criminal. In the United Kingdom, for instance, the City of Sanctuary movement has depended on the map as a tool to celebrate this movement as hospitable (see Figure 5.2). Unlike Figure 5.1, which positions sanctuary as an illegal practice, the City of Sanctuary map elicits a sense of hope. Here each sanctuary city across the United Kingdom is represented by the symbol of two bodies holding hands, forming what appears to be the shape of a home or some kind of shelter.

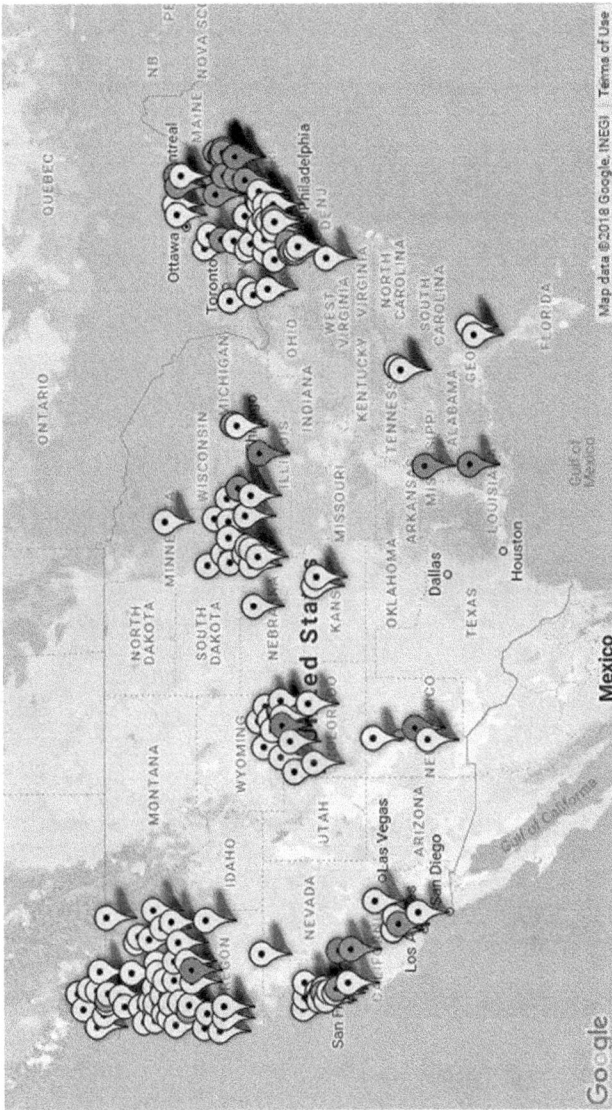

Figure 5.1 Sanctuary communities in the USA.

Figure 5.2 City of Sanctuary map, UK 2018.

Although these images are distinct in how they narrate sanctuary movements (as hostile/hospitable), they are connected in one important way. Both images imagine sanctuary as existing *within* the boundaries and strictures of the sovereign nation-state. In the first map we see sanctuary held within the territorial frame of the United States of America. In the second, sanctuary is snuggled into a familiar map of the United Kingdom. These maps reify, indeed unify, a statist way of seeing, or what James Scott refers to as 'seeing like a state' (1998), that is, a way of knowing the world through a top-down lens which assumes the state as sovereign.

I would argue that these maps take the imposition of colonial borders and boundaries that dispose and displace millions worldwide as given. In this way these sanctuary maps (seemingly designed to elicit different views) both serve to naturalise and entrench a statist political way of being. In each case the state is presented as an island that has no links to other spaces or political formations, be they other states, territories, or authorities. What this framing problematically elides is the way in which sanctuary may be experienced at *other scales*, across other registers, which in fact undermine and challenge the nation-state, and which challenge statist modes of political belonging.

At this point, I would like to turn to a different cartographic representation. The image shown in Figure 5.3 was created through a participatory, collaborative and – as described by the organisers – a 'crafty' mapping workshop. This workshop was led by Sanctuary Health – a grassroots movement founded in 2012 which, in its own words 'is committed to building cross-sectoral alliances of mutual support to advance the migrant-justice movement on unceded Coast Salish territories' (also known as Vancouver, BC, Canada). This activity was organised to provoke conversation and imagination around what a sanctuary might look and, indeed, feel like.

Strikingly, this map does not fit neatly within the colonial frame 'Canada'. Nor does this map allude to the colonial urban referent 'City of Vancouver'. In the absence of these statist strictures and place-names, the sticker reads 'sanctuary city'. It seems that this is an invitation to consider other ways of imagining place in terms that exceed colonial geopolitical imaginations. Perhaps, for instance, we might acknowledge this place as the unceded territories of the Musqueam (xʷməθkʷəy̓əm), Tsleil-Wauthuth (Səl̓ílwətaʔ/Selilwitulh) and Squamish (Skwxwú7mesh Úxwumixw) nations.

While the scale through which sanctuary is imagined in this map is 'the city', this urban space bears little relationship to colonial statist hierarchical conceptions. This image illustrates the urban as a metabolic

Figure 5.3 Access without Fear.

system rather than a contained geographical region. This metabolic understanding is illustrated through the buildings' (one notably identified with an 'H' which we might imagine to designate a hospital) connection to an intricate, subterranean root system that resembles lungs. In this map, beyond the horizon of familiar urban infrastructure, we also see mountain ranges. To my mind, this map evokes an expansive notion of urbanism – as that which exceeds tidy municipal lines and urban/rural distinctions. And, more importantly, this image allows us to imagine more expansive modes of political belonging that extend to the more-than-human world.

In addition to challenging colonial understandings of the urban, this visual defies official tourist maps of 'Vancouver' that are on every block of the city, directing pedestrians towards shopping centres and notable monuments. It juxtaposes 'official' cartographic representations that mark the city as a final achievement of welcome and multiculturalism. Instead, the words 'access without fear' in this image imply a limit. These words perform a call for, rather than a celebration of, a right to the city.

Critically this cartographic representation poses 'sanctuary' as a *process*, rather than a unified thing or place to be found on a familiar map. Sanctuary here is framed as an intimate movement that implies complex relationships. These relationships bleed across surface boundaries, and also seep and extend below the surface into the soil, water, and lands that sustain life. To reduce all of these connections to a pin on a map would be to erase the very heart of the sanctuary movement, which is pictured at the centre of the image.

Although many scholars (Carney et al., 2017) have increasingly referred to a sanctuary movement being 'scaled up' (beyond the city, to the nation, the international, or the planetary), this map reminds us how sanctuary is also functioning as a relational practice that actually *cuts across* these hierarchical territorial imaginaries. To retain a more expansive cartographic understanding of sanctuary, it seems, is vital if we are to imagine a more expansive politics.

I would like to consider one further image. Figure 5.4 was created by an asylum seeker living in Glasgow, who refers to himself as 'Nomad'. This image, again, does not fit neatly within conventional geopolitical frames. According to Nomad this is a map, though not an officially recognised one (Bagelman, 2016). This image intentionally does not conform to the grid. Rather, its circularity is meant to convey a sense of ambivalence about the sanctuary city in which he lives (Bagelman, 2016). At once, Nomad suggests, this circular map represents a feeling of inclusivity, and yet it also indicates a sense of containment or even imprisonment (Bagelman, 2016).

The question marks subtly drawn over the buildings in this map represent, to Nomad, an experience of waiting (Bagelman, 2016). As a person whose has been seeking refugee status for over eight years, waiting is an inherent part of his urban life. This map captures the intimate 'slow violence' that cannot be seen when we view sanctuary from above – as a little pin placed on the map. The protracted experience of waiting and waiting cannot be seen when we view sanctuary from

Figure 5.4 Illustration by 'Nomad', artist and asylum seeker.

a fixed, abstract, statist, Archimedean standpoint. Indeed, such a statist way of seeing blurs the 'attritional violence' that Nomad experiences and that – in its absence – 'is not typically viewed as violence at all' (Nixon, 2011: 2).

As feminist geographers have long argued, when we begin our analysis from the level of the state or region, and take such constructs as ontologically secure, we risk obscuring violence happening at other scales that are part of this production (Andrijasevic, 2010; Hyndman, 2004; Mountz and Loyd, 2013). Refusing this abstraction and erasure, this map illuminates both the spatial complexities of sanctuary and its attendant temporal violence. It draws us into the intimacies of sanctuary, as experienced by one who, without legal citizenship, is unable to fully access his urban environment (unable to access health services, education, or employment) without fear of deportation.

I suggest that both of the maps (Figures 5.3 and 5.4) explored in this section provide experiential and embodied ways of knowing sanctuary through their crafty representations. As many creative geographers have pointed out, craft can play a critical role in resisting conventional understandings of space, and can become sites and materials for performing alternative spatio-political configurations (Harvey et al., 2012). These maps address not simply the 'where is sanctuary?' but the 'how is sanctuary?' How is this process felt and practised? Sanctuary here is depicted through what Donna Haraway refers to as 'situated' ways of knowing and seeing (1988). These situated artistic interventions, it seems, are vital to understanding sanctuary in more complete terms: both in terms of its limits, and also in how it holds possibilities for a more expansive form of political belonging that exceeds the nation-state.

Sanctuary *détournement*

The second example of how art is playing a politically affective role in shaping sanctuary struggles today is through what I am calling sanctuary *détournement*. In French this term means 'diversion' or 'rerouting', and it was popularised as a political tactic in the 1950s by the Lettrist International and later adopted by the Situationist International movements. Famously, this concept and practice has also been taken up by the culture-jamming actors of the 1980s. Broadly speaking, the impulse animating this practice is to hijack familiar images, symbols, and icons and reroute them in creative and subversive ways (Debord, 1967).

With this practice in mind, I would like to turn attention towards a 'Transportation not Deportation' campaign that used *détournement* tactics to politicise the intensifying securitisation practices of Vancouver's transportation network on unceded territories. Two grassroots organisations, Sanctuary Health and No One Is Illegal, organised this campaign after Lucia Vega Jimenez, a Mexican woman living undocumented in the city, was stopped by transit police on her daily commute.

Lucia was intercepted by an armed transit patrol for 'not sounding
Canadian'. Shortly thereafter she was sent to an underground detention
centre (below Vancouver Airport), where she committed suicide in
her holding cell.

This terrible loss catalysed growing concern about the ways in which
border enforcement permeates beyond the edge of the nation-state
into the capillaries of everyday urban life wherein certain bodies are
subjected to intensified securitisation. This incident also exposed
the way in which border enforcement seeps below the surface, into
subterranean geographies. In this context, services such as transport
become less spaces of refuge, and more privatised border checkpoints
that funnel people with precarious status into dangerous carceral
geographies.

In order to publicise this intensification and blurring of border
enforcement into and below urban space, No One Is Illegal and
Sanctuary Health decided to stage an intervention. To do so, these
migrant justice organisations decided to detour, or reroute, some
imagery familiar to most commuters living in or visiting Vancouver.

Figure 5.5 shows, of course, a transit ticket. Vancouver's private
transit company, Translink, issues thousands of these little pieces of
paper every day. Commuters shove these tickets in jacket pockets,
and they can be found littering many streets. Despite its ubiquity this

Figure 5.5 Translink faresaver ticket.

object often remains an unnoticed part of the urban landscape. Given the everydayness of this object, No One Is Illegal and Sanctuary Health decided that subverting it might provoke conversation about mobility in the city. They did this in two principal ways, as shown in Figures 5.6 and 5.7. The purpose of detourning these familiar objects was to destabilise or detour the equally familiar narrative that frames Translink as a helpful service that simply connects people. The detourned image exposes how Translink (with its armed police, an annual police budget of over 30 million dollars, and a Memorandum of Understanding with the Canadian Border Services Agency) is less in the business of connecting everybody, and more in the business of stopping and criminalising *certain* types of bodies.

These mock tickets, which circulated through the city, left plenty of travellers confused. Some wondered whether this was an 'official' ticket that enabled travel. This affective politics of confusion incited conversation and increased awareness regarding the securitisation of transportation. In so doing, this art intervention exposed what Louise

VANCOUVER'S TRANSIT POLICE
ONLY ARMED TRANSIT POLICE IN THE COUNTRY

REFERRALS TO CBSA

TRANS/LINK 2013: **328**

1 in 5 resulted in an immigration investigation

Transit should not be a border checkpoint.
Transportation not Deportation!

Figure 5.6 Vancouver's transit police – protest reworking of Translink ticket.

Figure 5.7 Fair check? Protest reworking of Translink ticket.

Amoore refers to as 'rituals of border security' (Amoore and Hall, 2010: 301). As a practice of *détournement* it cast critical light on the presence of, and practices of, transit police as border guards. Moreover, this art drew critical attention to the quotidian objects and processes, such as vehicles and transportation infrastructure, that we often overlook as apolitical. Here, the politics of transportation (or what William Walters (2015) refers to as 'viapolitics') was revealed to be an inexorable part of the bordering regime. After months of tireless organising, Sanctuary Health and No One Is Illegal successfully ended the collaboration between Translink and the CBSA in 2015.[2]

Sanctuary zines

Related to this politics of *détournement*, sanctuary zines are also animated by an urge to reroute and repurpose familiar imagery and objects. Zines are a visual and textual mode of storytelling and are inexpensive, easy to make, and easy to distribute (Bagelman and Bagelman, 2016). Zines are often a collection of daily ephemera and repurposed images from dominant print media brought together to communicate an idiosyncratic story. Through simple acts of cutting and pasting, the zine is a relatively democratic artform: you do not have to identify as an 'artist', you do not have to own a computer or have access to a printing press to create or share this DIY work (Bagelman and Bagelman, 2016). Many trace the emergence of zines to the 1920s when artistic and philosophical movements such as Surrealism used small runs of self-published material decorated with collage and bricolage as a public forum for ideas.

Figures 5.8 and 5.9 show a double-page spread from a zine created by the UK-based human rights organisation Right to Remain. As

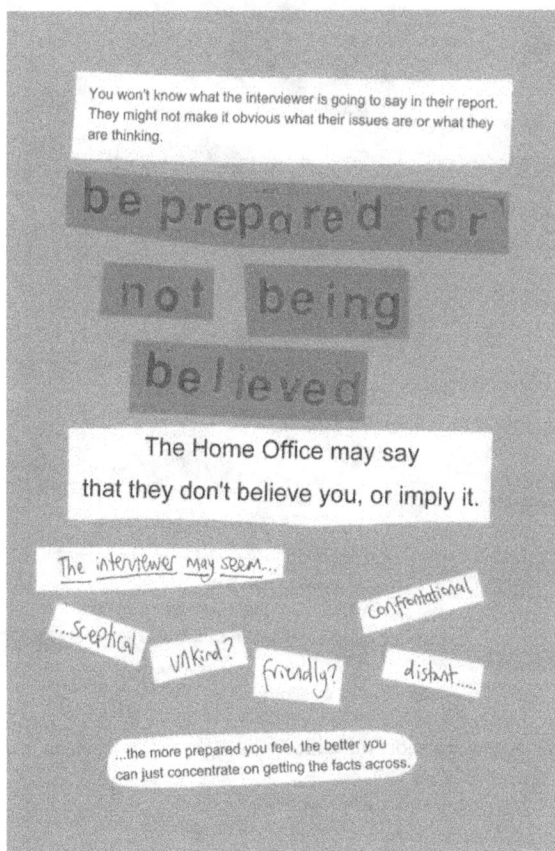

Figure 5.8 'Be prepared for not being believed' – Right to Remain zine front cover.

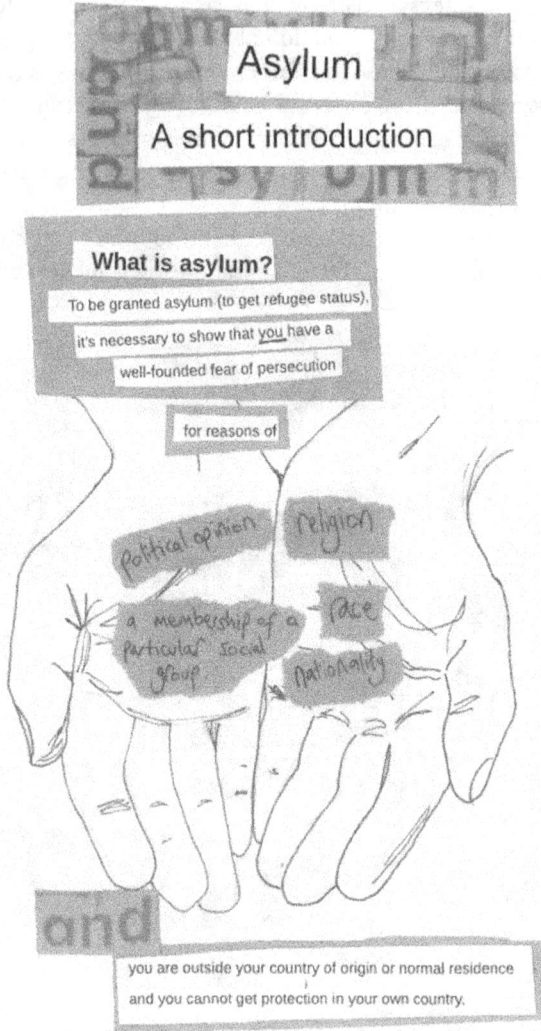

Figure 5.9 'Asylum: a short introduction' – Right to Remain zine front cover.

stated by Right to Remain, 'the content of the zine is based on Right to Remain's toolkit, Early Asylum Support Sheffield workshops and contains beautiful images and illustrations, making it accessible for people with only limited English language levels' (Right to Remain, 2018). The zine is freely available to asylum seekers, and unlike other more 'professional' resources, this zine was designed to be a more accessible resource and guide for asylum seekers preparing for their interviews to gain legal status.

In these images we see official language, used by the Home Office, cut out and pasted alongside intimate testimonies of having to traverse immigration rituals. These little booklets make visible the maze-like, and often painful, realities of dealing with state bureaucracy. They identify the cyclical traumas associated with exile. This circularity is precisely what is often cut out of official immigration interview processes – or what Mark Salter refers to as the 'confessionary complex' (2006: 168) – which demand that asylum seekers present their experiences in linear terms to the sovereign.

As an analogue and intimate form of expression, these booklets carve a place for political voices that are often eclipsed in dehumanising state rituals, which reduce the complex life histories of asylum seekers to a series of events to be confessed. While these zines provide an intimate account of immigration, they do not enact an individualised intimacy that might reduce state violence to an individual problem. Rather, these zines illuminate the structural violence inherent within immigration regimes. These zines expose the global political logic that renders certain lives precarious and what Nicholas De Genova calls 'deportable' (2002).

Sanctuary music

In addition to crafty maps, detourned objects and zines, the sounds of sanctuary also function as a political medium through which hostile immigration practices are being challenged. The album shown in Figure 5.11, 'Austin Songs of Protest from a Sanctuary City', was recorded in a BBQ shack on 18 November 2016 as songs of protest. The songs, which include titles such as 'The Spaniard' and 'Irrational Anthem', loudly contest Donald Trump's Senate Bill 4 to de-fund sanctuary. These songs (which can be found at the independent music

Figure 5.10 'Telling your story…' – Right to Remain zine front cover.

site https://austinsongsofprotest.bandcamp.com/releases) stir a variety of feelings and waves of emotion. Blending punk, folk, and classical music, this album elicits a range of responses.

In a similar vein, the song (and accompanying video) 'City of Sanctuary', created by UK-based artist Sam Slatcher, provides an interesting example of how music conjures a vivid notion of sanctuary (https://www.youtube.com/watch?v=auCmemjDluk). This video and

Figure 5.11 'Austin Songs of Protest from a Sanctuary City', album cover.

song features the journey of St Cuthbert's dead body, as a 'sleeping refugee' fleeing the Viking invasion of 875, to what would later become known as 'Durham'. It softly makes reference to the city's famous 'Sanctuary Knocker' for those fleeing legal prosecution, the miners' hall that became a sanctuary for the miners' strike in 1984, and to the Syrian refugee students who have recently fled to County Durham. This song serves to widen our political imaginaries by powerfully situating the practice of sanctuary within broader genealogies of sanctuary. The almost lullaby-like quality of this song is haunted both by violent histories, which were the conditions of possibility for exile, and yet the hopefulness of welcome. In listening to these pieces, I am left to wonder about the soundscapes of sanctuary. Might greater attention to the audio dimensions – often overlooked in academic work on sanctuary – teach us something about sanctuary activism? How do these chords and lyrics irritate, energise, and activate us? While listening to these albums online (far from the BBQ shack and the city of Durham), I sense a connection to distant geographies and I wonder what role these auditory waves of affect might play in building a more intricately, intimately connected movement?

Poetry: intimate geographies

The final form of artistic practice I examine is poetry, and in particular the following piece written by Kader Belouni entitled 'Sanctuary';

> Every day I sleep,
> Every day I wake,
> I don't know when I will be out.
> I am in limbo…
> It is not easy.
> You wake up, you don't know.
> You go to sleep, you don't know.
>
> 3 years 9 months – I wait.
> No idea which day I will put my feet outside.
> It was a stress.
> No, it was much more than stress.
> Some ask: is sanctuary a prison?
> The criminal knows what day he gets out.
> I do not know.
> I make no crime.
> Poem by Abdelkader (Kader, for friends) Belaouni (in Bagelman, 2016)

Much like the zines explored previously, this form of expression holds open the possibility of understanding sanctuary from the perspective of those who know it most intimately: people with precarious status. Reflecting on histories of migrant justice, as Megan Carney, Ricardo Gomez, Katharyne Mitchell, and Sana Vannini have argued, it is in part this ability to hold space for such nuance that 'poetry has been having all along a prominent role in voicing migrants' resistance' (2017: 18). Vitally, such forms of expression gesture at the complexities of sanctuary movements, complexities that might be lost when we see sanctuary as simply a designation or policy. While we have become familiar with an approach to sanctuary that understands this practice from city, rural, national, or planetary scales, what this expression offers is a more granular and quotidian account of sanctuary as a personal experience of protracted waiting and of feeling criminalised for one's existence. Similar to the sanctuary maps explored previously, this poem allows us to glean insight into the other registers of sanctuary as a complex lived reality that belies simplistic framings.

Artivism: an agonistic field

What, if anything, connects the diverse artful expressions explored in this chapter? I suggest that each of these expressions might be understood as political forms of artivism. Here, I borrow from film-maker M. K Asante's understanding:

> The artivist (artist + activist) uses her artistic talents to fight and struggle against injustice and oppression – by any medium necessary. The artivist merges commitment to freedom and justice with the pen, the lens, the brush, the voice, the body, and the imagination... (Asante, 2008: 39)

The above statement suggests that the artivist enacts powerful modes of political expression. The artivist is one who does not wait to be heard, but rather *takes* the opportunity to express herself. And she is not confined to singular tools to make herself heard, seen, and felt. Rather, she uses various *media*, 'any medium necessary', to create change and to expand our imaginations. The artivist, according to Asante, is engaged in powerful acts of artivism. For Asante, artivism is not confined to a particular geography but is a verb – an active process of taking new places (and exposing invisibilised places) through struggles against injustice.

That art can be a powerful form of resistance to oppression is not a new idea. With regard to sanctuary, art is almost inexorably entwined with some of its earliest recorded expressions. Art has often been deployed in advancing sanctuary through song, theatre, and murals. For instance, in the ancient Greek play *The Suppliants* by Aeschylus (470 BC) we hear suppliant women theatrically performing their case for asylum to King Pelasgus of Argos. In the following passage we hear the suppliant women who are fleeing forced marriages perform their cases:

> Think, and become wholeheartedly
> our pious sponsor (πρόξενος)
> do not betray the fugitive (τὰν φυγάδα)
> who comes from afar, set in motion
> by an impious expulsion

The Suppliants (418–423)

The women in this play seek to make their case through song and dance. Using irony, pointing out contradictions in the king's rule, and using their bodies and voices, these women do not at all appear the sort of demure, agentless women that the term 'suppliant' might imply. In an analysis of this play, Christopher Collard suggests that by embodying such theatrical performance, the 'suppliants are indeed difficult for Pelasgus to handle' (Aeschylus, 2008: xxi).

Art has historically been mobilised as a tool and celebration of freedom under subjugation and is at the very heart of various political movements and understandings of the political. bell hooks writes beautifully about art, arguing that its function 'is to do more than tell it like it is, it is to imagine what's possible' (2018). Similarly, Audrey Lorde argues in 'Poetry Is Not a Luxury' that art 'is a vital necessity of our existence. It forms the quality of the light within which we predicate our hopes and dreams towards survival and change' (1984).

The political theorist Hannah Arendt also famously examines the role of art as a form of politics. Though her understanding of the role of art belies simplistic reading, for our purposes here it is fruitful to point to the ways in which Arendt conceives art as a modality through which we carve out expansive forms of political belonging. In particular, she highlights that the art of narrative (or 'storytelling') is a lively and essential medium that provokes an understanding of the complex, and sometimes contradictory, qualities of our political lives. Art, she says, has this special ability precisely because it 'reveals meaning without committing the error of defining it' (1973b: 107). Art bleeds across simplistic, operationalised distinctions.

The forms of sanctuary art explored in this chapter, I argue, resonate with these words offered by Asante, Arendt, hooks, and Lorde. They enact a politics of the possible; they hold open a space for imagining how our worlds might be otherwise. As is the case with Kader Belouni's poem, the practices of sanctuary are not reducible to a fixed definition nor policy, but are a complexly lived landscape constituted by exclusion and welcome. Perhaps it is for this ability to hold space for this *both–and* that sanctuary artivism remains important political work. I would like to further suggest that these forms of artivism resemble what Engin Isin refers to as creative 'acts of citizenship', that is, a form of citizenship not delimited to a legal definition but, rather, processes that

> transform forms (orientations, strategies, technologies) and modes (citizens, strangers, outsiders, aliens) of being political by bringing into being new actors as activist citizens (claimants of rights and responsibilities) through creating new sites and scales of struggle. (Isin, 2008: 39)

Though art holds this possibility for transformation, this is not to say that artivism promises a transcendental, emancipatory potential. We should remain attentive to and critical of the many ways in which art is mobilised to repress through softer, insidious modalities of control. In the first instance, many of the expressions explored here could be read as a governmental strategy. The zines, for example, could be seen as an instrument through which migrant justice organisations assuage the concerns of asylum seekers and even normalise a hostile asylum process. By providing a 'guide' for a more hopeful future these zines might be read in terms of what Lauren Berlant refers to as 'cruel optimism' (2011) – that is, an aspirational politics which – without actually shifting structural violence – in fact becomes a mechanism of oppression.

We also do not need to look far to see how explicitly right-wing agendas are being mobilised through art. While crafty maps, zines, and poetry may effect a sense of welcome, these forms of expression are also used to entrench draconian politics and policies. This is painfully clear in the zine shown in Figure 5.12, which is used to deter migrants. This 18-page digital zine portrays Afghan asylum seekers, attempting to reach Australia, in distress in an offshore detention centre. This graphic booklet was launched on the Department for Immigration and Border Protection website and the Customs and Border Protection website as part of a deterrence policy.

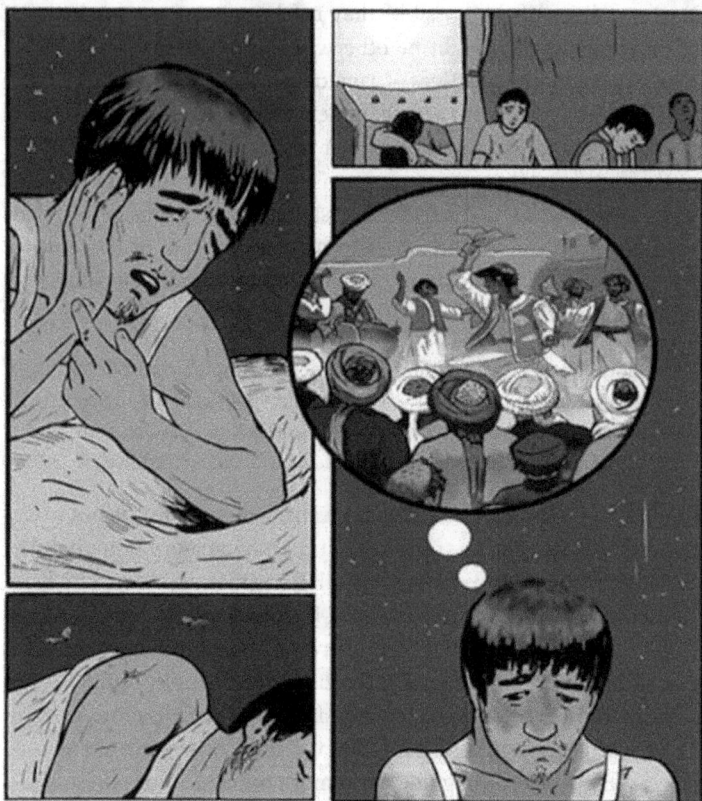

Figure 5.12 Page from a digital zine produced by the Australian Department of Home Affairs.

The point of my engaging in this artful field and investigating some sanctuary expressions is not to acritically celebrate these modes of politics, but to highlight the variegated discursive fields that shape how sanctuary is practised. In so doing my aim is to contribute to a growing field of visual political work that reminds us to question the images we consume, and to become more intentional about how we engage with and circulate these representations in our daily lives (Bleiker et al., 2013). For instance, as educators in the classroom we might ask: what maps do we use to visually convey an understanding of sanctuary? I also hope that by paying attention to the various artful expressions of sanctuary, we might widen our gaze beyond traditional actors. These artful expressions reminds us that sanctuary is not simply mayors and other elected officials and organisers getting things done, but rather a contested terrain wherein residents (with and without legal citizenship) intervene in creative ways. It is, to borrow Michel Foucault's language, an agonistic and relational field, rife with opportunities for shifting the order of things.

Global intimacies of sanctuary

Through what scale should we understand these forms of sanctuary artivism? Within sanctuary scholarship there is a tendency to imagine sanctuary through the scales of the urban (Filipcevic Cordes, 2017; Ridgley, 2008), national (Darling, 2010), international (Bauder, 2017), and – increasingly – planetary (Carney et al., 2017). For instance, in his article 'City sovereignty: urban resistance and rebel cities reconsidered', Vojislava Filipcevic Cordes makes the persuasive case that we should consider sanctuary at the urban scale, that sanctuary is not simply haphazard activity but rather a collective form of action that becomes realised through shared urban living. Jonathan Darling, calling upon the geographer Doreen Massey, carefully argues that urban sanctuary efforts in the UK cannot be understood as bound to particular cities, but rather are part of a more interconnected, and 'outward-looking', national movement. Harald Bauder argues in his recent article 'Sanctuary cities: policies and practices in international perspective' that this outward-looking quality is not only within national sanctuary contexts, but *across* them. What we see today, as the title of this piece implies, is an international movement. In a recent, joint-authored piece, 'Sanctuary planet', this scale is extended further. This article provides a direct call to imagine sanctuary as a planetary movement (Carney et al., 2017). In each of these cases, we see an appeal to view sanctuary as a kind of movement that links various actors, at different scales.

While understanding sanctuary through the scale of the urban, national, international, or even planetary helps expand our political horizons, I suggest that these frames cannot adequately capture the complex forms of political belonging that emerge in the forms of sanctuary explored in this chapter. Many of the examples explored

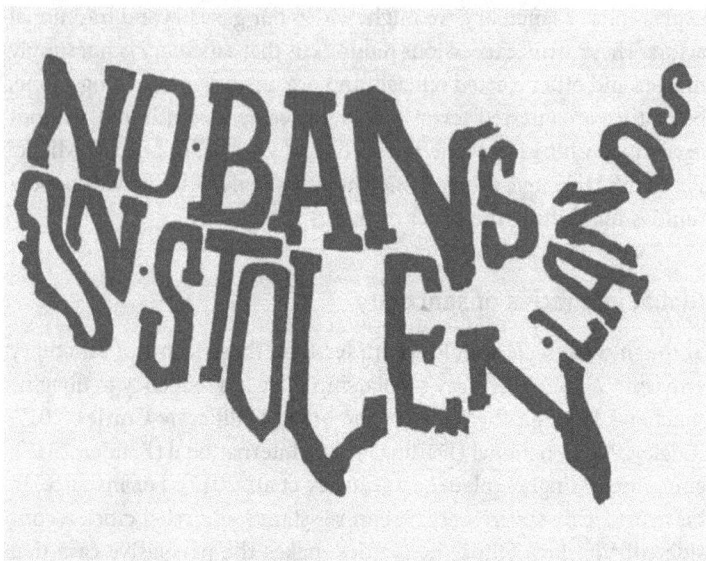

Figure 5.13 Dylan Miner, 'No bans on a stolen land'.

here are illuminating forms of belonging that do not fit neatly within the city/nation/planetary. When we hear people singing 'No Ban on Stolen Land' as a sanctuary protest song, are we hearing a politics expressed through the *national* scale? And what about art that detourns colonial maps, like Nomad's visual of the sanctuary city – does this fit within the *urban* scale? Or what about the map produced by the Indigenous artist Dylan Miner (Figure 5.13) – should we view this through a statist lens or…?

These forms of art, it seems, illuminate forms of political belonging that are excessive and directly confrontational to a statist scalar logic and politics. Figure 5.13, in particular, illuminates solidarities emerging between migrant and Indigenous communities that stand (sometimes uncomfortably) together to challenge the sovereignty of the state and settler colonial logics of the city.

As we witness sanctuary expand in exciting ways through forms of sanctuary artivism, I think that we need to develop more expansive ways to articulate and engage with these politics. I would like to suggest that a different analytical lens might be helpful in approaching diverse sanctuary expressions; namely, the global-intimate (Pratt and Rosner, 2006). Building on feminist geographical scholarship, I understand the global-intimate as a lens that attends to the ways in which our lives take shape in particular localities and also how these intimate lives are globally connected to extended geographies (Conlon and Heimstra, 2017; Pratt and Rosner, 2006). The analytical task set out here is to trace how people and places are connected through political processes – such as globalising capitalism – often in highly uneven and exploitative ways. I want to point to a few main ways in which I think this lens is vital in helping us understand and carefully build sanctuary movements today.

First, retaining the language of the global-intimate is important because it explicitly draws our attention to the lived, felt, visceral dimensions of both the need for and expressions of sanctuary. In practice, approaching sanctuary through a global-intimate lens means being attentive to how movements are being organised (not just the spectacular major moment, that is, the moment that a city is designated 'safe' by an official ordinance). It draws our attention to the *slow* work and (often gendered) emotional labour that goes into building and sustaining places of safety for people with precarious status. I am thinking here of the sustained energy that goes into listening, being silent with and holding space for people who have experienced trauma resulting from exile. Or the emotional labour that goes into organising public vigils for lives lost due to hostile border control. I am also thinking of the quiet organising that goes into finding temporary homes for people facing deportation orders, or the fierce work of fundraising that is done to support legal cases for people in precarious situations. These acts are perhaps not always seen or heard – but they are vital to a sanctuary movement that seeks to make all residents feel welcome. All of this work, I think, is not peripheral to but rather the beating heart that animates sanctuary.

Additionally, attending to intimacy compels us to ask not only 'what is sanctuary' but *how* is sanctuary enacted and felt by those with precarious status? And, importantly, how are the limits of sanctuary's sacred promise experienced by those who do not hold legal rights? Placing primacy on intimacy ensures that we keep asking these questions. An intimate register keeps our focus on building a movement that remains in step with those who are most immediately impacted by intensifying hostile border politics. Moreover, examining the intimacies of sanctuary, I think, repositions people with precarious status as experts with diverse knowledge and reorients us towards hard questions such as how can we bring these voices to the fore in ways that create safe platforms, and that support communities in the ways they wish to be supported?

To think about intimacy is not to suggest turning attention away from wider geopolitical forces of capitalism, colonialism, and the many other isms. Rather, this global-intimate lens insists on tracing and exposing the ways in which our everyday lives are both inexorably entwined with wider forces and struggles while remaining responsible to our everyday relationships (Conlon and Heimstra, 2017). As Geraldine Pratt has shown in her decades-long work with temporary foreign workers in Canada, the global-intimate exposes how a reliance on cheap care-labour in one place (namely Vancouver) produces the displacement of women elsewhere (namely the Philippines) (Pratt, 2013). And this lens provides an entry into sensing the myriad ways in which sanctuary organising is responding to uneven global relations. For instance, it exposes how sanctuary is doing the political work of linking purportedly distinct crises (environmental, economic, colonial) across seemingly disparate geographies. This global-intimate lens calls upon us to acknowledge how these modes of organising are being performed across multiple sites, often at the same time. At once we are called to grasp, for instance, the street protests, the policies, the fundraising, the doctor refusing to ask about status, the lobbying of governmental officials, the sanctuary school reading-lists, the meals quietly being made together. Rather than prioritising some of these modes of political activity as higher and designating some as lower, the relational lens of the global-intimate incites us to interrogate how these politics are functioning together to promote more generative places. As an analytical lens, the intimate-global provides us with a more nuanced way to stay with – and even contribute to – these complex sanctuary expressions that upend familiar spatial hierarchies and oppositions to make space for the complex ways we inhabit our worlds.

I conclude by making a call to pay greater attention to these artful expressions, for these practices illuminate and prefigure more textured and intersectional struggles that exceed traditional modes and scales of political belonging. These artful practices, in the words of artivist Marisa Franco (2017), should be taken seriously for 'they do not simply recreate what existed, but instead expand, reimagine and breathe life into its possibilities'.

Notes

1 I approach definitions not as a foundational logic upon which we build an unshakable argument. Rather, drawing on bell hooks, I see definitions as 'vital starting points for the imagination'. Such points of reference are important because, as hooks states, 'what we cannot imagine cannot come into being. A good definition marks our starting point and lets us know where we want to end up. As we move towards our desired destination we chart the journey, creating a map' (hooks, 2018: 14).

2 For more information visit https://transportationnotdeportation.wordpress.com/tag/translink (accessed 12 November 2018).

References

Aeschylus (2008) *Persians and Other Plays*, trans. Christopher Collard (New York: Oxford University Press).

Ahmed, S. (2004) 'Collective feelings: Or, the impressions left by others', *Theory, Culture & Society*, 21:2, 25–42.

Amin, A., and N. Thrift (2013) *Arts of the Political: New Openings for the Left* (Durham, NC: Duke University Press).

Amoore, L., and A. Hall (2010) 'Border theatre: on the arts of security and resistance', *Cultural Geographies*, 17:3, 299–319.

Anderson, B. (2006) 'Becoming and being hopeful: towards a theory of affect', *Environment and Planning D: Society and Space*, 24:5, 733–752.

Andrijasevic, R. (2010) 'The cross-border migration', in *Migration, Agency and Citizenship in Sex Trafficking* (Basingstoke: Palgrave Macmillan), 26–56.

Arendt, H. (1973a) *Men in Dark Times* (New York: Harcourt Brace).

Arendt, H. (1973b) *Origins of Totalitarianism* (New York: Harcourt Brace Jovanovich, new edn).

Asante, M. K. (2008) *It's Bigger Than Hip Hop: The Rise of the Post-hip-hop Generation* (Basingstoke: Macmillan).

Bagelman, J. (2013) 'Sanctuary: a politics of ease?', *Alternatives: Global, Local, Political*, 38:1, 49–62.

Bagelman, J. (2016) *Sanctuary City: A Suspended State* (New York: Palgrave Macmillan).

Bagelman, J., and C. Bagelman (2016) 'Zines: crafting change and repurposing the neoliberal university', *ACME: An International Journal for Critical Geographies*, 15:2, 365–392.

Bauder, H. (2017) 'Sanctuary cities: policies and practices in international perspective', *International Migration*, 55:2, 174–187.

Berlant, L. (2000) 'The subject of true feeling: pain, privacy and politics', in S. Ahmed, J. Kilby, C. Lury, M. McNeil, and B. Skeggs (eds), *Transformations: Thinking Through Feminism* (London: Routledge), 33–48.

Berlant, L. (2011) *Cruel Optimism* (Durham, NC: Duke University Press).

Bleiker, R., D. Campbell, E. Hutchison, and X. Nicholson (2013) 'The visual dehumanisation of refugees', *Australian Journal of Political Science*, 48:4, 398–416.

Braun, B. (2005) 'Environmental issues: writing a more-than-human urban geography', *Progress in Human Geography*, 29:5, 635–650.

Carney, M., R. Gomez, K. Mitchell, and S. Vannini (2017) 'Sanctuary planet: a global sanctuary movement for the time of Trump', *Environment and Planning D: Society and Space*, http://societyandspace.org/2017/05/16/sanctuary-planet-a-global-sanctuary-movement-for-the-time-of-trump/ (accessed 5 December 2017).

Closs Stephens, A. (2016) 'The affective atmospheres of nationalism', *Cultural Geographies*, 23:2, 181–198.

Conlon, D., and N. Heimstra (eds) (2017) *Intimate Economies of Immigration Detention: Critical Perspectives* (London: Routledge).

Darling, J. (2010) 'A city of sanctuary: the relational re-imagining of Sheffield's asylum politics', *Transactions of the Institute of British Geographers*, 35:1, 125–140.

Debord, G. (1967) *The Society of the Spectacle* (Berkeley, CA: Bureau of Public Secrets).

De Certeau, M., and P. Mayol (1998) *The Practice of Everyday Life. Volume 2: Living and Cooking* (Minneapolis, MN: University of Minnesota Press).

De Genova, N. P. (2002) 'Migrant "illegality" and deportability in everyday life', *Annual Review of Anthropology*, 31:1, 419–447.

Dibrell, R. (2018) 'Sanctuary communities', *Houston Chronicle*, www.chron.com/search/?action=search&searchindex=solr&query=%22sanctuary+communities%22&isRedesign=&page=2 (accessed 12 March 2018).

Filipcevic Cordes, V. (2017) 'City sovereignty: urban resistance and rebel cities reconsidered', *Urban Science*, 1:3.

Franco, M. (2017), 'Radical expansion of sanctuary', *Truthout*, https://truth-out.org (accessed 1 September 2017).

Haraway, D. (1988) 'Situated knowledges: the science question in feminism and the privilege of partial perspective', *Feminist Studies*, 14:3, 575–599.

Harvey, D. C., H. Hawkins, and N. J. Thomas (2012) 'Thinking creative clusters beyond the city: people, places and networks', *Geoforum*, 43:3, 529–539.

hooks, b. (2018) *All about Love: New Visions* (New York: William Morrow).

Hyndman, J. (2004) 'Mind the gap: bridging feminist and political geography through geopolitics', *Political Geography*, 23:3, 307–322.

Isin, E. F. (2008) 'Theorizing acts of citizenship', in E. F. Isin and G. M. Nielsen (eds), *Acts of Citizenship* (London: Zed Books), 15–43.

Lippert, R. K. (2004) 'Sanctuary practices, rationalities, and sovereignties', *Alternatives: Global, Local, Political*, 29:5, 535–555.

Lorde, A. (1984) 'Poetry Is Not a Luxury', in *Sister Outsider: Essays and Speeches* (Freedom, CA: Crossing Press), 36–39.

Mancina, P. (2012) 'The birth of a sanctuary-city: a history of governmental sanctuary in San Francisco', in R. K. Lippert and S. Rehaag (eds), *Sanctuary Practices in International Perspectives: Migration, Citizenship and Social Movements* (Abingdon: Routledge), 205–218.

Mancina, P. (2016) 'In the Spirit of Sanctuary: Sanctuary-City Policy Advocacy and the Production of Sanctuary-Power in San Francisco, California', PhD thesis, Vanderbilt University, https://etd.library.vanderbilt.edu/available/ etd-07112016-193322/unrestricted/Mancina.pdf (accessed 18 November 2018).

Massey, D. (2005) *For Space* (London: Sage).

Massey, D. (2013) *Space, Place and Gender* (Chichester: John Wiley & Sons).

Massumi, B. (2015) *Politics of Affect* (Chichester: John Wiley & Sons).

Mountz, A., K. Coddington, R. T. Catania, and J. M. Loyd (2013) 'Conceptualizing detention: mobility, containment, bordering, and exclusion', *Progress in Human Geography*, 37:4, 522–541.

Mountz, A., and J. M. Loyd (2013) 'Constructing the Mediterranean region: obscuring violence in the bordering of Europe's migration "crises"', *ACME*, 13:3, 173–195.

Nixon, R. (2011) *Slow Violence and the Environmentalism of the Poor* (Cambridge, MA: Harvard University Press).

Pratt, G. (2013) 'Unsettling narratives: global households, urban life and a politics of possibility', in L. Peake and M. Rieker (eds), *Rethinking Feminist Interventions into the Urban* (London: Routledge), 122–138.

Pratt, G., and V. Rosner (2006) 'The global & the intimate', *Women's Studies Quarterly*, 34:1, 13–24.

Ridgley, J. (2008) 'Cities of refuge: immigration enforcement, police, and the insurgent genealogies of citizenship in US sanctuary cities', *Urban Geography*, 29:1, 53–77, DOI: 10.2747/0272-3638.29.1.53.

Right to Remain (2018), https://righttoremain.org.uk/right-to-remain-group-launched-in-sheffield/ (accessed 4 December 2018).

Salter, M. B. (2006), 'The global visa regime and the political technologies of the international self: borders, bodies, biopolitics', *Alternatives*, 31:2, 167–189.

Scott, J. C. (1998) *Seeing Like a State: How Certain Schemes to Improve the Human Condition Have Failed* (New Haven, CT: Yale University Press).

Walters, W. (2015) 'Migration, vehicles, and politics: three theses on viapolitics', *European Journal of Social Theory*, 18:4, 469–488.

Williams, R. (1977) *Marxism and Literature* (Oxford: Oxford University Press).

Part II

Urban struggles

6

Understanding local government's engagement in immigrant policy making in the US

M. Anne Visser and Sheryl-Ann Simpson

In 2006 the municipal government of Hazleton Pennsylvania became the first city in the US to enact a so-called Illegal Relief Act (IIRA) (Varsanyi, 2010). Proponents of the Act were explicit that their aim was to make it as difficult as possible for undocumented residents to live and work in the city. In addition to describing these residents as 'illegal', proponents also claimed that undocumented residents were a burden on the city's social services and a threat to the broader security of the community. While the IIRA was enacted with the goal of regulating undocumented residents out of the city, the Act did not focus on arrests or detentions. Instead, the IIRA contained strong penalties for employers who hired and landlords who housed undocumented residents. Additionally, the IIRA declared English to be the official language of the city with the aim of limiting access to government services and information for non-English speakers.

Hazleton's anti-immigrant legislation functioned as a 'local regularisation' (LR), a policy that responds to the presence, or the possibility of arrival, of undocumented residents with conditional provisions that impact these residents' opportunities for economic participation (Visser, 2017). LRs encompass a range of policy types including local engagement with federal immigration laws, employment verification laws, anti-solicitation ordinances, regulations about housing, and language access laws. LRs might be inclusive, favourable to the expanded participation of undocumented residents, or unfavourable, excluding undocumented residents from economic life through measures that also impact on their opportunities for social and political participation.

Hazleton was just one of dozens of cities that proposed or enacted LRs in and around 2006, a period of increased immigration policy making activity for local governments around the US.

In this chapter we examine the increased activity of municipal, county, and US state governments through the analysis of a unique database of over 3,000 LRs passed from 1980 to 2014 (Visser, 2017). We examine the character, timing, and location of policy adoption, and compare patterns between these scales. While LRs have been examined in the past, it has usually been through specific case studies, examinations of particular domains, or comparisons across limited time periods, usually during the early 2000s (see, for example, Walker and Leitner, 2011; Steil and Vasi, 2014; Walker, 2014). By examining a country-wide, longitudinal database of LRs we are able to attend to patterns that emerge between scales and across time. Additionally, by focusing on the entire country the database captures action in 'ordinary' cities (as well as US states and counties), developing urban theory that is attentive to a full range of local settings (Robinson, 2002).

Examining the US is informative, as the immigrant community in the country is growing and becoming more diverse in terms of site of emigration, race and ethnicity, and formal status. Additionally, the geography of immigration is shifting, with increasing rates of foreign-born residents in secondary cities and suburban locations (Jones-Correa, 2001). The federated organisation of the US government also means that there are three scales below the central government, each with different capacities and interests in the area of immigration. While our analysis is primarily descriptive, the patterns that emerge can also be used to refine hypotheses around the motivations of local state actors to engage in questions of immigration in general, and irregular immigration specifically.

The conditions that surrounded the passage of the IIRA in Hazleton highlight some of the major debates around local state actors' motivations for engaging in immigration policy making. A city of just over 20,000 people in 2006, Hazleton had become a site of secondary migration for emigrants from Spanish-speaking Caribbean, Central American, and South American countries such as the Dominican Republic. While many of the new residents in Hazleton had first settled in larger centres such as New York, Philadelphia, and areas in New Jersey, they were drawn to the smaller city by a lower cost of living and employment opportunities in the processing and logistics service industry. This included positions at a Cargill meat-packing plant and various retail warehouses (Martinez, 2011). Yet racialised nationalist narratives described these new Latino residents as the cause of crime and overcrowding in the city, rather than acknowledging their economic engagement.

In highlighting the 'illegality' of undocumented residents present in their city, proponents of the Act also drew attention to a perceived failure of the federal government to secure international borders. The IIRA, however, did not focus on detention and removal, and instead focused on regulating residents' practices within the city. These practices included the ability to engage and participate in the economic and social spheres, and to occupy and animate space in the city (Dikeç, 2005; Kallio, 2012; Phillips and Robinson, 2015). Further, this approach was a declaration that the city had no responsibility to take on the costs of providing social services to these residents.

Hazleton gained broad attention because it was the first city to enact a type of restrictive policy at a high point of immigration debates in the US. But there were dozens of ordinary cities around the country that proposed or passed Acts similar to Hazleton's. While complex and diverse in their own right, cities such as Hazleton (or San Bernardino in California, the first city to propose an IIRA although it was not enacted) are not often featured in urban theorising (Robinson, 2002). Therefore, examining local action in a range of cities, including secondary cities such as Hazleton, can provide new insights into the relationships between immigration and cities more generally.

In addition to conditions in a particular place, multi-scalar processes have also been found to be important motivators for local actions (Filomeno, 2017). Taking the example of Hazleton, IIRA proponents specifically pointed to the failure of the federal government to secure borders and enforce immigration laws to justify their need to act around immigration. At the same time, the city was never able to enforce the Act, as it was overturned by federal courts in 2007. While Hazleton's policy was enacted in seeming opposition to federal actions, the relationships between different scales of government around issues of immigration vary from cooperation initiated from central or lower levels of government, through to direct conflict and subsequent disconnect between policies and programmes at different scales (Ridgley,

2008; Scholten and Penninx, 2016; Caponio and Jones-Correa, 2017; Newton, 2017).

While the analysis in this chapter does not focus directly on the causes or motivations for adopting LRs, by examining patterns across the country and over time our analysis strengthens the development of hypotheses around the motivations for adopting LRs. In doing so, we argue that, in spite of the attention paid to the inclusive character of local immigration actions, a strong majority of LRs enacted at all scales are unfavourable, and exclude undocumented residents from opportunities for participation in formal social, political, and economic spheres. Additionally, the patterns between scales and over time suggest an important role for federal governments in directing local action. In the following sections we further define local regularisation policies and examine current understandings of the motivations for local governments to engage in immigration policy making, including characteristics of immigrant residents alongside non-immigrant residents, communities, institutions, and structures. We then analyse longitudinal LR data from the US, and end with a discussion of the ways in which these longitudinal patterns might inform further research into immigration policy making. Finally, recentring the discussion on both local scales of government and the relationships between scales has the potential to offer new perspectives on the conditions shaping the everyday life of immigrant residents in the US.

Local regularisation

Local regularisations are part of a group of state actions that focus on the regularisation of the labour market either through provisions that reinforce and regulate the exclusion of undocumented residents, or through temporary, place-bound status to allow for participation (Visser, 2017). Whether favourable and inclusive of undocumented residents' participation, or exclusionary and unfavourable to participation, LRs operate through a range of strategies that impact on undocumented residents' opportunities for social and political alongside economic participation.

The database (see Visser, 2017) analysed in this chapter includes LRs in four policy domains: 1) policies related to local engagement with federal immigration enforcement; 2) employment identification enforcement; 3) solicitation of informal work in public spaces; and 4) local language policies. While policies in each domain have the potential to impact on the economic engagement of undocumented immigrant residents, they do so through distinct mechanisms. These include interventions that relate directly to formal legal status, and interventions focused on cultural and social membership in place (Simpson, 2015). Understanding local immigration policy making through the idea of local regularisation is an opportunity to examine the ways in which the local state shapes and conditions immigrant residents' experiences of immigration, settlement, and incorporation in terms of both formal status and broader practices of membership and citizenship (Staeheli et al., 2012; Bauböck, 2015). Before unpacking these relations in more detail, we shall briefly outline these policy domains of LRs examined in this chapter.

Local engagement with federal immigration enforcement

The US federal government's Priority Enforcement Program (originally the 287(g) programme, enacted in 1996 with major amendments in 2008 and 2014) allowed local governments to engage in immigration enforcement activities by authorising local law enforcement agents to make inquiries into immigration status as part of more routine local police duties, and to cooperate with and report to federal immigration agents. These so-called 'Secure Community' arrangements extend the capacity of US federal immigration enforcement by having local governments fund an increase in personnel involved in formal immigration enforcement, and expanding the spaces and circumstances under which undocumented residents might encounter this enforcement. Favourable actions in this domain include local governments passing legislation to prohibit the use of funds to support the enforcement of federal immigration laws, or revoking Secure Community arrangements.

Employment identification enforcement

Unfavourable employment identification enforcement policies include the requirement to comply with the federal Real ID Act of 2005, and policies that comply with the US federal E-Verify policies. The Real ID Act mandates the type of identification documents and other verification that must be used to prove an employee's eligibility for regular employment. These policies exclude forms of verification that undocumented residents can obtain, including tax ID numbers, or local identification that does not require proof of federal status. E-Verify is a database that allows employers to compare identification information provided by potential employees with databases maintained by the Department of Homeland Security and Social Security Administration to confirm documented status and employment eligibility. In 2007 the US federal government moved to make the use of E-Verify mandatory for federal contractors. Favourable policies in this domain might prohibit Real ID programmes, support the use of local identification mechanisms for work authorisation, or implement temporary worker programmes. As such, this group of policies also relates to the relationships between formal immigrant enforcement responsibilities at the federal and local levels, but focuses on the workplace as the site of enforcement as opposed to public spaces or home settings.

Solicitation of informal work in public spaces

One strategy to cope with irregular status is to seek work in the informal sector (Kim, 2015). Informal work falls out of step with formal employment regulations or protections, and might include work where wage or workplace safety regulations are not met, contingent employment, work where employees are not formally registered, as well as employment that does not comply with tax statutes (Visser, 2017). One of the most publicly visible elements of the informal economy in the US has been day labour, where potential employees seek work in public places, including at street corners and in parking lots (Varsanyi, 2008). Informal work is usually in low-paying, manual labour positions, for example, in residential construction, private household work, and landscaping. Over 90 per cent of day labourers in the US are immigrant residents, including many undocumented workers (Valenzuela et al., 2005). Rather than focusing on formal immigration enforcement, policies targeting day labour sites seek to regulate the presence and actions of immigrant residents in public spaces. Through the regulation of public action, these policies also shape opportunities for economic participation for a largely immigrant, mixed-status workforce. While unfavourable policies ban or restrict public solicitation, favourable policies might include the establishment of centres for day labourers, or revoking anti-solicitation ordinances.

Local language policies

The US has no national language policy, and so language policy LRs create local cultures of incorporation in which access to government information, services and public participation are expanded or restricted. Unfavourable policies in this domain include English-only ordinances, which mandate that public documents will not regularly be available in additional languages. Favourable policies promote regular multilingual access to government documents. Language ordinances do not deal directly with questions of formal status or immigration enforcement, but do shape the opportunities for full local membership. By targeting language specifically, these policies also highlight the symbolic and racialised character of US immigration debates. Whether favourable or unfavourable, these laws conjure a specific, well-defined image of immigrant residents in general, and undocumented residents in particular. Language skills become the defining factor in identifying members and non-members. In reality of course, the English-language skills of all residents in the US vary wildly, and as such, language laws, by limiting or increasing their opportunity for full participation in political, economic and social life, have material impacts on non-English-speaking residents with a variety of immigration statuses, including US citizens.

Examining the patterns of LRs across these four policy domains builds a stronger understanding of the increasingly varied and complex conditions of enforcement and opportunities faced by undocumented residents. At the same time, examining the actions of local governments, including the highly politicised issue in public discourse in the US, also helps to explain what motivates local political actors to engage with the politics of immigration in general, and the question of irregular migration in particular. In the next section, we outline a series of local and multi-scalar theories around the motivation for engagement.

Local state motivations in immigration policy making

Any understanding of the motivations for local state engagement in immigration should take a relational perspective – one that engages with the ways in which place shapes and conditions the relationships between states and residents (Phillips and Robinson, 2015). In mapping out an agenda to examine place effects in processes of immigration, Robinson (2010) describes the need to examine the characteristics of both immigrant and non-immigrant residents, alongside the culture of the place, its history and collective identity, and the material opportunity structures in place. Furthermore, immigration policy making is a complex, multi-scalar process (Caponio and Jones-Correa, 2017); therefore understanding the motivations of local governments to act also necessitates an understanding of the influences between scales of government.

Resident characteristics and narratives

Part of the explanation around the motivation for local immigration policy making, including LRs, centres around the characteristics of immigrant residents, including their national, ethnic, and racial characteristics. The location and density of settlement has also been posited as an explanation for local state action around immigration. Ellis, for example, explains that '[d]ispersed immigrant populations have their cultural and physical presence diluted whereas concentration of the foreign-born crystallises native feelings of loss of numerical dominance, declining control over territory, and a fear of being overrun' (2006: 54). This explanation, however, overlooks the characteristics and narratives that exist in place.

An examination that primarily relies on the characteristics of immigrant residents, and the idea that the presence of immigrant residents is in and of itself disruptive, localises the practice of methodological nationalism. Glick Schiller and Çağlar describe methodological nationalism as an approach in which 'state borders' are taken as 'societal boundaries' creating 'a mode of logic that makes immigrants the fundamental threat to social solidarity' where 'natives are assumed to uniformly share common social norms' (2009: 180). A relational approach, as Robinson (2010) suggests, will also take into account the characteristics and narratives of established residents (see also Bolt et al., 2010). As an example, in the US, 'illegal immigration' has been tied to Latino residents for as long as there has been legislation requiring authorisation to enter the country. Hernández (2010) documents the ways in which policing the US–Mexico border region became the primary way in which the Border Patrol, established in 1924, could operationalise its sprawling mandate to police immigration (see also Mehan, 1997; Chavez, 2013). A century later this relationship persists, and, as in Hazleton, the presence of Latino residents becomes a signifier of immigration generally, and irregular migration specifically. And the conflation of Latino and foreign happens in inclusive as well as exclusionary narratives around immigration. In Hazleton this narrative was employed by anti-immigration proponents, who presented themselves as the defenders of small town life and values, a life that new residents were said naturally to disrupt (Martinez, 2011). As we discuss in the next section, in addition to demographic questions and cultural narratives, economic narratives and material opportunity structures have also been identified as potential motivators for local engagement in immigration policies and the adoption of LRs.

Economic needs and opportunities

Immigrant workers and Latino residents are over-represented in low-wage jobs in the US. Additionally, increased economic inequality and the polarisation of the US labour market has led to greater competition generally, including the perception of 'ethnic competition' in the labour market (Visser and Meléndez, 2011, 2015; Visser, 2017, 2018). Studies suggest that even the perception of a relationship between immigration and economic insecurity can drive public opinion on immigration policies (Pantoja, 2006; Wilkes et al., 2008).

Greater economic instability is also related to a broad rescaling of welfare responsibilities (Brenner and Theodore, 2002), including welfare competencies being downloaded or devolved to lower levels of government, or offloaded to non-governmental actors (Beckwith, 2007). Further, individuals are incentivised to find market-based solutions to social welfare questions (Katz, 2001). At the same time, inclusive attitudes towards immigrant residents are bolstered when economic security is reinforced through universalist, as opposed to liberal or residual, welfare states (Crepaz and Damron, 2009).

Yet the character of welfare support, and in turn relationships between states and immigrant residents, is not simply determined by the scale at which this support is delivered (Keating, 2009). Motivated by ideas around efficiency, local state actors may make general investments in human capital to increase economic performance (Keating, 2009). 'Market citizenship' approaches informed by the assumption that 'unconstrained mobility and non-discrimination is all that is needed for social integration' (Bauböck, 2015: 73) would lead to reduced support. Local state actors might also compete to selectively attract migrant residents who were seen as skilled or creative (Jørgensen, 2012), or simply use the presence of immigrant residents as an economic development tool. Some local state actors employ the image of immigrant communities to brand themselves as growing, cosmopolitan, and global places (Glick Schiller and Çağlar, 2013; Harwood and Lee, 2015; Lee, 2016). The variety of economic motivations and actions that local governments take on highlights the distinct set of local interests in processes of immigration.

Distinct local interests

From one perspective, the main distinction from central governments that might motivate local government action is the cost of settlement. As Ellis describes:

> while the US Government takes responsibility for entry (and has a rela- tively unselective set of criteria for admittance), [US] states and localities bear the cost of absorption. This friction has generated [US] state demands for greater resources from the federal government as well as local and [US] state initiatives to deny services to immigrants. (2006: 56).

This explanation certainly fits with the narrative of cities such as Hazleton, where the burden of undocumented immigrant residents on schools and other social services, for example, was invoked to support local policies unfavourable to undocumented residents.

From another perspective, a sense of responsibility to residents can drive local government action. Looking specifically at bureaucratic actors, for example, Jones-Correa (2008) and Marrow (2009) examine bureaucratic incorporation in suburban and rural sites in the US. Bureaucratic incorporation describes the role of bureaucrats in organisations such as formal education systems, libraries, emergency medical service agencies, and social welfare agencies responding to immigrant residents, including undocumented residents, in inclusive ways. Organisations in both cases altered and extended services to include all residents. These efforts also involved interaction with political actors to advocate for a redistribution of funding that would support these extended services. Particularly, for the most inclusive sectors such as elementary and secondary education, and emergency medical services, inclusionary actions were described through bureaucratic norms that focused on ideas of equal worth, and a broad definition of the public to be served that included all residents, regardless of formal status (Jones-Correa, 2008; Marrow, 2009; Kim et al., 2018).

These bureaucratic norms also relate to a local sense of citizenship that defines local membership and citizenship through principles of domicile, and a responsibility to provide services to, and be accountable to, residents by virtue of the ties and connections they have to a municipality (Bauder, 2014; Bauböck, 2015). This broader ethics of inclusion (Darling, 2013) motivates sanctuary city policies, which extend access to services and potentially decision making to residents without formal federal status. The capacity and political will to act on principles of inclusion and domicile citizenship also relate to the broader institutional relationships and governance communities that develop around local immigration policy making.

Institutional arrangements and governance communities

Institutional explanations for local state engagement in immigration policy making focus on the relationships between local state and local non-governmental organisations (NGOs). Distinct from the type of lobbying or civil society actions that advocate specifically for particular policies or state actions (Benjamin-Alvarado et al., 2009), the focus of these institutional explanations is on ongoing relationships, influence, and resource exchange. Frasure and Jones-Correa (2010), for example, highlight the ways in which local NGOs are able to exchange resources such as the ability to carry out service delivery, or connect and communicate with immigrant and other diverse communities, for state resources and authority. 'There is a powerful logic at work behind these relationships that lends them […] stability', declare Frasure and Jones-Correa, that '[e]ach set of actors benefits from the relationship' (2010: 474).

One of the possible challenges in the relationship between local governments and local organisations is that close ties can lead to a vassal relationship, wherein local NGOs play the role of a shadow state, assigned responsibilities for social services without the power or independence to advocate around broader questions of inequity (Martin, 2004; Trudeau and Veronis, 2009; Frasure and Jones-Correa, 2010). Empirical research into the work of local NGOs, however, highlights the ways in which these organisations navigate and negotiate multiple positions in relation to the state (Elwood, 2006). There are examples of immigrant-serving organisations using relationships with the state as an opportunity for direct negotiation; collaborating with immigrant residents to identify and advocate for immigrant community interests; 'mistranslating' state narratives, for example, by promoting the ideal of a public responsibility for social welfare with their clients at the same time that states are supporting the privatisation of welfare; or promoting norms around multiculturalism as state policy making becomes more expressly exclusionary or nationalistic (Theodore and Martin, 2007; Simpson, 2015).

Finally, an institutional approach attends to the impact of state–local NGO relationships over time, including the types of policy legacies and path dependencies they engender (Zincone and Caponio, 2006). Piccoli (2016), for example, examines the variations in regional healthcare access for undocumented immigrant residents in Italy, Spain, and Switzerland. He concludes that much of the variation between regions can be explained through the characteristics of established links between NGOs and governments. These links define the means and character of health delivery and, more broadly, the character of regional citizenship, including the willingness and ability to include undocumented residents as members deserving of healthcare. While the focus of Piccoli's analysis is healthcare, he notes that regional citizenship characteristics would influence other areas of social welfare too. Alongside the relationships between actors at the local scale, the relationships between state actors at different scales has also been proposed as playing an important role in shaping motivations for local state actors to engage in immigration policy making (Filomeno, 2017).

Multi-scalar governance

Alongside other complex social policy and membership questions, immigration policy making is a multi-scalar process with interactions between scales of government (Caponio and Jones-Correa, 2017). In addition to local governments looking to the central government for action and direction around immigration, the federal government in the US has increasingly involved local governments to carry out immigration enforcement (Newton, 2017). Arrangements such as the 287(g) programme, which authorised local governments to directly engage in immigration enforcement, are examples of the types of coordinated policy making that defines multi-level governance (Scholten and Penninx, 2016; Caponio and Jones-Correa, 2017).

At the same time, local actions also come in the form of direct responses or rebukes to central government policies, narratives, and programmes. In examining primarily larger European cities and their inclusionary policies and programmes, Scholten and Penninx note that 'politicized debates at the national level can have a performative effect at the local level' (2016: 100), and posit that these cities have become more active and entrepreneurial in their actions around immigration to counter central government actions and narratives. As already noted, in Hazleton local actors also described their anti-immigration policies as a response to federal policies, in this case perceived inaction around enforcement. Whether inclusionary or exclusionary, the results of these entrepreneurial actions have decoupled central and local policies and policy making processes (Scholten and Penninx, 2016). There are multiple possible outcomes from the decoupling of policies at different scales, including the potential for greater conflict between governments (Newton, 2017; Spencer, 2018), alongside official, but quiet, local policy implementation designed not to draw the attention of additional scales of government, for example policy enacted through collaboration with local NGOs (Spencer, 2018). Finally, decoupled policy making can lead to a patchwork of rules surrounding and experiences for immigrant residents, and horizontal diffusion of policies (McCann and Ward, 2013; Cook, 2015; Newton,

2017). Hazleton's unfavourable policies, for example, used as a blueprint the policy of San Bernardino, the first city to propose this type of policy (Martinez, 2011).

Policy entrepreneurship can also develop into local activism, when local state policies can 'reasonably be understood as deliberate attempts to spotlight unfavourable laws and policies in hopes of stimulating change' (Riverstone-Newell, 2013: 16). While there has been less evidence of such policy activism in the local actions and literature around immigration, Riverstone-Newell (2013) examines local responses to the Patriot Act, passed by the US federal government after attacks in New York and Washington on 11 September 2001, which increased state surveillance and detention powers. She finds that municipal anti-Patriot Act activism had an effect on the actions of US states, and an accumulation of municipal actions increased the probability of the higher level of government adopting a similar policy. Rather than higher levels of government simply setting the agenda, the relationships between scales of government is multidirectional, shaped through local conditions (Jørgensen, 2012).

While immigration in the US is clearly defined as a federal policy domain, local governments, municipalities, counties, and US states have thus become increasingly active in law and policy making that impacts the lives of immigrant residents generally, and undocumented residents specifically. Rather than simply the addition of immigrant residents, a relational approach to studying immigration geographies (Robinson, 2010; Philips and Robinson, 2015) and the motivations for increased local immigration policy making supports an examination of the ways in which demographics, cultural narratives, economic opportunities, local institutions, and multi-scalar relationships interact to direct the probability and direction of local action.

Examining immigration policy making through this more expansive lens highlights the existing heterogeneity within states, which in turns reframes immigration away from being an existential national crisis into just one of many social welfare and membership puzzles facing local governments. In this understanding, the experience of immigration, and the opportunities afforded to immigrant residents, is contingent on local conditions. As such, local conditions and actions become a key site of inquiry around immigration.

In this section, we do not propose to solve the question of the exact mechanisms through which local governments are motivated to act. Rather, in response to the framework of conditions and actions established so far throughout this chapter, by examining what is happening at multiple scales, longitudinally, and across the entire country, we aim to uncover patterns that can help to refine these theories around motivations.

Local regularisation across scales

In this section we analyse the patterns for 3,441 LRs across four domains adopted between 1980 and 2014. These policies are drawn from a larger LR database (see Visser, 2017) and we included policies with complete data, including dates, in our analysis. The larger database was compiled through a systematic search of databases created by the National Immigration Law Center, National Council of La Raza and LatinoJustice, which was supplemented by additional municipal code databases Municode, General Code, Code Publishing and American Legal Publishing. Visser (2017) provides a full description of this dataset including how LRs were identified, coded, and categorised.

Across the country a strong majority of LRs were adopted after 2006 and were exclusionary or unfavourable in character. There was, however, a great deal of variation in terms of the type and character of LRs passed at different scales and over the course of the study period. To explore this in more depth, we focus on three spatial contexts – US states, counties, and municipalities.

US states

As the largest scale of government below the central government, US states have general authority in areas such as education, providing key identification documents used for employment verification, and transportation. US state governments, however, vary in relation to their governance capacities, historical contexts, and populations. For example, the most populous state, California, has over 39 million residents, full-time legislators, and according to the US Census Bureau a foreign-born population of 27 per cent. Wyoming, at the other end of the spectrum, has a total population of under 600,000 people, part-time lawmakers, and a foreign-born population of 4 per cent.

In spite of this variation, a strong majority, 86 per cent of the fifty-six US state LRs in the database, were unfavourable to undocumented residents' economic participation. LRs at this scale were also heavily skewed towards policies in the employment ID verification domain (71 per cent), with the remainder split between language policies (14 per cent), and solicitation (14 per cent). The timing of US state policies matched general trends across the country, including an increase after 2006, with 23 per cent of all policies at this scale passed in 2007 alone. There was also a shift in the character of policies after 2006 from the solicitation domain to the employment ID domain.

Pre-2006 policy making by US state governments primarily focused on informal interventions in larger states, or states with growing immigrant and Latino populations, for example California, Texas, and Georgia. Post-2006 policy making at this scale of government shifted. First, a wider range of US states passed immigration-related policies, for example New York, Iowa, Alaska, and Texas, in just 2006 and 2007. Second, there was a shift to policies focused on formal interventions that directly responded to federal policies, including the adoption of the Real ID Act and expansion of the E-Verify and Secure Cities programmes discussed above. The federal government explicitly described its policies in this domain as an attempt to standardise practices across the country, and US states were largely willing to cooperate with the federal mandate. This desire and willingness for coordination highlights a shift towards multi-level governance approaches to immigration enforcement during this period (Newton, 2017).

Counties

There are 3,142 counties across the US, with an average of sixty counties per US state. While the role of counties varies across the US states, in almost all cases they play a role in law enforcement, and in most US states they also participate in service delivery, ranging from infrastructure, housing, and economic development to involvement in health and education services.

There were 2,959 county LRs included in the database, and in thirty-six US states all counties had passed some type of LR by 2014. Counties were the most active scale of government passing the most LRs. Only eight of the policies included in the database were favourable. Ninety-eight per cent of the LRs were related to the relationship of local governments to federal immigration legislation and enforcement, including Secure Community Acts, which authorise county police forces to engage in immigration enforcement. Few policies were passed before 2000. The majority of policies were adopted after 2006, with 28 per cent of LRs at this scale adopted in 2011 alone.

While counties were the most active, they were in many ways the least entrepreneurial (Scholten and Penninx, 2016) of all local scales of government during the study period. Action at this scale was almost entirely directed towards compliance and cooperation with central government policies. In spite of the important role that counties play in social welfare delivery, they passed almost no LRs focused on cultural incorporation. Because of the patchwork of jurisdictions in the US, however, county actions potentially play a strong role in the lives of immigrant residents, including undocumented residents. Crossing over county lines can change undocumented residents' membership status, as local law enforcement officers become immigration officers in the counties with Secure Community arrangements, exposing undocumented residents to increased surveillance. Additionally, and particularly in the west and south of the USA, a substantial proportion of the population lives in unincorporated areas. These are areas without municipal governments where county governments provide a wider range of services. They are often areas with high numbers of low-income residents and, particularly in California, high numbers of Latino and immigrant residents (Flegal et al., 2013).

Finally, preliminary analysis combining LR information with data from the US Census Bureau suggests that across the study period, the presence of Latino residents in a county, regardless of immigration and citizenship status, is a stronger predictor of counties passing a restrictive LR than the presence of immigrant residents. When the data was further disaggregated, we found that counties with no Latino residents have a higher probability than counties with just a small population to pass LRs; and with the highest numbers of Latino residents the probability of passing an LR drops considerably. Rather than crystallising nationalist sentiments (Ellis, 2006: 54), the presence of foreign-born populations has less effect on policy making than the perception of immigration embodied by Latino residents (Mehan, 1997; Hernández, 2010). Further, even here the non-linear relationship (higher probabilities of LRs with no Latino residents as compared to a few, and lowest probabilities with the highest concentrations) suggests the need for further examination of the ways in which narratives and demographics interact (Chavez, 2013; Phillips and Robinson, 2015).

Municipalities

US municipalities include cities, towns, and villages, and are the most intimate scale of government. While their competencies vary, and are generally defined by the governments of US states, a municipality's greatest responsibilities are in service delivery. These services might include education, parks and recreation, policing, waste management, libraries, and local economic development.

The pattern of LRs in cities is distinct from the other two sub-federal governments in the US. First, only a limited number of municipalities enacted any sort of LR. From the almost 650,000 municipalities in the US, only 313 LRs were identified in the database, 242 LRs with complete data including dates between 1980 and 2014. All LRs were adopted by cities, as opposed to smaller municipalities such as towns and villages, and in thirteen states no municipal LRs were enacted.

The content of policies was also distinct from those passed by US states and counties. For the municipal LRs, 28 per cent were positive; 42 per cent were in the language domain, and 64 per cent in the language domain were positive. The remaining policies were split almost evenly between employment identification (27 per cent) and public solicitation (29 per cent). The timing of policies was also distinct from the other scales of government, with 21 per cent of municipal LRs in the database adopted before 2000. Earlier policies were 80 per cent anti-solicitation laws.

Municipalities varied from other scales of local government, with a significantly smaller proportion of government action, greater diversity across the policy domains, and distinct patterns over time. Importantly, post-2000 policy making in cities was more likely to be favourable and in the domains associated with informal incorporation, as compared to the other scales of government. As such, municipal LRs impact on membership opportunities broadly, and affect a wide range of residents, including immigrant residents with both regular and irregular status, and even US citizens who may share characteristics with the public imaginary of 'an immigrant'. In the US this imaginary largely includes residents with limited English skills and residents with Latin American or Hispanic heritage. Finally, the lack of municipal action raises the question of the motivation of the cities that did adopt LRs, especially given their limited official power in this area.

Preliminary analysis suggests that larger city populations were related to an increased probability of a city adopting an LR. This correlation suggests that the capacity of cities to act might be limited by their policy-making and programme-delivery capacities, as smaller cities, towns, and villages might not have the administrative capacity to take entrepreneurial actions in these policy areas (Jørgensen, 2012). Another probable limitation is financial ties between municipalities and the higher levels of government. Transfers from US state and federal governments make up a larger proportion of municipal revenues, which likely figures into municipal actors' calculations about how entrepreneurial they can afford to be in pursuing decoupled immigration policy making.

Discussion and conclusion

In this chapter we have examined data from a longitudinal database of local regularisation policies passed across the US between 1980 and 2014. Through a descriptive analysis of this database we identified key patterns in the data that build a stronger understanding of the local conditions for undocumented immigrant residents. While LRs are policies that specifically impact on opportunities for participation in the economic sphere, the range of strategies employed in LRs, which include both formal and informal interventions, make this an important lens through which to understand the broad range of interactions between local state actors and immigrant residents.

Understanding the variations in local actions around immigration is an important tool to begin to understand patterns, changes, and the mechanisms driving these changes in policy making and politics around immigration, settlement, and incorporation. Understanding these patterns and patterns of change is particularly important as the landscape of immigrant policy making continues to shift in the US, and as the result of the 2016 presidential election has reignited highly politicised debates around immigration, immigrant resident settlement, and incorporation. As an example, the state of California was one of the earliest adopters of unfavourable LRs, but on 1 January 2018 California's SB54 came into effect, making it the first 'sanctuary state'. The federal Justice Department has already moved to sue the California government, claiming that the law obscures and conflicts with federal law. At the same time the president continues to threaten to withhold federal grants from any local sanctuary jurisdiction.

While a great deal of the literature around local government engagement with immigration policy making has focused on inclusive policies in cities as potential or actual sites of sanctuary (Jones-Correa, 2008; Marrow, 2009; Scholten and Penninx, 2016), our main finding is that a strong majority of LRs at all scales were unfavourable, increasing the exclusion of undocumented residents. Even at the municipal scale, 72 per cent of policies were unfavourable. Additionally, at the scale of US states and counties, policies were specifically focused on engagement in the enforcement of formal federal immigration policies and programmes. For these local governments the focus was on security from, rather than sanctuary for, immigrant residents.

In terms of the motivation for passing LRs, the timing of policies, with a sharp increase at all scales of government after 2006, indicates an increase in multi-level governance around immigration enforcement in the US (Scholten and Penninx, 2016; Caponio and Jones-Correa, 2017; Filomeno, 2017; Newton, 2017; Spencer, 2018). Particularly at the scale of US states and counties, most local policies directly responded to federal programmes such as E-Verify and 287(g), later renamed Secure Communities. This coordinated policy making resulted in local governments providing the resources needed to implement federal immigration enforcement, including detention and deportation, and the exclusion of undocumented residents from employment and social participation.

After 2000, while other scales of government increasingly adopted unfavourable policies, municipal governments increased their favourable policy making. Particularly as municipalities are the least economically and politically independent scale of government, this pattern of decoupled policy making (Scholten and Penninx, 2016) supports theories that distinct municipal interests motivate inclusive immigration policy making. These interests include a local sense of citizenship informed by an ethics of inclusion, and responsibilities to all residents (Darling, 2013; Bauder, 2014; Bauböck, 2015). In addition to local interests, the finding that cities, and indeed larger cities, were more likely to pass any policy at all highlights the difficulty for ordinary cities to act in the sphere of immigration (Robinson, 2002). This opens a research opportunity for in-depth examinations of the cases of smaller municipalities that did pass LRs, and of cities that proposed but did not adopt them (see, for example, Martinez, 2011). These case studies could also help to build a stronger understanding around economic motivations, and the institutional arrangements that facilitate both inclusionary and exclusionary policy making (Pantoja, 2006; Wilkes et al., 2008; Frasure and Jones-Correa, 2010). Finally, attention to a wider range of municipalities would supply additional points of comparison to understand the interactions between Anglo-American narratives and demographic change described in greater detail above.

The patterns at the municipal scale are distinct from the other scales of local government, but do not warrant unbridled optimism around cities as sites for inclusion and membership for immigrant residents. Aside from the limited policy making and the largely exclusionary actions of cities, a strong majority of the favourable or inclusive municipal action focused on informal interventions. Policies around multilingual access to government information or services are certainly welcoming, but they do not provide sanctuary, and the ability to engage and participate is in many ways conditional on formal status (Staeheli et al., 2012; DeFilippis and Faust, 2014; Sandoval, 2015). Further, as Hudson (this volume) discusses, a focus on service provision and decoupled policy making without direct engagement of the levels of government with formal authority in matters of immigration amounts to an acceptance of formal conditions of exclusion.

For undocumented residents the shifting politics of local engagement means navigating a patchwork of policies and citizenship regimes. One's membership, access to resources, and the criminalisation of one's body shifts when moving between cities, counties, and US states. Rather than disrupting a homogeneous polity unambiguously defined by a border, immigrant residents confront existing heterogeneity within and between cities, counties, and US states, which shapes experiences of immigration, settlement, and incorporation. Further focusing on this heterogeneity draws attention to the ways in which questions around immigration are just one part of a broader set of governance puzzles related to questions of shifting roles for the provision of social welfare between levels of government, as well as general questions around engagement and participation. Focusing on the local aspects of immigration policy making builds a stronger understanding of the experience of immigration and the experience of contemporary citizenship more broadly.

Acknowledgements

Invaluable research assistance was provided by Laura Daly, Dakota Smith, Daniel Rodriguez, and J. Marcos Garcillazo.

References

Bauböck, R. (2015) 'The three levels of citizenship in the European Union', *Phenomenology and Mind*, 8, 66–76.
Bauder, H. (2014) 'Domicile citizenship, human mobility and territoriality', *Progress in Human Geography*, 38:1, 91–106.
Beckwith, K. (2007) 'Mapping strategic engagements: women's movements and the state', *International Feminist Journal of Politics*, 9:3, 312–338, DOI: 10.1080/14616740701438218.
Benjamin-Alvarado, J., L. DeSipio, and C. Montoya (2009) 'Latino mobilization in new immigrant destinations: the anti-H.R. 4437 protest in Nebraska's cities', *Urban Affairs Review*, 44, 718–735.
Bolt, G., A. S. Özüekren, and D. Phillips (2010) 'Linking integration and residential segregation', *Journal of Ethnic and Migration Studies*, 36:2, 169–186.
Brenner, N., and N. Theodore (2002) 'Cities and the geographies of "actually existing neoliberalism"', *Antipode*, 34:3, 349–379.
Caponio, T., and M. Jones-Correa (2017) 'Theorizing migration policy in multilevel states: the multilevel governance perspective', *Journal of Ethnic and Migration Studies*, online earlyview, DOI: 10.1080/1369183X.2017.1341705.
Chavez, L. (2013) *The Latino Threat: Constructing Immigrants, Citizens, and the Nation* (Palo Alto, CA: Stanford University Press).
Cook, I. R. (2015) 'Policy mobilities and interdisciplinary engagement', *International Journal of Urban and Regional Research*, 39:4, 835–837.

Crepaz, M. M. L., and R. Damron (2009) 'Constructing tolerance: how the welfare state shapes attitudes about immigrants', *Comparative Political Studies*, 42:3, 437–463, DOI: 10.1177/0010414008325576.

Darling, J. (2013) 'Moral urbanism, asylum, and the politics of critique', *Environment and Planning A*, 45:8, 1785–1801, DOI: 10.1068/a45441.

DeFilippis, J., and B. Faust (2014) 'Immigration and community development in New York City', *Urban Geography*, 35:8, 1196–1214.

Dikeç, M. (2005) 'Space, politics, and the political', *Environment and Planning D: Society and Space*, 23, 171–188.

Ellis, M. (2006) 'Unsettling immigrant geographies: US immigration and the politics of scale', *Tijdschrift voor Economische en Sociale Geografie*, 97:1, 49–58.

Elwood, S. (2006) 'Beyond cooptation or resistance: urban spatial politics, community organizations, and GIS-based spatial narratives', *Annals of the Association of American Geographers*, 96:2, 323–341.

Filomeno, F. A. (2017) *Theories of Local Immigration Policy* (Basingstoke: Palgrave Macmillan).

Flegal, C., S. Rice, J. Mann, and J. Tran (2013) *California Unincorporated: Mapping Disadvantaged Communities in the San Joaquin Valley* (Oakland, CA: Policylink).

Frasure, L. A., and M. Jones-Correa (2010) 'The logic of institutional interdependency: the case of day laborer policy in suburbia', *Urban Affairs Review*, 45:4, 451–482.

Glick Schiller, N., and A. Çağlar (2009) 'Towards a comparative theory of locality in migration studies: migrant incorporation and city scale', *Journal of Ethnic and Migration Studies*, 35, 177–202.

Glick Schiller, N., and A. Çağlar (2013) 'Locating migrant pathways of economic emplacement: thinking beyond the ethnic lens', *Ethnicities*, 13:4, 494–514.

Harwood, S. A., and S. S. Lee (2015) 'Immigrant-friendly community plans: rustbelt efforts to attract and retain immigrants', in M. Burayidi (ed.), *Cities and the Politics of Difference* (Toronto: University of Toronto Press).

Hernández, K. L. (2010) *MIGRA! A History of the U.S. Border Patrol* (Berkeley, CA: University of California Press).

Jones-Correa, M. (2001) 'Comparative approaches to changing interethnic relations in cities', in M. Jones-Correa (ed.), *Governing American Cities: Inter-Ethnic Coalitions, Competition, and Conflict* (New York: Russell Sage), 1–14.

Jones-Correa, M. (2008) 'Race to the top? The politics of immigrant education in suburbia', in D. S. Massey (ed.), *New Faces in New Places: The Changing Geography of American Immigration* (New York: Russell Sage), 308–40.

Jørgensen, M. B. (2012) 'The diverging logics of integration policy making at national and city level', *International Migration Review*, 46:1, 244–278.

Kallio, K. P. (2012) 'Political presence and the politics of noise', *Space and Polity*, 16:3, 287–302.

Katz, C. (2001) 'Vagabond capitalism and the necessity of social reproduction', *Antipode*, 33:4, 709–728.

Keating, M. (2009) 'Social citizenship, solidarity and welfare in regionalized and plurinational states', *Citizenship Studies*, 13:5, 501–513.

Kim, A. J. (2015) 'From the enclave to the city: the economic benefits of immigrant flexibility', *Local Environment: The International Journal of Justice and Sustainability*, 20:6, 706–727.

Kim, A. J., J. M. Levin, and N. D. Botchwey (2018) 'Planning with unauthorized immigrant communities: what can cities do?', *Journal of Planning Literature*, 33:1, 3–16.

Lee, S. (2016) 'The fantasy and reality of selling diversity: using immigration to manage global insecurities', paper presented at the Association of Collegiate Schools of Planning, Annual Conference, November.

Marrow, H. B. (2009) 'Immigrant bureaucratic incorporation: the dual roles of professional missions and government policies', *American Sociological Review*, 74:5, 756–776.

Martin, D. (2004) 'Nonprofit foundations and grassroots organizing: reshaping urban governance', *The Professional Geographer*, 56, 394–405.

Martinez, A. (2011) 'The politics of Latino belonging: law, scale, and identity in municipal anti-immigrant ordinances in the United States', PhD dissertation, Rutgers, the State University of New Jersey.

McCann, E., and K. Ward (2013) 'A multi-disciplinary approach to policy transfer: geographies, assemblages, mobilities and mutations', *Policy Studies*, 34:1, 2–18.

Mehan, H. (1997) 'The discourse of the illegal immigration debate: a case study in the politics of representation', *Discourse & Society*, 8:2, 249–270.

Newton, L. (2017) 'Immigration politics by proxy: state agency in an era of national reluctance', *Journal of Ethnic and Migration Studies*, 44:12, 2086–2105, DOI: 10.1080/1369183X.2017.1341714.

Pantoja, A. (2006) 'Against the tide? Core American values and attitudes toward US immigration policy in the mid-1990s', *Journal of Ethnic and Migration Studies*, 32:3, 515–531.

Phillips, D., and D. Robinson (2015) 'Reflections on migration, community, and place', *Population, Space and Place*, 21, 409–420.

Piccoli, L. (2016) 'Left out by the state, taken in by the region? Explaining the regional variation of healthcare rights for undocumented migrants in Italy, Spain, and Switzerland', *Working Paper*, 10, National Center of Competence in Research – The Migration-Mobility Nexus, and University of Neuchatel, Neuchâtel, Switzerland.

Ridgley, J. (2008) 'Cities of refuge: immigration enforcement, police, and the insurgent genealogies of citizenship in US sanctuary cities', *Urban Geography*, 29:1, 53–77, DOI: 10.2747/0272-3638.29.1.53.

Riverstone-Newell, L. (2013) 'The diffusion of local bills of rights resolutions to the states', *State and Local Government Review*, 45:1, 14–24.

Robinson, D. (2010) 'The neighbourhood effect of a new immigration', *Environment and Planning A*, 42, 2451–2466

Robinson, J. (2002) 'Global and world cities: a view from off the map', *International Journal of Urban and Regional Research*, 26:3, 531–554.

Sandoval, G. F. (2015) 'Immigrant integration models in "illegal" communities: Postville Iowa's shadow context', *Local Environment*, 20:6, 683–705.

Scholten, P., and R. Penninx (2016) 'The multilevel governance of migration and integration', in B. Garcés-Mascareñas and R. Penninx (eds), *Integration Processes and Policies in Europe* (IMISCOE Research Series) (Berlin: Springer), 91–108, DOI: 10.1007/978-3-319-21674-4_6.

Simpson, S. (2015) 'Negotiating places of incorporation: comparing the practices of community development organisation in immigration and incorporation', *Journal of Ethnic and Migration Studies*, 41:12, 1978–2000.

Spencer, S. (2018) 'Multi-level governance of an intractable policy problem: migrants with irregular status in Europe', *Journal of Ethnic and Migration Studies*, 44:12, 2034–2052, DOI: 10.1080/1369183X.2017.1341708.

Staeheli, L. A., P. Ehrkamp, H. Leitner, and C. R. Nagel (2012) 'Dreaming the ordinary: daily life and the complex geographies of citizenship', *Progress in Human Geography*, 36:5, 628–644.

Steil, J. P., and I. B. Vasi (2014) 'The new immigration contestation: social movements and local immigration policy making in the United States, 2000–2011', *American Journal of Sociology*, 119, 1104–1155.

Theodore, N., and N. Martin (2007) 'Migrant civil society: new voices in the struggle over community development', *Journal of Urban Affairs*, 29:3, 269–287.

Trudeau, D., and L. Veronis (2009) 'Enacting state restructuring: NGOs as "translation mechanisms"', *Environment and Planning D: Society and Space*, 27:6, 1117–1134.

Valenzuela A., A. L. Gonzalez, N. Theodore, and E. J. Melendez (2005) *In Pursuit of the American Dream: Day Labor in the Greater Washington, DC Region* (Los Angeles: Center for the Study of Urban Poverty).

Varsanyi, M. W. (2008) 'Immigration policing through the backdoor: city ordinances, the "right to the city," and the exclusion of undocumented day laborers', *Urban Geography*, 29:1, 29–52.

Varsanyi, M. W. (ed.) (2010) *Taking Local Control: Immigration Policy Activism in U.S. Cities and States* (Stanford, CA: Stanford University Press).

Visser, M. A. (2017) 'Reshaping migrant labor market geographies: local regularizations and the informal economy', *Population, Space, and Place*, 23:7, DOI: 10.1002/psp.2025.

Visser, M. A. (2018) 'Restructuring opportunity: employment change and job quality in the US during the Great Recession', forthcoming, *Socio-Economic Review*, DOI: https://doi.org/10.1093/ser/mwy002.

Visser, M. A., and E. J. Meléndez (2011) 'Puerto Ricans in low wage jobs and labor markets: the issues, trends and policies', *CENTRO Journal*, 23:11, 3–28.

Visser, M. A., and E. J. Meléndez (2015) 'Working in the new low wage economy: understanding participation in low wage employment in the recessionary era', *Working USA*, 18, 7–29.

Walker, K. E. (2014) 'Immigration, local policy, and national identity in the suburban United States', *Urban Geography*, 35:4, 508–529.

Walker, K. E., and H. Leitner (2011) 'The variegated landscape of local immigration policies in the United States', *Urban Geography*, 32:3, 156–178.

Wilkes, R., N. Guppy, and L. Farris (2008) '"No thanks, we're full": individual characteristics, national context, and changing attitudes toward immigration', *International Migration Review*, 42:2, 302–329.

Zincone, G., and T. Caponio (2006) 'The multilevel governance of migration', in R. Penninx, M. Berger, and K. Kraal (eds), *The Dynamics of International Migration and Settlement in Europe: A State of the Art* (IMISCOE Joint Studies) (Amsterdam: Amsterdam University Press).

7

Resisting the camp: migrants' squats as antithetical spaces in Athens's City Plaza

Valeria Raimondi

From EU to Greece: regulating migrant spatialities

The current so-called refugee crisis has led to difficulties in several European Union (EU) member states that, since 2015, have struggled to cope with the increased influx of migrants. This situation has led to repeated attempts to implement migration policies that have created division in the EU itself. This is due, among other things, to the uncertainty caused by the redefinition of the increasingly contested asylum system (Campesi, 2018a; Klepp, 2010). However, the measures that Europe has taken to face this crisis have often proven unable to create an effective reception for arriving migrants, in part because they have centred on closing and reinforcing the EU's external borders. Some countries have reacted to the crisis with the voluntary reactivation of border controls, leading to a (re)fragmentation of the European Schengen area. On the one hand, this may suggest a return of national borders; on the other, the European Commission's response goes in the direction of a post-national management of Europe's borders, as exemplified by the proposal of a new border agency on 15 December 2015 (Campesi, 2018b). The proposal clearly states the need for a reinforcement, in the short term, of the role of the European Border and Coast Guard Agency (Frontex) while, in the long term, it forecasts a transformation of Frontex itself into a genuine border agency, allowed to 'step in ... to ensure that action is taken on the ground even when a Member State is unable or unwilling to take the necessary measures'.[1] This represents a fundamental break in the evolution of the control devices of the European border, moving closer to establishing a supranational border force, enabled to act independently of the consent of the member states, and consequently posing a challenge to forms of democratic control.

Since the beginning of the crisis, the Euro-Mediterranean area has therefore been slowly transformed into one of the world's most advanced laboratories for post-national border management – a space in which Europe has tried to use all its hegemonic capabilities to adapt the migration policies of neighbouring countries to the needs of its internal policy (Heller and Pezzani, 2016). The progressive extra-territorialisation and externalisation of such migration control practices has resulted in the production of a 'buffer zone', aimed at protecting the EU's external borders. However, the sovereign authority of the EU is not played out only on the supranational level, but also invades a range of narrower spatialities. More precisely, in the areas directly influenced by the landing of migrants, EU policies established border zones (such as the Greek islands close to the Greek–Turkish border), characterised by the presence of camps and hotspots. With the camps and hotspot system, EU countries tangibly manifested their power over the *lives* and *bodies* of people who do not fall into the category of (European) citizen and, as such, are labelled as 'ungrateful … undeserving, unwelcomed others who are not entitled to climb the steps towards properly authorised citizenship status' (Moulin, 2012: 55).

These processes are exemplified by the establishment, on 18 March 2016, of the agreement between the European Union and Turkey and the effect it has had on thousands of people trying to reach Europe, mainly from Syria, Afghanistan, Iran, Pakistan, but also from North African countries. Concisely, the agreement allows Greece to return to Turkey 'all new irregular migrants' arriving in the country after 20 March 2016, with the following three major conditions:

- For every Syrian returned to Turkey from the Greek islands, another Syrian will be resettled from Turkey into the EU, taking into account the UN Vulnerability Criteria;
- The fulfilment of the visa liberalisation roadmap will be accelerated vis-à-vis all participating Member States with a view to lifting the visa requirements for Turkish citizens at the latest by the end of June 2016, provided that all benchmarks have been met;

- The EU [...] will further speed up the disbursement of the initially allocated 3 billion Euros under the Facility for Refugees in Turkey and ensure funding of further projects for persons under temporary protection. (Council of the EU, Press Release, 144/16)

The first main consequence of the deal was that, from the summer of 2016 until the spring of 2017, only 1 per cent of asylum applications in Greece were approved, as Turkey was declared a 'safe country' and hence deportations from 'hotspot islands' back to Turkey were enabled.

The rejection of asylum applications, along with the contextual closure of the so-called Balkan route, resulted in more than 62,000 migrants being stranded across Greece, mostly in the hotspots on the islands, and throughout fifty-one institutional or extempore camps all over the country.[2] The hotspots are part of the system of devices created by the EU to control the flow of migrants and to make a first selection of incoming migrants. All migrants are taken to these centres (located near landing areas in Greece and Italy), fingerprinted and

Figure 7.1 A 'no border' wall in Lesbos, August 2017.

registered, and subsequently categorised as 'category 1' or asylum seeker (and therefore liable to relocation), or 'category 2', irregular access. In its function as an arbitrary filter, the hotspot is seen as a way to overcome the rule of law and suspend international refugee law. Since resettlement has not kept pace with arrivals to the hotspots, the conditions in overcrowded refugee camps have deteriorated and migrants are neglected in squalid conditions, hidden away from locals and tourists on the Greek islands and on the outskirts of the mainland's cities (Tazzioli, 2017; Garelli and Tazzioli, 2017).

Rather than being the result of incompetence or lack of resources,[3] the inhumane conditions of the camps – along with the high denial rate of asylum applications – can be considered part of a deterrence strategy, meant to discourage people from crossing the Aegean. The process of constructing these border zones betrays the real *logic* behind them: rather than being places for reception, the camps are devices for enclosing and confining refugees and asylum seekers, preventing contact with local society and reflecting a logic in which citizens and 'irregular migrants' should not meet each other. Further, keeping people confined inside the camps automatically transforms migrants into bodies to be cared for, for as long as their presence is tolerated within European territory. In doing so, confinement serves to deny the decision-making agency and political capacity of migrants.

In this chapter, I investigate a specific time of migration: the *im*mobility – or the 'temporality of waiting' – of the prolonged moment during which migrants are stuck in the net of EU migration policies (Mezzadra, 2015). This work aims at shedding light on practices that are at the same time against and beyond the aforementioned logic, and present themselves as 'alternatives' to this reception system. In particular, I focus on a specific form of migrants' response initiative: self-managed and self-organised squatting initiatives, arranged with the support of local solidarity networks. These creative – and often highly effective – practices of struggle highlight the agency of migrants, as well as an understanding of their expectations and claims. Moreover, such self-organised reception is seen as an alternative form of enacting citizenship (Mezzadra, 2011), while the general sociopolitical context in which these practices are 'enacted' is composed of political subjectivities who by themselves overtly challenge and reject the frame of the nation-state. The hypothesis at the heart of this chapter is that these experiences not only fulfil migrants' material needs, but also articulate their demands in a political way, revealing the precarious nature of migrants' lives, in opposition to the institutional reception system that tries to keep migrants physically outside this sociopolitical context. These practices of self-organisation could thus constitute forms of self-provided 'alternative' welfare, capable of extending and renegotiating the legal and social status of the 'citizen' (Mezzadra, 2004).

In making this case, the chapter draws on empirical research that was conducted in Athens from December 2016 to September 2017. During these months of fieldwork, I was actively involved in the life of 'City Plaza Accommodation and Solidarity Space', a migrants' squat in central Athens. My involvement took several different forms, from participation in the place's activities to actually living there for a period of time. Moreover, so as not to see City Plaza as an isolated space and in order to locate it in its broader local context, research practice extended beyond it, exploring other places and engaging with different practices throughout the city. As a result, in this chapter I focus on City Plaza as the main case study through which practices of self-organisation are illuminated.

The chapter is structured as follows: a conceptual discussion brings together notions of migration, citizenship, and urban space. The urban sphere is central to the dynamics investigated because migrant squatting must be considered in relation to other forms of urban activism, and as such it represents a continuation of wider urban struggles for rights of citizenship in the European context. I then introduce the idea of squats as spaces that are 'antithetical' to the official political narrative of the camp, and the political subjectivities that originate from them. Looking at migrant squatting through the lens of the autonomy of migration makes the transformative power of these experiences more explicit as they enact and make visible 'more intimate scales of political mobilisation' (Darling and Bauder, this volume). The subsequent two sections elaborate on the specific local dynamics that are relevant for the study presented here: the intersecting crises and merging struggles in Greece, and in Athens more precisely. In the chapter's main empirical part, I present the City Plaza squat in Athens as a case of 'autonomous geography' and discuss the political character of this endeavour, stressing the role of the squat in supporting migrant struggles and providing refugees and asylum seekers with a discursive space of political legitimation.

Migration, citizenship, and the urban

This chapter integrates perspectives from the autonomy of migration literature and critical citizenship studies, as well as emphasising the role of the urban scale in rethinking the politics of the refugee crisis. To begin, the disruptive power of migrants becomes evident at the transnational level; the very moment of crossing national borders marks the beginning of migrants' struggles. Beyond border crossing though, the struggles continue and take diverse forms at narrower scales, such as the urban. If the presence of migrants continuously decomposes and recomposes borders, as De Genova argues (2015), in cities such disruptive powers may become even more unsettling, for borders and their crossing are transferred into the city through processes of rescaling (Darling and Bauder, this volume; Lebuhn, 2013).

Seen as 'crucial sites where rights are claimed and social and environmental injustices are denounced' (Rossi and Vanolo, 2012: 133), cities allow us to consider migrant practices 'that involve struggles around fundamental social and political issues – namely mobility, residence and citizenship rights' (Nyers, 2015: 1). The notion of citizenship is pivotal here. It helps us draw attention to how migrants and refugees enact themselves as political subjects by demanding rights they do not have; in this way they may perform 'acts of citizenship' (Isin, 2008). According to De Genova (2015: 4), 'transnational migrations constitute a central dynamic in the contemporary social production (and transformation) of urban space'. Cities provide the physical and social ground for developing new spatial imaginaries, practices, and experiences, in which migrants' subjectivities are enacted. It is this enactment of migrant subjectivities that renders 'breaking' the citizen/non-citizen dichotomy possible, which is one aspect of rescaling the migrant struggle as an urban struggle (Bauder, 2016; Darling, 2017). With regard to this chapter, the occupations of migrants and their supporters are considered active elements of migrant struggles at the urban scale, as these practices have the subversive power to overturn the logic of *denying* the migrant subject, a logic that is enacted through the socio-spatial confinement of the camps.

In my attempt to weave together migration and citizenship, especially in reference to urban space, I looked at migrant practices through the 'gaze of autonomy', as Mezzadra suggests (2011). The concept of autonomy is thus pivotal, and, when looked at with this gaze, occupied spaces can be reread as 'autonomous geographies' – as 'spaces where people desire to constitute non-capitalist, egalitarian and solidaristic forms of political, social, and economic organization through a combination of resistance and creation' (Pickerill and Chatterton, 2006: 1). More generally, the idea of autonomy – a key concept in modern emancipatory politics – is not only a theoretical lens, but also the tool to actually ground research practice, by researching spaces that sought to realise a form of thinking and doing free from the 'presupposition of inequality' (Rancière, 2017). Put differently, these are spaces that implement practices and forms of organisation free from hierarchical constraints and beliefs.

Citizens and non-citizens in antithetical spaces

Attempting to rescale border struggles as *urban* struggles, this chapter focuses on and deploys empirical evidence from one of the city's various spatialities: the migrants' squat. To achieve this, I suggest that we interpret the squat in relation to another type of space, this time not within the urban fabric but rather on its fringes: the camp. Conceptually placed in opposition to the camp, the squat is hereby seen as an *antithetical space* – antithetical in the sense that it involves practices and performs social meanings that, in many senses, oppose in a politically conflictual way its institutional counterpart. To elaborate on the relationship between these antithetical spaces, it is essential to start from the challenge 'to theorize citizenship as an institution in flux embedded in current social and political struggles that constitute it' (Isin, 2009: 370).

To begin, the camp performs spatially the citizen/non-citizen dichotomy: by keeping refugees and asylum seekers confined in peripheral areas, it denies them the right to move, to act freely, to be part of the *public*, the latter being located away, *outside*. In other words, kept distant from the public eye, migrants in camps are denied the privileges entailed in the category of 'citizenship' and are thus made non-citizens: passive objects of the migration process. Nevertheless, there exist spaces antithetical to 'the idealized image of the camp, as a distant and legitimate "other" of the city' (Darling, 2017: 182): the squats located in the cities. In other words, the enclosed and politically sterile camp, where every effort of struggle is immediately suppressed violently, is in contrast to the squats and the 'subversive socialities' that they render possible. In this sense, these antithetical spaces offer the ground for critically reflecting upon the spatial dimensions of citizenship.

Whereas the camp system contributes to actualising the citizen/ non-citizen dichotomy, urban struggles, in the form of autonomous experiences, allow us to overcome the exclusive uses and connotations that are normally intrinsic in the concept of 'citizenship'. This arises in two main ways: first, with a spatial artifice that does not accept and reproduce the alienation and seclusion of the camp; and second, by giving the possibility of political enactment to migrant subjectivities. The process of breaking the dichotomy consists in 'making what was unseen visible, in getting what was only audible as noise to be heard as speech' (Rancière, 2001: n.p.). It is the presence of refugees and asylum seekers at the very centre of the city that functions as an ongoing reminder of their existence in the everyday lives of citizens.

In this way, the squats offer 'experiences of informality' (Darling, 2017) through which migrants acquire their lost visibility. Visible in the city, the migrant subject becomes an active one – a political subject capable of writing a different script and creating a new scene: an activist citizen (Isin, 2009: 381). Thus, if migrants are confined in the camps in order to depict them as passive *objects* of the migration process, the experiences of self-organised reception prove that instead they are (or can be) active subjects capable of putting into action new practices of resistance; they are not a 'nuisance', but people with skills and capabilities, and most of all, with personal aspirations (Mezzadra, 2015). Far from being 'practices of managed resettlement' from the camp to the city (Darling, 2017: 182), the experiences of self-organised reception challenge the exclusive nature of citizenship by enlarging the latter's privileges to those who would have no access to them otherwise, through grassroots actions aimed at establishing a sort of welfare from below.

Drawing once again on Rancière, as the recognition of a subject as a 'political being' goes along with the 'refiguration' of the space he or she belongs to, the contraposition of the logics of the camps and the squats becomes more evident. In fact, in Rancière's words, 'in order to refuse the title of political subjects to a category ... it has traditionally been sufficient to assert that they belong to ... a space separated from public life' (Rancière, 2001: n.p.) – in our empirical terms, the camp. The politicisation of these categories, Rancière continues, happens through the re-qualification of those places (the camps), that is, 'in getting them to be seen as the spaces of a community, of getting themselves to be seen or heard as speaking subjects (if only in the form of litigation)' (Rancière, 2001: n.p.). Along with the subversive socialities they produce, and characterised by fluid and anti-hierarchical forms of relations, the squats – supported by the social movements that generated (and may often maintain) them – ought to be seen as a continuation of the struggles for European and global rights of citizenship that have a long history in Europe, from the *sans papiers* in France in 1996, to the 'Kein Mensch ist illegal' ('No one is illegal') and 'NoBorder' movements. All together, these struggles contribute to 'the formation of a new "gaze" and sensitivity on migration, as well as of a new epistemic community challenging the boundaries of established migration and border studies' (De Genova et al., 2015: 58).

As spaces of autonomous geographies, migrants' squats can be considered as the empirical manifestation of the process of rescaling border struggles as urban struggles (De Genova, 2015). Such a perspective allows us to rethink the subjectivity of both the citizen and the migrant – not separately but dialectically. This chapter will turn to one of these autonomous geographies, putting at the core of the research the social practices of refugees and asylum seekers, in the everyday life of their attempt to counter the surveillance regime of institutional reception. Before that, it is crucial to locate this autonomous geography in its local context.

Intersecting crises ...

In Greece the 'refugee crisis' is not being inscribed upon a spatial tabula rasa; rather, it arrived where another deep crisis – this time named 'socio-economic' – had already become 'a generalised state of exception' (Dalakoglou, 2013: 35) affecting the whole society, in the aftermath of the 2008 global financial crisis. For the case of Athens specifically, Maloutas (2014) highlights how this crisis's effects are spatialised: urban inequalities are widening through a violent redistribution of wealth and income. Along with them, the economic crisis has spread uncertainty in Greece – together with a feeling of anger shared by a large part of the population – which has resulted in a wave of demonstrations and actions all over the country, of which the most famous is the occupation of the capital's main square of Syntagma (for example, see Arampatzi, 2017; Dalakoglou and Agelopoulos, 2017; Hadjimichalis, 2013; Kallianos, 2013), triggering a series of spontaneous measures to cope with both the 'humanitarian' and political consequences of the crisis itself.

The adaptive responses and counter-strategies produced by the crisis resulted in particularly relevant urban scenarios, characterised by the presence of self-organised spaces aimed at compensating for the crumbling of welfare generated by the crisis. The refugee crisis hit an economically distressed country that was itself adapting to a crisis of austerity and economic shock, and thus was 'equipped' with autonomous structures and a highly combative social ground.

This antagonistic and well-structured environment turned out to be essential as the migrants' situation worsened in the summer of 2015. During the 'summer of migration', thousands of asylum seekers landed on the Greek islands and were then relocated to the mainland. Due to the lack of proper reception structures, migrants were housed in poorly equipped structures or makeshift camps in peripheral areas of major Greek cities, often lacking adequate facilities to host a population composed of 40 per cent minors. Most of the migrant population who managed to leave the camps (or did not have access to them initially because of a lack of space) moved to the city centres, looking for improvised accommodation and waiting to find alternative routes to move towards other EU countries.

Therefore, what we observe in Greece is a critical, productive intersection of two crises: the socio-economic crisis and the refugee crisis. Among other connections, this intersection resulted in a parallel merging of different struggles. The solidarity movement among Greek citizens – fighting for their social rights on a daily basis – has therefore embraced the struggle of asylum seekers, resisting the constraints of European migration policies. Particularly in the active Athenian sociopolitical context, citizens developed new forms of representation, different political perspectives, and innovative practices of democracy and citizenship. All this developed in an urban environment where among all the different groups affected by the socio-economic crisis, migrants were often in the worst condition (Maloutas, 2014).

The situation of daily precariousness for refugees and asylum seekers – especially those living on the streets – was exacerbated by the constant threat of assault from far-right xenophobic groups, which increasingly gained ground in Greek society, as evidenced by the success of the Golden Dawn party in the 2012 elections, and confirmed in the elections of 2015 (Bampilis, 2018). Most of the migrants who remained stuck in Greece after the closure of the border with Macedonia moved to the Greek capital, the city that most of all is suffering the severe consequences of the social and economic crisis in the country. At a spatial level, the far right has benefited from the situation and has appropriated stigmatised Athenian neighbourhoods – such as Aghios Panteleimonas, where City Plaza is located – in order to, first, legitimate their presence and, then, perform their hatred against foreign residents (Koutrolikou, 2015; see also Triandafyllidou and Kouki, 2014).

Regarding the so-called institutional reception, Athens hosts five government-sponsored accommodation facilities, where the majority of asylum seekers are accommodated while waiting for the asylum relocation process (this may take from six to eighteen months). All the camps are located in semi-abandoned industrial areas on the outskirts of the city, and lack proper facilities and connections to the city centre. Some of these facilities are tangible examples of the overlapping of crises: built to house the Olympic Games in 2004, the former Olympic airport 'Ellinikò' and related structures fell into disuse, and were then reopened to accommodate asylum seekers. Due to the poor conditions of the structures, the camps were evacuated in June 2017 and approximately 1,400 migrants were forcedly moved to Thebes, 100 km north of Athens.

Far from being a sanctuary city, Athens presents instead some relevant experiences of 'autonomous practices of welcome'. Having been a 'hub' for incubating social movements during the Greek 'age of resistance', the Greek capital offers a peculiar sociopolitical landscape, where activism and solidarity manifest themselves through autonomous spaces and alternative processes. Most of these practices take shape in the neighbourhood of Exarcheia, characterised by an antagonistic sociopolitical environment.

... and struggles merging

Already beginning in the summer 2015, the presence of refugees and asylum seekers has been remarkable in the public spaces of Athens. Many of those who did not end up in the city's peripheral camps settled in squares, such as Victoria Square, and parks, such as Pedion tou Areos (both of which are close to one another) (Kasparek, 2016). That summer is recognised as the starting moment of the solidarity movement in Athens, when activists from leftist and anarchist groups began mobilising to offer support to the migrant population in need. In September 2015, and as a response to the situation, the first squat – Notara 26 – was opened in Athens, in Exarcheia neighbourhood,

Figure 7.2 'Freedom for political prisoners and urban guerrilla fighters', banner hanging on the wall of the Polytechnic School in Exarcheia.

accommodating a small number of migrants. The following year, the closing of the Balkan route brought the 'refugee crisis' to a climax and signalled an urgent need to host migrants and refugees around the country.

Exarcheia is a peculiar neighbourhood in the centre of Athens, a headquarters for anarchist and leftist groups – whose presence is extremely powerful in the area – that includes a number of *aftonoma stekia* (autonomous centres) and squats (see Cappuccini, 2018). This neighbourhood is characterised by the production of conflictual urbanity and strategies of opposition, that on the one hand leads to a closure from the 'outside', but on the other hand contributes to consolidating a neighbourhood 'resistance identity', open to the inclusion of new subjectivities. The strategies consist in a combination of insurrectionist violent practices and the opening of neighbourhood assemblies, cultural centres, and cooperatives that have become the 'backbone of social and political resistance in the city' (Kritidis, 2014: 90). This sociopolitical context provided a fertile ground for the development of a network of solidarity experiences, such as self-organised kitchens, healthcare centres, social centres, and community assemblies that shape this multicultural, politically radical urban fabric. These experiences had long existed in Exarcheia[4] and expanded after the 2008 economic crisis (Dalakoglou and Agelopoulos, 2017). The result is a sort of 'solidarity economy' within the neighbourhood, which prepared the area well for the influx of migrants. In Exarcheia the walls are scrawled with the vocabulary of anti-authoritarianism, written in Arabic and English, Pashto and Greek, offering a vision of a post-border future.

We might thus suggest that in Exarcheia all voices are potentially audible (and are struggling to become audible), regardless of the 'categorisation' and the social group of belonging (i.e. migrants, the homeless, precarious workers, the unemployed, LGBTQI+, students, and others). In the struggle to claim rights these groups often overlap, and the resulting 'hybridisation' increases the strength and visibility of the movement rather than decreasing it. Presently there are almost a dozen squats that provide food and social services in Exarcheia, with approximately 2,500 migrants living in those spaces.[5] The anarchist identity of the Greek activists makes these places sites of political opposition to the state, where the challenge to EU migration policies is overtly manifested. Moreover, organising these facilities in, and therefore bringing migrants to, the city centre has above all the function of opposing the logic of denying the presence of migrant subjects in the city, perpetrated by the institutions of the camp system. As stated by the activists, these squats are born and reproduce themselves first as spaces of struggle, in which everyday activities (such as collective decision making, provision of food and accommodation, site-security, education, and healthcare) are secondary to the ideological goal. City Plaza Hotel, discussed in the section below, is one prominent member of this network and exemplifies key aspects of this thinking.

City Plaza, a 'refugee accommodation and solidarity space'

On 22 April 2016 a group of politically active people with experience in self-organised practices occupied the abandoned City Plaza Hotel and turned it into a space for accommodating refugees and asylum seekers. Rather than an empty hotel, City Plaza became a home for 400 people. Although to contextualise City Plaza in terms of its social and political organisation is a difficult task, the place is characterised by some as a radically egalitarian project. In general, it is made up of three main groups: the Greek activists; foreign people who have fled war, poverty, or persecution; and international activists who express their solidarity practically by joining the place and supporting its activities. Approximately 100 families live there. Each family has its own room, and three meals per day are provided to all the inhabitants, along with hygiene products, clothes, and everything needed for a dignified life. As with other migrants' squats in Athens, City Plaza refused any kind of economic and logistical support from local authorities and NGOs. City Plaza's funding depends exclusively on donations from individuals and solidarity groups (from Greece and all over Europe) and is run on an entirely voluntary basis, with dozens of activists and volunteers coming to support the squat from all over the world.

Contrary to any camp, dignity, safety, and privacy are essential components of City Plaza. Different kinds of activities and services are guaranteed inside City Plaza: there is a healthcare space with a medical team of volunteer doctors and nurses; a range of language courses in addition to English, German, and Greek; educational and

Figure 7.3 The view of City Plaza from Acharnon Street.

recreational activities for children; and legal advice concerning asylum
and relocation. As a result of the multiplicity of such functions and
the inclusive ways they are carried out, people perceive City Plaza as
their 'home', something that allows them to feel 'settled' in the city
and help establish a sense of normality in everyday life.

Not only a refuge: City Plaza as a political space

City Plaza – along with the other migrants' squats – is not only a
'space of refuge', because material provision and the coverage of basic
needs are only one side of the place's dynamics. 'Our idea was not to
make a thousand City Plazas', said one of the founders. The squat,
she explained, has an expansive definition of the term 'refugee' that
includes migrants fleeing war, political persecution, extreme poverty,
and environmental devastation; it represents a rejection of the legal
distinction between different kinds of motives for migration. The
'residents' – this is what the migrant component is called among the
inhabitants of City Plaza – are either people waiting for formal

resettlement after having had their asylum applications approved, or people who have left refugee camps elsewhere in Greece. One activist thus characterised City Plaza as an 'antagonistic political example meant to shame both the state and the NGOs'.

Therefore, City Plaza is also a space for political struggle against current migration policies and is intended to support the local anti-fascist movement. First of all, it (as with other migrants' squats more broadly) presents itself as a (standing) rebuttal – shouted quite loudly – to government policies that deliberately mistreat refugees and migrants. As one activist noted, 'If we can do it without institutional funding, without any kind of resources from the state or from NGOs [then this proves that] they [the state and NGOs] choose to have the camps'. In the words of another activist, the place has had since its inception overt political intentions: 'We wanted to set a good example of housing in order to say no to the way they are building the camps', he said. 'There is an alternative: treating refugees like humans.'

Three different levels of assemblies take place in City Plaza and structure its organisation, both in terms of its temporality and its spatiality. First are 'house meetings' every second week, in which all residents are called to participate in order to collectively discuss organisational issues regarding cooking and cleaning shifts, food and other supplies, and children-related issues, as well as problems that might arise from the complex cohabitation. Parallel translations in Arabic, Farsi, and English aim to make the assembly equally inclusive for all residents. Second, there is a weekly 'solidarity meeting' of (but not limited to) the activists, where the functioning of shifts is discussed and 'external' volunteers can propose their ideas for activities for City Plaza. And third, a 'coordination meeting' takes place once a week in order to address explicitly political issues, such as participation in demonstrations and other political actions. These actions include the organisation of a nationwide demonstration on 17 March (the date of the signing of the EU–Turkey deal) against EU migration and border policies. In September 2017 the assembly decided to support a hunger strike organised by refugees living in the camps of Athens, giving them logistical and media support and offering medical care. Solidarity is not only in support of migrants: in April 2017 an anniversary party was organised at City Plaza and the proceeds were allocated to the former workers of the hotel, to symbolically pay the salaries they never received due to the bankruptcy of the business.

With most of the assemblies and activities being attended both by activists and residents, the final aim of City Plaza is to put into practice a conception of everyday life that empowers migrants, providing them with the tools and practical knowledge necessary to continue their journey and get in touch with activists and migrants in other countries, contributing to enlarging the solidarity network. Events such as movie screenings, activities specifically tailored for women, and talks open to the wider public reflect the political ideas crystallised in situ and embed them in everyday life, attempting to connect these ideas to the wider city as they do so. Such practices seek to defy social, sexual, and political norms and deal with cultural difference in a way contrary to what happens in the camps, where even the queue to get food or to access bathrooms is often organised according to national groupings.

Whereas participation in maintenance-related activities – such as cleaning, cooking, and guarding shifts – is equally shared among all residents, participation in clearly political activities depends on

Figure 7.4 A 'house assembly' in City Plaza.

individual choice. By and large, it is the younger residents with already
acquired political experience from their own countries who engage
in practices of 'migrant counterconducts' (Inda, 2011). The nature
of these practices can vary substantially, from street protests, rallies,
and demonstrations in front of government buildings, to distributing
political flyers inside or around the camps and performing supportive
actions for other struggles, such as the hunger strikes of migrants
in the camps. In this way, City Plaza as a political space expands its
spatialities and embraces broader actions in the city, drawing connections between struggles in different spaces and at different spatial
scales. An example of this is the mutual support between City Plaza
and the 'open assembly' of the former port workers of Perama – a port
city and a suburb of Piraeus – or the organisation of the assembly of
the migrants' squats in Athens.

There is a continuously changing dynamic concerning the participation of residents in migrant counter-conducts, which is not simply
restricted to younger residents. The three assembly types mentioned
above should be seen as intersecting with each other. During the
assemblies and their subsequent practices, the boundaries between
'activists' and 'refugees' are not clearly drawn. Rather, the two subjectivities overlap, exchange elements, and produce new subjectivities. For
example, the political role of migrant residents may be significantly
reinforced, resulting in engagements with migrant counter-conducts
by people who would not have expressed such a will previously. 'We
want to show to refugees that they are not only a problem but also
part of the solution. Here they take care of themselves and also of
other people living here', said an activist. 'We learn from them [the
refugee residents] how to evolve our languages and how to break the
borders of our minds and political beliefs, and lower them so we can
listen to them.' This interplay of different subjectivities involves asym-
metries of power that are acknowledged and critically reflected upon.
Activists are aware of their (potent) role to give visibility to subjectivities
and issues, and assemblies provide space for engaging in dialogues
necessary to deal with such power relations. Therefore, the link between
the different political agencies – principally of the activists and the
residents – is often negotiated in practice.

Moreover, it is continuously acknowledged that not all those
(migrants) who live in City Plaza are aware of the informality of the
situation when they arrive. Quite often the 'Greek/local organisers'

Figure 7.5 Demonstration organised by City Plaza residents and activists against EU migration policies, September 2017.

take on a difficult task: to explain in detail to newcomers the risks as well as the 'privileges' and, above all, the responsibilities involved in this cohabitation. As a Greek activist explained: 'When people come here [City Plaza], we explain the rules. First rule: no violence here. Second rule: you have to live with people from 14 countries. Third rule: self-organisation does not mean that you can do whatever you want.' Thus, the place gains further complexities that have to be negotiated. The founders insist that their aim is to find common purposes, not to indoctrinate those living in the place, most of whom, as an activist acknowledges, 'don't come here because they are leftist'. On the other hand, some of the residents are Arab Spring activists who arrive with their own discourse of justice, rights, and dissent already well formulated.

Spatial connections

The physical location of City Plaza reflects, and is significant for, the project's political character. City Plaza is *inside* the city, a fact that contrasts with the location of camps that exist at the margins, both social and spatial, of Greek society. Indeed, the migrants living in City Plaza have the chance to develop relations with the rest of the city and use public space for recreational and other activities. 'All kids in Plaza go to school', an activist explains. 'The main point is that they are here *in the city*. In camps, they are far and there are no buses.' In the city centre, and especially adjacent to Exarcheia, City Plaza crosses policy-established boundaries and relocates refugees and asylum seekers within the urban socio-spatial fabric. In this way, City Plaza relates to the various other places of solidarity in the city, such as solidarity kitchens, local assemblies, and social centres, and thus critically contributes to the shaping of the local political scene. As one activist noted, 'It was clear since the beginning that we didn't come here [to City Plaza] to solve the problems of refugees, the refugee crisis.' Although not solving the 'refugee problem', the activists admit that the location gives this issue a significant visibility.

More precisely, the close proximity to Exarcheia should not obscure the local dynamics. City Plaza is in one of the city's most politically conservative neighbourhoods, Aghios Panteleimonas, which has been a former stronghold of the fascist Golden Dawn party. Through the aforementioned visibility, the squat, along with the activities and social dynamics it renders possible inside and around it, contrasts to its neighbourhood. As such, it operates as a material challenge to the conservative remnants of far-right practices that have taken place there. This contrast is taken into account by residents. According to another activist, 'This place [City Plaza] ends up being a safe space also for the neighbourhood.' If the last statement is true for most of the inhabitants of the neighbourhood (migrants who have settled here since the beginning of the 1990s), given the social and political context of the area it is possible that Greek residents perceive City Plaza as a dangerous intrusion that could cause violent xenophobic reactions from right-wing groups.

With the motto 'we struggle together, we will live together', City Plaza created a local network that includes other migrants' housing squats, trade unions, schools, hospitals, and social spaces involved in the common struggle to demand social and political rights against anti-refugee government policies. As described previously, this is how the squat's spatialities relate to other parts of the neighbourhood and the city. However, it is critical to emphasise how the transnational network of solidarities shaped in and around City Plaza contributes to extending the place's dynamics. For it not only provides economic support but also plays an active political role, as every month dozens of activists from all over the world stay at City Plaza and participate in its activities.

Regarding the practices of counter-conduct, it should be highlighted that there are important differences between those taking place in the camps and in the squats. In the case of the latter, these practices mainly include demonstrations throughout the city, whereas in the case of the former they take more risky forms, with migrants being subjected to violent repression by the police. In camps, struggles are often individualised through practices that primarily involve the only 'tool' left to migrants: their own bodies. Shifting from resistance to revolt, hunger strikes in camps have become the practice of counter-conduct most common but most risky for the lives of asylum seekers.

At the same time, a series of threats of eviction, generated by the Greek government and the Police Department, has put all forty-six squatted places in and around Exarcheia in a state of precariousness. However, such threats have also served to further stress the political character of these spaces. Specifically, the City Plaza collective has responded to the most recent threat of eviction by turning it into a chance to explicitly express the political stance that leads the initiative through issuing an official statement. Through both their actions, and this statement, the appropriation (not ownership) of an abandoned building counters the dehumanising and discriminating practices of the EU and the Greek state; an empty urban space is transformed into a politically meaningful place in order to respond to people's needs and to offer a foundation for other forms of political claim. The statement reads:

> [We] take full responsibility for transforming an empty abandoned building into a home of solidarity and dignity for over 1,500 refugees over 20 months to date at a time when the state and the NGOs involvement has left a wake of wretchedness, imprisonment, and racism. The right of empty and unused buildings to remain empty and unused is, in our view, clearly subordinate to the right of thousands of people to dignity. For this reason, we sought to transform a dark and deprived

corner of Acharnon [the street where City Plaza is located] into a place full of life, creativity, and resistance.

We would like to point out once more that we are not claiming ownership of the building, we are simply using it. Refugee Accommodation Space City Plaza is a workshop of solidarity and resistance. All of us who are taking part in it have the power and determination to guard it against the threats of the state and the shadow state. We will continue to fight against the anti-refugee policies of the Greek government and the EU, against the EU-Turkey deal and against racism and xenophobia. (23 January 2018, Acharnon 78, Athens, Refugee Accommodation and Solidarity Space City Plaza, official statement)

Conclusion

Due to its geographical position, Greece is one of the EU's main arrival countries for asylum seekers, and one of those suffering most from European migration policies. Until the closure of its northern border with Macedonia, Greece had functioned as a corridor for those en route to wealthier northern European countries. Since the summer of 2015 an increasing number of migrants have been stuck in the country, and more and more people have been relocated to overcrowded camps and hotspots, both on the Greek islands and on the mainland. With many migrants and asylum seekers travelling to Athens and living in precarious and dangerous conditions camped informally around the city, a powerful solidarity movement mobilised to support the migrants in need. This mobilisation has resulted in the opening of several occupied spaces, where migrants live together with Greek and international activists.

In this context, the experiences of self-organised reception fill the gap between the institutional regime and the refugee's viewpoint. Above all, they serve to dismantle the rhetoric built around the figure of the refugee that is aimed at 'neutralising' her or him as an active and autonomous subject. Rather than labelling migrants as 'empirical anomalies' with regard to the predominant narratives of citizenship, by providing a discursive space of political legitimation these non-hierarchical spaces of multicultural encounter, crystallised in the form of the squat, create a frame where new practices of citizenship can find expression. As the case presented in this chapter – the City Plaza project in Athens – illustrates, the autonomous geographies thus activated allow us to (temporarily) eliminate from our vocabulary the terms 'reception' and 'integration' (intended as a pedagogical process) to instead make room for attempts to construct shared places. Moreover, the presence of migrants inside our cities forces us to rethink the future of the spaces we live in every day, offering a new perspective to look at those spaces. Although 'confined' to the particular area of the neighbourhood of Exarcheia, where activism and practices of struggle are well rooted, thanks to the networks built by migrants and activists these spaces stretch, and cover the whole of Europe (and beyond). The 'gaze of autonomy' applied at the urban level highlights the antithetical character of migrants' squats as political spaces created through struggle. As the creation of space goes hand in hand with the process of political subjectification, the creation of antithetical spaces goes with the creation of antithetical subjectivities. In the case of refugee squatting this implies the recognition of the migrant subject as an active political subject, capable of putting into action new practices of struggle and resistance.

Notes

1 'A European border and coast guard to protect Europe's external borders', Strasbourg, 15 December 2015, europa.eu/rapid/press-release_IP-15-6327_en.pdf.
2 The deal also led to a coercive 'voluntary' returns programme, that is, leaving refugees stranded in inhumane conditions in Greek and Turkish jails for months.
3 Since the beginning of the 'crisis' in June 2015, Greece has been given $803 million in humanitarian aid for refugees and migrants, making it the most expensive humanitarian response in history in terms of cost per beneficiary.
4 Today's situation is the result of a longer struggle, begun in the 1970s with the resistance against the military junta, and culminating in the occupation of the Polytechnic School on 17 November 1973.
5 Obviously, there are no official data available. This estimate was calculated based on information received from each squat.

References

Arampatzi, A. (2017) 'Contentious spatialities in an era of austerity: everyday politics and "struggle communities" in Athens, Greece', *Political Geography*, 60, 47–56.

Bampilis, T. (2018) 'Far-right extremism in the city of Athens during the Greek crisis', in D. Dalakoglou and G. Agelopoulos (eds), *Critical Times in Greece: Anthropological Engagements with the Crisis* (London: Routledge), 59–72.

Bauder, H. (2016) 'Possibilities of urban belonging', *Antipode*, 48:2, 252–271.

Campesi, G. (2018a) 'Seeking asylum in times of crisis: reception, confinement, and detention at Europe's southern border', *Refugee Survey Quarterly*, 27:1, 1–27.

Campesi, G. (2018b) 'European Border and Coast Guard (Frontex): security, democracy, and rights at the EU border', *Oxford Research Encyclopedia of Criminology and Criminal Justice*, http://criminology.oxfordre.com/ (accessed 8 July 2018).

Cappuccini, M. (2018) *Austerity and Democracy in Athens: Crisis and Community in Exarchia* (London: Springer).

Dalakoglou, D. (2013) 'The crisis before "The Crisis": violence and urban neoliberalization in Athens', *Social Justice*, 39:1, 24–42.

Dalakoglou, D., and G. Agelopoulos (eds) (2017) *Critical Times in Greece: Anthropological Engagements with the Crisis* (London: Routledge).

Darling, J. (2017) 'Forced migration and the city: irregularity, informality, and the politics of presence', *Progress in Human Geography*, 41:2, 178–198.

De Genova, N. (2015) 'Border struggles in the migrant metropolis', *Nordic Journal of Migration Research*, 5:1, 3–10.

De Genova, N., S. Mezzadra, and J. Pickles (2015) 'New keywords: migration and borders', *Cultural Studies*, 29:1, 55–87.

Garelli, G., and M. Tazzioli (2017) 'The biopolitical warfare on migrants: EU naval force and NATO operations of migration government in the Mediterranean', *Critical Military Studies*, 4:2, 181–200.

Hadjimichalis, C. (2013) 'From streets and squares to radical political emancipation? Resistance lessons from Athens during the crisis', *Human Geography*, 6:2, 116–136.

Heller, C., and L. Pezzani (2016) 'Ebbing and flowing: the EU's shifting practices of (non-) assistance and bordering in a time of crisis', *Near Futures Online*, 1:1, http://nearfuturesonline.org/ebbing-and-flowing-the-eus-shifting-practices-of-non-assistance-and-bordering-in-a-time-of-crisis/ (accessed 5 December 2018).

Inda, J. X. (2011) 'Borderzones of enforcement: criminalization, workplace raids, and migrant counterconducts', in V. Squire (ed.), *The Contested Politics of Mobility: Borderzones and Irregularity* (Basingstoke: Palgrave Macmillan), 74–91.

Isin, E. F. (2008) 'Theorizing acts of citizenship', in E. F. Isin and G. M. Nielsen (eds), *Acts of Citizenship* (London: Zed Books), 15–43.

Isin, E. F. (2009) 'Citizenship in flux: the figure of the activist citizen', *Subjectivity*, 29:1, 367–388.

Isin, E. F., and G. M. Nielsen (eds) (2008) *Acts of Citizenship* (London: Zed Books).

Kallianos, Y. (2013) 'Agency of the street: crisis, radical politics and the production of public space in Athens 2008–12', *City*, 17:4, 548–557.

Kasparek, B. (2016) 'Routes, corridors, and spaces of exception: governing migration and Europe', *Near Futures Online*, 1:1, http://nearfuturesonline.org/routes-corridors-and-spaces-of-exception-governing-migration-and-europe/ (accessed 5 December 2018).

Klepp, S. (2010) 'A contested asylum system: the European Union between refugee protection and border control in the Mediterranean Sea', *European Journal of Migration & Law*, 12:1, 1–21.

Koutrolikou, P. (2015) 'Socio-spatial stigmatization and its "incorporation" in the centre of Athens, Greece', *City*, 19:4, 510–521.

Kritidis, G. (2014) 'The rise and crisis of the anarchist and libertarian movement in Greece, 1973–2012', in B. Van der Steen, A. Katzeff, and L. van Hoogenhuijze (eds), *The City Is Ours: Squatting and Autonomous Movements in Europe from the 1970s to the Present* (Oakland, CA: PM Press), 63–94.

Lebuhn, H. (2013) 'Local border practices and urban citizenship in Europe: exploring urban borderlands', *City*, 17:1, 37–51.

Maloutas, T. (2014) 'Social and spatial impact of the crisis in athens-from clientelist regulation to sovereign debt crisis', *Région et Développement*, 39, 149–166.

Mezzadra, S. (2004) *I confini della libertà: per un'analisi politica delle migrazioni contemporanee* (Rome: DeriveApprodi).

Mezzadra, S. (2011) 'The gaze of autonomy: capitalism, migration and social struggles', in V. Squire (ed.), *The Contested Politics of Mobility: Borderzones and Irregularity* (Basingstoke: Palgrave Macmillan), 121–142.

Mezzadra, S. (2015) 'The proliferation of borders and the right to escape', in Y. Jansen, R. Celikates, and J. de Bloois (eds), *The Irregularization of Migration in Contemporary Europe: Detention, Deportation, Drowning* (New York: Rowman & Littlefield), 121–135.

Moulin, C. (2012) 'Ungrateful subjects? Refugee protests and the logic of gratitude', in P. Nyers and K. Rygiel (eds), *Citizenship, Migrant Activism and the Politics of Movement* (London: Routledge), 54–72.

Nyers, P. (2015) 'Migrant citizenships and autonomous mobilities', *Migration, Mobility, & Displacement*, 1:1, 23–37.

Pickerill, J., and P. Chatterton (2006) 'Notes towards autonomous geographies: creation, resistance and self-management as survival tactics', *Progress in Human Geography*, 30:6, 730–746.

Rancière, J. (2001) 'Ten theses on politics', *Theory & Event*, 5:3, n.p.

Rancière, J. (2017) 'Democracy, equality, emancipation in a changing world', address given at B-FEST (International Anti-authoritarian Festival of

Babylonia Journal), 27 May, www.babylonia.gr/2017/06/11/jacques-ranciere-democracy-equality-emancipation-changing-world/ (accessed 5 December 2018).

Rossi, U., and A. Vanolo (2012) *Urban Political Geographies: A Global Perspective* (London: Sage).

Tazzioli, M. (2017) 'Containment through mobility: migrants' spatial disobediences and the reshaping of control through the hotspot system', *Journal of Ethnic and Migration Studies*, 44:16, 1–16.

Triandafyllidou, A., and H. Kouki (2014) 'Naturalizing racism in the center of Athens in May 2011: lessons from Greece', *Journal of Immigrant & Refugee Studies*, 12:4, 418–436.

8

Rescaling citizenship struggles in provincial urban England

Ben Rogaly

Following the United Kingdom's vote to leave the European Union (EU) in June 2016, the National Theatre of Great Britain commissioned a new play, *My Country: A Work in Progress*. The play was based on the words of people recorded across the UK giving their views of the country in the light of the referendum campaign and the result. Director Rufus Norris admitted to counting the precise number of pro-Leave versus pro-Remain lines in the script in order to ensure that the play tilted towards a Leave perspective, because he estimated that a disproportionate number of theatregoers would have voted Remain. The script contains very few mentions of specific places, but it does refer to Peterborough, a small cathedral city in England, with the line 'Peterborough is overwhelmed by migrant workers'.

Peterborough has a reputation among local authority policy makers across England as a city to which large numbers of work-seeking EU nationals headed following the enlargement of the EU in 2004 (Jones, 2013). Situated on the main London–Edinburgh railway line and just 45 minutes from London on the fastest trains, Peterborough has also been visited regularly by national-level politicians and journalists seeking to investigate the impact of immigration in the UK as a whole or to make announcements about national immigration policy initiatives (Burnett, 2012: 4; Rogaly, 2016: 663). Analysis of the most recent Census in 2011 appears to bear out the city's reputation regarding the increased number of non-UK EU nationals: the proportion of Peterborough's population self-identifying in the Other White[1] category rose from 3 per cent in 2001 to 10.6 per cent at the time of census, while over half of the 20.6 per cent of the population born outside the UK had arrived since 2004. In the lead-up to the 2015 general election, the then leader of the anti-EU United Kingdom Independence Party Nigel Farage referred to Peterborough on national radio:

> Well, go to Peterborough, you know ... go and see the fact that we don't have integration ... And what's happened, unsurprisingly, in some ways, what's happened with very large numbers of people coming, is you get quarters and districts of towns and cities that get taken over by one particular group...[2]

Yet the picture of migration, citizenship, and rights in the city of Peterborough and its surrounding rural areas is, unsurprisingly, more complex than its reputation as a major reception city for international migrant workers, or Farage's portrayal of the consequences of this, might suggest.

In this chapter I argue, through the example of Peterborough, that a focus on urban citizenship struggles can provide grounds for hope in contemporary England, in spite of highly divisive national-level debates before, during, and after the 2016 referendum. At the same time it is important not to romanticise the potential of city-wide or neighbourhood-level citizenship as inherently offering greater inclusivity and equality in terms of rights and representation, as opposed to when citizenship is understood entirely as defining a person's relationship to a nation-state (Antonsich and Matejskova, 2015; Hudson, this volume; Visser and Simpson, this volume). Moreover, struggles at the scale of the city or the neighbourhood take place in a national context. At the time of writing there is widespread resentment across the UK following decades of neoliberal urbanism and the intensified austerity of the period following the 2008 banking crisis (Cook et al., 2011; Crewe, 2016). Moreover, since the 2016 referendum EU nationals in the UK have experienced continuing uncertainty over their future rights. This period overlaps with ongoing, plural, shifting forms of racism, including a post-9/11 growth in anti-Muslim racism (Virdee and McGeever, 2017) and a 'xeno-racism ... that is meted out to impoverished strangers even if they are white' (Sivanandan, 2001: 2; Gidley, 2018). In seeking to explore this apparent contradiction in a *provincial* city I am inspired by Les Back's (1996) concept of the 'metropolitan paradox' developed in the global city context of London, where, in an ethnographic study conducted in the 1990s, he argued that racisms coexisted side-by-side with spaces and moments of urban conviviality and everyday multi-culture.[3]

At the national level, the Leave campaign in the referendum repeatedly used the slogan 'take back control', emphasising the importance that the campaign attached to the UK's sovereignty, including over immigration policy. The referendum thus also, in part, like Nigel Farage's approach to the general election the year before, contributed to an ongoing struggle over citizenship. This struggle was most notable regarding whether it would be the free movement requirements of the EU, or the national policy of the government of the UK, that determined which EU citizens could enter the country and on what, if any, conditions. My longitudinal ethnographic engagement with a single study location provides a rare glimpse into continuity and change in citizenship struggles at the scale of a provincial city and of certain neighbourhoods within it, while attending to the relationships between these and more generalised national and international struggles. Like Visser and Simpson in this volume, my approach highlights relations between scales across time. However, as will become clear, my place-based methods have more in common with the 'grounded engagement' referred to by Bagelman in this volume.

The next two sections of the chapter explain, in turn, what I mean by citizenship struggle and by a relational approach to scale. I go on in three subsequent sections to describe my research in Peterborough, explore an earlier citizenship struggle there that foreshadowed the outcome of the 2016 referendum, and exemplify hopeful acts of subnational citizenship. The final section briefly concludes.

Citizenship and struggle

Citizenship is an amorphous concept. Some have even suggested that it 'risks losing its meaning … [through a] combination of overuse and confusion' (Anderson and Hughes, 2015: 1; Bloemraad and Sheares, 2017: 854). Yet in this chapter I will analyse multiple dimensions of citizenship[4] together, rather than attempting to slice it up into different 'types'. *Struggles* over citizenship are thus treated here as plural. They include struggles over labelling and categories – how people are spoken about and referred to in prevalent discourses in online and print media, as well as in physical locations such as workplaces, schools, and public outdoor space. Equally, they incorporate struggles over the distribution of resources, and over representation and meaningful involvement in decision-making processes (Allen, 2011: ix; Kuge, this volume).

Noting the renewed anti-migrant moral panic that followed the UK granting nationals of newly acceded EU states access to its labour market in 2004, and that then surged following the 2008 financial crisis, Fitzgerald and Smoczynski (2015) argue that this situation led not only to the stigmatisation of nationals of central and eastern EU states, but also to a fightback. Focusing on the experience of Polish migrants in particular, Fitzgerald and Smoczynski extend their argument to other EU nationalities, stating that the notion of the 'Polish migrant' operated as a 'floating signifier' that related to 'a broader Eastern European migrant community' (2015: 340–341). The fightback, as a form of citizenship struggle, consisted of 'resist[ing] social exclusion' including through

> the proliferation of ethnic on-line media that provide[d] comprehensive information on the rights of EU citizens … Respondents that were equipped with greater cultural capital resources (language skills, education) were significantly less likely to be interpellated as a 'deviant migrant' … *Polish migrants' strategy of fighting back … clearly calls for further research* (Fitzgerald and Smoczynski, 2015: 355, emphasis added).

Balibar proposes more generally that 'struggles [over citizenship] are always necessary', whether over 'an exclusion from recognition (or dignity, or rights, or property, or security, or speech, or decision-making)', because 'the subproletariat or underclass of the insecure, immigrants, and especially youth … are *pushed* or *left outside* representation' (2012: 438, 441, author's emphasis). The kind of dialectic referred to by Balibar is echoed in Staeheli et al.'s review of the ways in which citizenship struggles have emerged in 'ordinary' life, with ordinary used in its double meaning as *both* 'standard and routine' *and* 'invok[ing] order and authority' (2012: 628).

Citizenship struggles are thus waged both from above, through the 'governmental reproduction of normative distinctions of citizen and non-citizen' (Darling, 2017: 728), and from below. Actors in contemporary contestations over citizenship in the UK include relatively recently arrived international migrants and longer-term residents of all ethnicities. Citizenship struggles are very often racialised, and, as in the USA, understanding them requires analysis of how 'race', faith identities, and immigration intersect (Ehrkamp, 2017). However, this is not a dialectical battle between two clearly defined opposing forces. Acts of citizenship emerging 'from below' have varying degrees of instrumentality, strength, and duration (Darling, 2017: 730–731; see also Bagelman, this volume). They may include resources deployed in everyday life and 'claims rooted in family, in community, and in an expanded range of moral universes ... [among them] values of care, mutuality, love, respect and other-regardingness' (Staeheli et al., 2012: 640).

Importantly, however, claims relating to 'family and community' may be deployed in reactionary ways, for example in efforts by long-term residents and/or majority white populations to 'take back control'. Thus as well as hitherto marginalised people and groups seeking greater enfranchisement and representation, the actors may include people and organisations seeking to exclude certain others from various aspects of citizenship, with 'acts and interventions ... that are actively *destructive* of other ways of being ... [for example] the affective politics of hate, the saliency of desires to retain and protect privilege, and the rejection of forms of solidarity that seek to extend concern to others' (Darling, 2017: 734, author's emphasis). Such positions reflect ongoing contests over the nation in the UK and elsewhere, as part of which 'claims about "proper" conventions may articulate exclusionary national identities, or inclusively seek to broaden the range of practices conceived as national *along with the people who practise them*' (Edensor, 2006: 533, emphasis added; see also Visser and Simpson, this volume).

The location of this chapter in a specific historical time-period – from the financial crisis of 2008 until 2017, the year after the referendum – avoids the 'empirical presentism' that Guarnizo (2012: 17) found characteristic of many contemporary studies of citizenship. Earlier periods are relevant to the analysis here too, with citizenship struggles in the UK often characterised in ways that carry echoes of the UK's relatively recent past as a coloniser (see Stoler, 2006; Rogaly and Taylor,

2010; Amin, 2012: 92; Mitchell, 2014).[5] Temporality is also important in ways not confined to *historical* time: not only may citizenship acts from below be fleeting (Darling, 2017: 731), but some of the actors themselves may see their presence in national, city, or neighbourhood space as transient. Moreover, people's intentions to stay in a particular place or national territory, degree of citizenship, and connection to places elsewhere are unlikely to be fixed (Andrucki and Dickinson, 2015). The modes of governance of recently arrived people, the degree to which their presence is constructed by themselves or others as transient, and the implications of the latter for whether and to what extent they are regarded as citizens are all subject to struggle (Canepari and Rosa, 2017: 2).

Scale, sub-national citizenship, and a relational understanding of place

Regarding the scales at which citizenship struggles occur, I am persuaded by Guarnizo's (2012) argument that the analysis of citizenship needs to move away from an either/or stance, towards a more relational understanding that *both* recognises the importance of scalar particularity *and* rejects the idea of a nested hierarchy of discrete scales. Guarnizo proposes that scales are always interwoven and interrelated. So citizenship struggles are not simply analytically rescaled from the nation-state back to the city,[6] but they occur *simultaneously* and in *related* ways at *multiple* scales (see also Jones and Fowler, 2007; Visser and Simpson, this volume). For EU nationals in the UK the process of negotiating Brexit has brought a heightened degree of uncertainty over the terms of their formal political citizenship, including their rights to reside, work, and invite family members to join them in the UK. The debate has revealed major differences between the UK's constituent nations and cities, with arguments made at various points by the Scottish government and the Greater London Assembly for more comprehensive citizenship rights for EU nationals (both current residents and future arrivals) than would be the case in the rest of the UK if some of the more restrictionist national positions were to be adopted. At the same time the status of EU nationals in the UK is, at the time of writing, subject to ongoing negotiations between the UK government and the twenty-seven other national governments that form the EU.

A relational, multi-scalar approach to examining citizenship struggles resonates, as Oosterlynck et al. argue, with a relational understanding of place, and with an emphasis on citizenship *practices*:

> Places themselves are open and fluid, and issues of recognition, redistribution and representation can be made visible and negotiated through the enactment of citizenship relating to that place. Places then become sites for the everyday agonistic negotiation of claims of diverse subjects. (Oosterlynck et al., 2016: 775)

Oosterlynck et al.'s call for attention to citizen practices in place allows for the possibility of situated solidarity between recent arrivals and longer-term residents, and between racialised minorities and majority populations (see also Askins, 2016; Back et al., 2018). In an environment characterised by neoliberal urbanism and austerity, this implicitly turns local citizenship struggles back to the question of class, resonating with Massey's (2011) suggestion that differently displaced people – including people who have *had* to move residence and people who have had no choice but to stay put – might come together in 'common anger'.

For Oosterlynck et al.,

> relationality as a starting point ... opens up perspectives for solidarity among heterogeneous populations who do not have anything in common apart from the place they share. In schools, parks, factories, offices, sports fields or neighbourhood centres, innovative forms of solidarity develop around the joint appropriation and the envisaged common future of a particular place. (2016: 775)

So any attempt to 'reinvent' urban citizenship (Bauböck, 2003) needs to avoid 'methodological cityism' (Pastore and Ponzo, 2016) by considering the relation between more localised, site-specific, and neighbourhood practices on the one hand and the scale of the city on the other. At the same time, such efforts should retain an analytical alertness to the connections between both of these and struggles over differential citizenship and the nation-state and supranational institutions beyond. Such an approach recognises the uneven social geography of the city, and its causes (Harvey, 2009), while also potentially providing a pathway to claiming a 'right to the city' from the ground up for all *residents*.

Residence in the city, *jus domicilii*, is also the basis for Bauder's (2014) exploration of the possibility of a *legal* urban citizenship, in contrast to the more commonly used grounds for citizenship based on parentage or place of birth. Both Bauder and Oosterlynck et al. – albeit in very different ways – thus offer urban counterweights to the uncontested transplanting of hierarchical forms of citizenship based on differentiated rights of residence, work, and access to social benefits that otherwise flow from unequal legal statuses produced by the nation-state. However, Hoekstra's (2015) comparative study of Amsterdam and The Hague shows that the implementation of a residence-based urban citizenship approach by city authorities is not necessarily equally inclusive of all residents. As she points out, for example, recent arrivals in The Hague are required to make an active choice to be a citizen while 'native majority members are exempted from such demonstrations of loyalty' (Hoekstra, 2015: 1811).

With these discussions in mind, I briefly describe the research project in Peterborough before illustrating a pre-Brexit tremor in the city through the example of a local struggle for 'indigenous' rights over place that could be seen as a small-scale precursor of the national campaign to 'take back control' in 2016. Noting the marked lack of representation for non-UK EU citizens in both cases, I then relate an experience of a more convivial everyday citizenship act in Peterborough, that, while not created as part of an instrumental struggle, nevertheless can be seen as part of a larger set of claims being made from below for a more inclusive place-based (sub-national) citizenship.

Researching citizenship struggles in Peterborough

From 2011 to 2017 I researched concurrent overlapping citizenship struggles in Peterborough, including over workplace justice in the intensive food and retail distribution centre sectors (Rogaly and Qureshi, 2017); over the right to determine the pace and nature of change in the physical environment of central neighbourhoods with long histories of initial settlement by international migrants;[7] and over the broader right to co-determine to whom the city belongs both in the present and in the future (Massey, 2011; Rogaly and Qureshi,

2013). All these were in turn interrelated with ongoing struggles at other scales.

Citizenship was not the sole focus of my work, but the research grant that first took me to Peterborough was part of what might be understood – from its name Citizen Power Peterborough (CPP) – as a would-be urban citizenship promotion scheme.[8] Emanating from an alliance between the director of the London-based think-tank the Royal Society of Arts (RSA) and the then leader of Peterborough City Council, the legacy of CPP is disputed. For example, Rutter suggests that during its three-year duration it was the 'largest' initiative 'involved in activities to build better relations between different ethnic groups and between new migrants and longer-settled residents' and that it thereby gave rise to 'social links and friendships ... that ... acted to resolve tensions in the centre of the city' (Rutter, 2015: 236). On the other hand, Rajkowska and Humm point to a more discordant aspect of the CPP's record, appearing to hold local actors responsible for the withdrawal of permission for an art installation commissioned by the RSA from Rajkowska, an artist based in London and Nowogród, Poland. Rajkowska faced extremely challenging personal circumstances at the time she was staying in Peterborough. Her experience caused her to conclude that 'there was no point in staying [in Peterborough] [...] having started to feel extremely ill-at-ease [there]' (Rajkowska and Humm, 2016: 12–13). Like her, I am an outsider to the city, but my relationship with Peterborough has been different. I have continued to be pulled back there, inspired by organisations and individuals already engaged in struggles for equality and against racism in an era of economic austerity (Rogaly, 2016: 668–669). This is in spite of my ambivalent relation to the CPP scheme itself (Rogaly, 2016: 664–666).

While living part-time in Peterborough for the first nine months of the research, and continuing to be a regular overnight visitor there up to the time of writing, a key question remaining at the forefront of my mind concerned exclusions from urban citizenship. The question was expressed in slightly different terms in the title of the original project: *Places for All?* The question mark in the title deliberately evoked a pluralistic vision for a right to this city based on residence – not formal political citizenship necessarily, but nevertheless in the spirit of Bauder's *jus domicilii*. The plural, *places*, opened up questions of difference between neighbourhoods in the city, as well as struggles over citizenship at the neighbourhood level.

Through this research, the anthropologist Kaveri Qureshi and I recorded oral history interviews with seventy-six individuals, of which sixty-one were life history interviews. The rest included key informant interviews and oral histories of particular events. The invitation to participate in the study was made on the basis that narrators were residents of Peterborough or one of its surrounding villages. It thus included both people born locally, and those who had moved there, whether relatively recently or decades earlier, from other parts of the UK or from other nation-states. The intention was to create and share locally a sense of Peterborough's multiple elsewheres (Rogaly and Qureshi, 2013) and how these contributed to making the city.

Peterborough is a multi-ethnic, multi-faith city. For example, a relatively high proportion of residents self-identified as Muslim in the 2011 Census – 9.4 per cent against a figure for England and Wales of 4.8 per cent. Moreover, since the 1950s the city has been the destination for tens of thousands of international migrants responding to job openings, including people arriving from Italy and south Asia (Cameron, 2012). Peterborough City Council welcomed east African Asian and Vietnamese refugees in the 1970s and early 1980s respectively; the city was also designated as a dispersal area[9] for asylum seekers at the turn of the millennium (Burnett, 2012: 7). Nevertheless, the largest single flow of migrants to the city was made up of mainly white British Londoners and Scots at the time of the building of the city's satellite 'New Town' areas in the 1970s and 1980s.

As a national programme of austerity was being rolled out, and swingeing cuts were made to the budget of Peterborough City Council (Rutter, 2015), we were interested in exploring commonalities between long-term residents and recently arrived people of all ethnic and national backgrounds. At the same time we wanted to understand the nature of everyday citizenship in the city for EU nationals, many of whom had come to work in local food factories and warehouses, without necessarily knowing whether they would seek to reside in the UK long term.

The life history narrators were adults[10] of a wide range of ages; thirty-three of them were women and twenty-eight were men. They were diverse in terms of country of birth, ethnicity, and nationality. While twenty-five were UK-born, fourteen had arrived in the UK since the mid-1990s and twenty-two had first entered the country between the end of the Second World War and 1995. Twelve participants were EU nationals – seven from Poland, two from Lithuania, and one each from Italy, Portugal, and Belgium.

Most of the narrators worked in or had retired from working-class occupations, corresponding to the above average proportion of people in Peterborough employed in elementary occupations or as process operatives[11] and/or in approximated social grades D and E.[12] While people moving to Peterborough have worked in a range of occupations, including, at various points in time, brick manufacture, fruit canning, and engineering work, the city's location adjacent to the highly productive soils of the Fens region to the east continues to make it a hub for workers employed in temporary agency work in the food sector, including in production, packing, and processing (Rutter, 2015: 9; Rogaly and Qureshi, 2017: 190–191). Understanding citizenship struggles in Peterborough in this period must therefore include an examination of the claims made by temporary migrant workers, including EU nationals, to rights and representation in the city. It also requires engagement with the changing dynamics of food sector capitalism.

Jason,[13] a white British Peterborough-born man in his fifties, who had witnessed the latter changes first hand across his own working life, referred to them as a process of 'commercialisation and industrialisation' (interview, 31 March 2017). His insider analysis concurs with existing academic work showing how the concentrated power of retail corporations indirectly drove down employment conditions in horticultural production and food processing in the UK, and, at the same time, increased demand for workers in sorting and packing roles through ramped-up imports of year-round supplies of the same varieties of fruit and vegetables (e.g. Rogaly, 2008; Scott, 2017). Beyond food, the shape of demand for temporary agency workers was also connected to the expansion of what another research participant referred to as 'huge sheds' on the edges of the city, owned by corporations such as Amazon, Ikea, DHL, and Tesco. Since the UK's vote to leave the EU and the beginning of the Brexit process, EU citizens

from central and eastern European countries have not sought work
in these sectors to the same degree, and national business organisations
have clamoured for the UK government to pay attention to emerging
labour shortages.[14]

Pre-Brexit tremors in a Peterborough neighbourhood

Brexit was a term that had not yet been invented in 2011, but my
fieldnotes from that year contained an early hint, a murmur, of what
its effects might be for EU nationals living and working in Peterborough.
On 9 December 2011 the then UK prime minister David Cameron
had deployed the British veto against EU treaty change to support
the ailing euro, and in the process had, according to the *Guardian*
newspaper, 'appear[ed] to query whether being in the EU would remain
in Britain's interests'. I had been discussing the anti-Muslim English
Defence League's attempted recruitment of Polish workers at a retail
distribution centre in Peterborough with a Polish worker there and
her partner. I wrote in my notebook that

> This all came up in the context of a discussion about the Cameron
> announcement on Europe and the niggling anxiety that they talked
> about this creating in the minds of accession country nationals who
> were settling/ considering settling. (author fieldnotes, 14 December
> 2011)

In some ways anticipating the national and EU-level debates during
and after the 2016 referendum over the future status of EU citizens
living in countries of the EU other than their own (Bulat, 2018), the
question of what kind of citizenship nationals of Central and Eastern
European EU member countries enjoy in Peterborough persisted in
the research since its inception.

Yet the most striking element of the city-level citizenship struggles
engaged in by non-UK EU nationals in Peterborough remains the
absence of institutionalised representation. A community organisation
worker interviewed for an earlier research project reported a similar
absence for recently arrived Kurdish people in the mid-2000s, and
the consequences of this for narratives about Kurdish residents and
thus for citizenship struggles with which they were engaged (Jones,
2011: 227–228). The importance of representation and its absence

is further illustrated by the emergence and demise of a dedicated reception and signposting organisation for newly arrived international migrants in the city: New Link. New Link began operating in 2004, sited in the part of the Lincoln Road area around which much private rental accommodation used by migrant workers was located. An oral history interview with one former New Link worker suggested that the original bid that won £2.2 million of funding from the Home Office arose out of long-term residents' reactions to the arrival of asylum seekers following Peterborough's designation as a dispersal area in 1999, and the large numbers of non-UK EU citizens who came to the city to seek work following the EU enlargement in 2004. In 2001–2

> tensions [had been] rising among settled residents and all the people coming in, because nobody knew who they were, so they thought everybody was a bogus asylum seeker … Then when the migrant workers started to come, it exacerbated it. So what then happened was we … put in a bid, which went into the Home Office with the Police, Health and City Council.

Yet according to the same narrator, the funding

> caused this massive problem with the politicians and the residents, because all this money was being used to help foreign people, and that was really the beginning of what became more interesting about it, because it was dealing with that that we learned so much.

Another oral history narrator provided fragments of the story of the citizenship struggle that led first to New Link being relocated in 2010, with a smaller team, to the main council offices at Bayard House in the city centre, and then to lose all its council funding the following year. The narrator was a white British long-term resident of the city with a leadership role in a campaign to shut down New Link. With hindsight, this local campaign can be seen to have been akin to elements of the national 'take back control' campaign in the 2016 referendum. In spite of the ethno-national diversity of the area, the campaign was led by a residents' association made up mainly of white British people, who portrayed themselves as asserting the rights of so-called 'indigenous' people in this particular area of the city, regardless of their own migration histories. The main message of the campaign was that newly arrived international migrants should not receive dedicated services, using a rhetoric that suggested an entitlement associated with both whiteness and British nationality. Moreover, the campaign was supported by sympathetic councillors, its language resonating with a police officer who had told Kaveri Qureshi and me in an interview that

> We always consider 'cohesion' … But not the white English majority, who increasingly feel that they're not getting a voice or resources, and are starting to feel like a minority themselves. (quoted in Rogaly and Qureshi, 2013: 427)

Prefiguring the surprise that Leave campaign leaders expressed at the Leave victory in the national referendum five years later, the local campaign leader told me of his disbelief at the speed of its success in an interview in 2011:

> Well things moved rapidly. With the council if it happens in six months that's lightning speed, but we've had real … even quicker than lightning in relation to how we've dealt with that. (7 September 2011)

Following an interview in the city council offices two months earlier I had noted:

> [A council officer] said [the council] were considering the use of compulsory purchase orders, [because] the 'indigenous' population were saying they've lost what there was and would like 'heritage and history reclaimed'. (author fieldnotes, 27 July 2011)

For those advocating for the rights of so-called 'indigenous' ethnic majority white British people in this part of Peterborough, the number of new arrivals, including non-UK EU nationals in the city, was *both* a genuine matter of concern *and* a surface issue obscuring a deeper unease with ethnic diversity and particularly the number of residents with Pakistani Muslim heritage, their role in the provision of homes of multiple occupation to the new arrivals, and the effect of this on the property market. Another sign of this was the letter sent in January 2010 from two councillors representing Peterborough's North ward to the leaders of the three main national political parties. The letter expressed the councillors' concerns both with many years of spending cuts leading to a reduction in the services that the council was able to provide, and with what they referred to as the 'dramatic' impact on those services of the growing number of non-UK EU citizens in Peterborough. Yet, tellingly, and in spite of one of the councillors, a former leader of the council, having energetically welcomed Ugandan Asian and Vietnamese refugees to the city in the 1970s and 1980s and having been instrumental in the addition of Urdu to the curriculum of the city's secondary schools, the passage about the impact on a school in North ward pointed to the low number of primary school reception class pupils who were 'white British'.[15]

Erel (2011) has argued that the relatively high number of new arrivals from central and eastern Europe had the effect of re-intensifying the racialisation of long-settled British south Asian heritage Muslims in Peterborough. This dynamic too prefigured national developments during and after the 2016 referendum campaign, when the highlighting of the case for ending the free movement of workers from the EU seemed to be read by some as legitimating a wider antagonism towards people who looked or sounded other than white British, in some cases leading to racist hate crimes against black and minority ethnic people, especially those visibly appearing as Muslim, regardless of how they had voted in the referendum (Burnett, 2016). The politically motivated elision between the argument against the free movement of (mostly white, Christian heritage) central and eastern European EU citizens and the play on popular racialised and anti-Muslim tropes (Virdee and McGeever, 2017) became explicit in the language of some Leave campaign leaders. Messages such as that conveyed by the notorious 'Breaking Point' poster that pictured large numbers of dark-skinned people, mainly male and implicitly Muslim, and the regular reference to the likelihood that Turkey would soon join the European Union and that Turkish nationals would have the automatic right to live and work in the UK, left no room for ambiguity.

Everyday citizenship acts in the provincial city

Running alongside, and against, local and national agendas of 'tak[ing] back control' and multiple forms of racism, recent arrivals to the city, their long-term resident allies, and anti-racist and pro-migrant

organisations have made individual and sometimes collective transformations in the experience of urban citizenship in Peterborough.
These have involved acts of citizenship that vary, echoing Darling
(2017), in terms of the degree to which they are instrumental, as well
as in strength and duration. Some such acts have been based around
language or country of origin and include the popular and well-attended
Lithuanian and Polish weekend language schools and national/linguistic
community-based websites, such as Polonia Peterborough and Nasze
Strony. In 2015 the city council attempted to increase its engagement
with Lithuanian, Latvian, Slovakian, and Czech communities in the
city, advertising four Community Connector posts. However, these
were restructured in 2017 and no longer provided a formal bridge
between the city council and specific national/linguistic communities
in the city. Representation thus remained very limited locally, and this
was compounded by the national exclusion of non-UK EU citizens
from the 2016 referendum vote.[16]

Yet while, as shown by Gilroy (2004), conviviality does not operate
outside racisms but is, rather, interwoven with them in specific space-
time configurations (see also Nayak, 2017), everyday acts of convivial
citizenship in Peterborough reveal the potential for a more hopeful
national politics. Egid, a Kurdish man whom I interviewed in 2017,
remembered working alongside Lithuanian people when he first arrived
in the UK in 2002. While he lived in Peterborough and they lived in
Grantham, all were transported daily by an agency to the cut-flower
plant where they worked. Egid recalled 'mad nights out' in both cities.
More recently he had married a Kurdish woman and both worked in
one of the city's large warehouses. Because they had a car they gave
lifts to and from work to three women (Polish and Lithuanian) and
formed a close family friendship with one of them, who was also a
neighbour. Egid and other current and former food factory and
warehouse workers I interviewed in 2017 all described how work in
these sectors had become increasingly intense over time, with raised
targets, fines, and even dismissals for under-performance. Yet the way
work was organised by certain companies and at particular worksites
continued to enable connections to be made across ethno-national
difference, providing increased potential for collective refusal to comply
with a particular supervisor or target. Narrators recalled refusing to
be ground down by repetitive, intensive, fast-paced, unhealthy, and

sometimes dangerous work. For example, Armins, a Latvian man, counted as many as sixty nationalities in a warehouse he had worked in for nine months soon after the 2008 financial crisis:

> I think making friends there and having conversations and being able to relate to each other ... was one of the best things about the warehouse. I'm a people person, I like to be surrounded by people ... just having nice conversations and even planning the future ... We were cheating, of course. We were standing behind these big boxes and talking <laughs>. And then our targets went down and then, yeah. But nobody actually cared. Those who were very scared about their targets, yeah, these people kind of were keeping to themselves. They didn't have a lot of people to talk to. But those who liked other people and yeah, we were actually cheating. And break times as well.

Such events, and the narration of them, can be seen as acts of citizenship, as demands to have a narrative, to build a life, and to be heard. They resonated with the earliest interviews that Kaveri Qureshi and I carried out in Peterborough in 2011, during which other workers criticised supervisory regimes that prevented more than minimal interaction at work and, like Armins, placed explicit value on the ethno-national diversity of food factory and warehouse workforces around Peterborough (Rogaly and Qureshi, 2017).

Towards the end of the same year, I had been invited to a party in the community centre on the ground floor of a block of social housing. The party itself can be understood as an act of convivial urban citizenship. I wrote about it in my fieldnotes the next day:

> I had been invited some weeks ago by Maria [a Polish research participant]. It was a party for St Andrews Day – that precedes Advent [and was held in the community room at her block of flats].
>
> There were about twenty people there in all – we were greeted on arrival by young Polish women in their twenties with three and four year old children. Two were married to Egyptian husbands – neither of whom were there. There was a fair amount of chaos – we were not offered drinks – people were helping themselves. The Buddhist son of Patrycja, another Polish research participant, was working his way through blue WKD vodka. Sarah's daughter Jo was there with her partner Enrique who is Argentinian. Jo has a job as a teaching assistant. She has travelled round India and Latin America – met Enrique in Argentina. Jo's sister also turned up later.

I pledged to interview Sarah again and also Sean [both of whom are white British]. Sean is a sixty year-old lorry driver who has lived in Peterborough all his life. He's married to Deirdre, from Sunderland. He's travelled a lot on his lorry and has no romance about Peterborough but lots to tell about his younger days – remembered delivering telegrams in the city beginning 1966 – in fact to the area where the flats we were partying in were built when it was just streets – a rough area then according to both Sarah and Sean. Deirdre, Sean's partner is a care worker.

We were sat down for the meal around a large table. I had already been given a sweet pastry and now it was time for borscht (beetroot) soup with meat dumplings accompanied by empañadas made by Jo with Quorn and herbs. There was chicken stew to follow with spices and tomatoes – I think Patrycja had cooked that. Then there was delicious Polish salad – lots of mayonnaise and pickle in it. A chocolate cake cut into squares in front of us and lovely Polish bread. Patrycja and Maria served the food. Really nice atmosphere – there was an elderly couple there too, at least one of whom was English.

I spoke with a Polish woman, Beata who was married to an Egyptian, with whom she'd had a son, now 27 months old. Beata, who is very tall with long blond hair, has become Muslim. She said she believes women who are Muslim should wear hijab but that her family are not ready for it. She's been to visit his family in Egypt and had a good time. She said she's learned Arabic cooking and that she likes cooking. She works in the same factory as Maria. Her husband is working through an agency – tonight he was driving a fork-lift truck in a warehouse. Beata's mother is currently living with them and looking after their son. Beata speaks to her son in Polish and to her husband in Arabic. They are waiting for English until he goes to school.

It was a lovely evening – I also had a conversation with Patrycja's son. He told me about the macho boys' culture on the line at the Japanese tie-up with Perkins Engineering where he works … The workers survey each other for mistakes that they can report on each other – the machismo is over turning out the perfect product. He claims to have found efficiencies in every part of the manufacturing process – to handle him, he claims, the company has given him a training role across all the parts of the process. He spent 3–4 weeks in Thailand in the summer including 2 weeks in his girlfriend's village.

My notes following the party concur with Oosterlynck et al.'s argument for the potential for solidarity rooted in common experiences of class and place (2016: 775) across differences in ethnicity, national identity, immigration status, and length of residence. As I wrote at the time 'This was bottom up integration in practice. Ordinary everyday working class conviviality across generations. Very gendered with Patrycja shouldering much of the cooking and Maria having to clear up quite a bit.'

Conclusion

These brief glimpses from my research in Peterborough show the interrelation between citizenship practices and struggles at a variety of sites and scales, including workplaces, neighbourhoods, and the city as a whole. They also suggest that possibilities for bottom-up conviviality coexist in localised citizenship acts that can be seen as an everyday 'politics of presence' (Darling, this volume), which is inclusive of people whose presence is temporary and who may be formally resident elsewhere. However, the chapter also showed how, in historically and geographically situated ways, convivial acts are located alongside and in relation to practices and discourses that promote division and a lack of mutual regard at multiple scales.

I want to emphasise that revisiting my first years of research in the city in 2011 and 2012 serves as a reminder that the push-back against both international migrants and ethnic minorities, particularly Muslims, that formed part of the Leave campaign in the 2016 referendum did not come out of the blue but was prefigured at different scales, especially throughout the whole period of austerity, declining wages, and deteriorating job quality that followed the 2008 financial crisis. Yet the referendum campaign and its result *has* significantly changed the context for citizenship struggles by EU nationals in the UK.

Such struggles have been researched in detail in Scotland by Botterill (2018) and are also borne out by my own ongoing work in Peterborough. Individual post-referendum experiences are neither uniform nor constant, but, while much national attention is paid to the ethnicised notion of working-class life that prioritises the experience of white British nationals within that class, it is important to mention the widespread evidence of hurt, of having been kicked in the solar plexus, that the Leave vote represented for many resident EU nationals. In Peterborough, where many non-UK EU citizens work and have made their homes and yet have no formal or informal representation in city decision making, struggles over urban citizenship continue. The more uncertain and hostile the national environment feels, the more people who have lived and worked in the city for many years consider a return to their country of origin. Which country or countries they feel are theirs is indeed, to take a different slant on the title of the post-referendum play I referred to at the start of the chapter, a work-in-progress.

Acknowledgements

I am grateful to Amy Clarke, Alison Davies, Mostyn Davies, Jay Gearing, Katy Hawkins, Kaveri Qureshi, Kirat Randhawa, and Mark Richards for helpful comments and discussions while I was writing this chapter, and to Harald Bauder and Jonathan Darling for their patience and excellent editorial suggestions. None of them are responsible for remaining errors or for the views expressed here. I am also grateful for funding for this work through two AHRC grants (AH/J501669/1; AH/N004094/1).

Notes

1 The second largest self-identification category in the 2011 Census (after White British), largely made up of non-UK EU nationals. See www.ons.gov.uk/people populationandcommunity/culturalidentity/ethnicity/articles/ethnicityandthela bourmarket2011censusenglandandwales/2014–11–13 (accessed 14 March 2018).

2 BBC Radio 4, Today programme, 2 April 2015.

3 In a study conducted in 2005–6 in Peterborough, Erel similarly identified 'both convivial and more conflictual modes of everyday life' and connected these to 'new migrations' (2011: 2053). For definitions of conviviality and everyday multi-culture, see, respectively, Wise and Noble (2016) and Gidley (2013).

4 These dimensions include both formalised political status and informal practices that are part of everyday 'social interactions and identity negotiations that become a micro-politics of daily life' (Bloemraad and Sheares, 2017: 854).

5 See Anderson (2016: ch. 10) for an explanation of the role of censuses, maps, and museums in producing categories for Dutch colonial rule in south-east Asia as well as for its undoing.

6 Guarnizo insisted on taking the citizenship concept back to its roots in cities of the ancient world.

7 Including many who arrived in the UK as Commonwealth citizens and only later became 'migrants' (Bhambra, 2016).

8 The research has been funded by two grants from the UK Arts and Humanities Research Council. The proposal for the first of these, *Places for All?*, responded to a national Research Fellowship competition, specifically linked to the Citizen Power Peterborough project. It was jointly written with a team of collaborating artists and academics: Mukul Ahmed, Teresa Cairns, Denis Doran, Liz Hingley, Raminder Kaur, and Kaveri Qureshi. The resulting project ran from 2011 to 2013. See www.placesforall.co.uk. Since October 2016 I have continued the research as part of a separate project, *Creative Interruptions*. See www.creativeinterruptions.com. Both sites were last accessed on 1 March 2018.

9 The policy of dispersal was implemented as part of the UK's Immigration and Asylum Act, 1999.

10 With the exception of one narrator who was 17 at the time.

11 Rising proportions of both categories in the workforce in the first decade of this century bucked a downward national trend (Dorling and Thomas, 2016).

12 33 per cent as against 23 per cent in the East of England region and 25 per cent in England as a whole according to the 2011 Census (Opportunity Peterborough Economic Intelligence Report, 2015). Approximated social grade is a socio-economic classification produced by the UK Office of National Statistics. See www.ukgeographics.co.uk/blog/social-grade-a-b-c1-c2-d-e (accessed 15 March 2018).

13 Unless otherwise requested in writing, research participants' names have been changed or omitted entirely.

14 See www.theguardian.com/politics/2018/feb/20/farmers-tell-gove-lack-of-migrant-workers-now-mission-critical and www.theguardian.com/uk-news/2018/feb/21/number-of-western-eu-nationals-in-uk-workforce-falls-by-5-percent (both last accessed 28 February 2018).

15 Letter published by the *Daily Mail*, 10 April 2010, and cited by Burnett (2012). See www.dailymail.co.uk/news/article-1264930/Peterborough-struggling-immigration-toll.html (accessed 1 March 2018).

16 Who has the right to vote in UK referenda is legislated for separately before each referendum. Non-UK EU citizens have the right to vote in local government elections in the UK but not in general elections.

References

Allen, D. (2011) 'Foreword', in I. Young, *Justice and the Politics of Difference* (Princeton, NJ: Princeton University Press, 2nd edn), ix–x.

Amin, A. (2012) *Land of Strangers* (Cambridge: Polity).

Anderson, B. (2016) *Imagined Communities: Reflections on the Origins and Spread of Nationalism* (London: Verso, rev. edn).

Anderson, B., and V. Hughes (2015) 'Introduction', in B. Anderson and V. Hughes (eds), *Citizenship and its Others* (Basingstoke: Palgrave), 1–9.

Andrucki, M., and J. Dickinson (2015) 'Rethinking centers and margins in geography: bodies, life course, and the performance of transnational space', *Annals of the Association of American Geographers*, 105:1, 203–218.

Antonsich, M., and T. Matejskova (2015) 'Conclusion: nation and diversity – a false conundrum', in T. Matejskova and M. Antonsich (eds), *Governing through Diversity: Migration Societies in Post-Multiculturalist Times* (Basingstoke: Palgrave), 201–209.

Askins, K. (2016) 'Emotional citizenry: everyday geographies of befriending, belonging and intercultural encounter', *Transactions of the Institute of British Geographers*, 41:4, 515–527.

Back, L. (1996) *New Ethnicities and Urban Culture: Racisms and Multiculture in Young Lives* (London: UCL Press).

Back, L., and S. Sinha, with C. Bryan, V. Baraku, and M. Yemba (2018) *Migrant City* (London: Routledge).

Balibar, E. (2012) 'The "impossible" community of the citizens: past and present problems', *Environment and Planning D: Society and Space*, 30, 437–449.

Bauböck, R. (2003) 'Reinventing urban citizenship', *Citizenship Studies*, 7:2, 139–160.

Bauder, H. (2014) 'Domicile citizenship, human mobility and territoriality', *Progress in Human Geography*, 38:1, 91–106.

Bhambra, G. (2016) 'Brexit, the Commonwealth, and exclusionary citizenship', *Open Democracy* (8 December 2016), www.opendemocracy.net/gurminder-k-bhambra/brexit-commonwealth-and-exclusionary-citizenship (accessed 9 November 2018).

Bloemraad, I., and A. Sheares (2017) 'Understanding membership in a world of global migration: (how) does citizenship matter?', *International Migration Review*, 51:4, 823–867.

Botterill, K. (2018) 'Rethinking "community" relationally: Polish communities in Scotland before and after Brexit', *Transactions of the Institute of British Geographers*, 43:4, 540–554, DOI: 10.1111/tran.12249.

Bulat, A. (2018) 'The rights of non-UK EU citizens living here are not a "done deal"'. This is why', *LSE Brexit Blog* (27 February), http://blogs.lse.ac.uk/brexit/2018/02/27/the-rights-of-non-uk-eu-citizens-living-here-are-not-a-done-deal-this-is-why/ (accessed 5 December 2018).

Burnett, J. (2012) *The New Geographies of Racism: Peterborough* (London: Institute of Race Relations).

Burnett, J. (2016) *Racial Violence and the Brexit State* (London: Institute of Race Relations).

Cameron, J. (2012) 'Postwar economic integration: how did a brick shortage change Peterborough', MA dissertation, Birbeck College, University of London.

Canepari, E., and E. Rosa (2017) 'A quiet claim to citizenship: mobility, urban spaces and city practices over time', *Citizenship Studies*, 21:6, 657–674.

Cook, J., P. Dwyer, and L. Waite (2011) 'Accession 8 migration and the proactive and defensive engagement of social citizenship', *Journal of Social Policy*, 41:2, 329–347.

Crewe, T. (2016) 'The strange death of municipal England', *London Review of Books*, 38:24, 6–10.

Darling, J. (2017) 'Acts, ambiguities and the labour of contesting citizenship', *Citizenship Studies*, 21:6, 727–736.

Dorling, D., and B. Thomas (2016) *People and Places: A 21st-Century Atlas of the UK* (Bristol: Policy Press).

Edensor, T. (2006) 'Reconsidering national temporalities: institutional times, everyday routines, serial spaces and synchronicities', *European Journal of Social Theory*, 9:4, 525–545.

Ehrkamp, P. (2017) 'Geographies of migration II: the racial-spatial politics of immigration', *Progress in Human Geography*, DOI: 10.1177/0309132517747317

Erel, U. (2011) 'Complex belongings: racialization and migration in a small English city', *Ethnic and Racial Studies*, 34:12, 2048–2068.

Fitzgerald, I., and R. Smoczynski (2015) 'Anti-Polish migrant moral panic in the UK: rethinking employment insecurities and moral regulation', *Czech Sociological Review*, 51:3, 339–361.

Gidley, B. (2013) 'Landscapes of belonging, portraits of life: researching everyday multiculture in an inner city estate', *Identities: Global Studies of Culture and Power*, 20:4, 361–376.

Gidley, B. (2018) 'Sivanandan's pessimistic hope in a degraded age', *Sociological Review Blog* (10 February), www.thesociologicalreview.com/blog/sivanandan-s-pessimistic-hope-in-a-degraded-age.html (accessed 5 December 2018).

Gilroy P. (2004) *After Empire: Melancholia or Convivial Culture* (Abingdon: Routledge).

Guarnizo, L. (2012) 'The fluid, multi-scalar, and contradictory construction of citizenship', in M. Smith and M. McQuarrie (eds), *Remaking Urban Citizenship: Organizations, Institutions and the Right to the City* (London: Transaction), 11–38.

Harvey, D. (2009) *Social Justice and the City* (Atlanta, GA: University of Georgia Press, rev. edn).

Hoekstra, M. (2015) 'Diverse cities and good citizenship: how local governments in the Netherlands recast national integration discourses', *Ethnic and Racial Studies*, 38:10, 1798–1814.

Jones, H. (2011) 'Uncomfortable positions: how policy practitioners negotiate difficult subjects', PhD thesis, Goldsmiths, University of London.

Jones, H. (2013) *Negotiating Cohesion, Inequality and Change: Uncomfortable Positions in Local Government* (Bristol: Policy Press).

Jones, R., and C. Fowler (2007) 'Placing and scaling the nation', *Environment and Planning D: Society and Space*, 25, 332–354.

Massey, D. (2011) 'Landscape/place/politics: an essay', https://thefutureofland scape.wordpress.com/landscapespacepolitics-an-essay/ (accessed 8 November 2018).

Mitchell, K. (2014) 'Difference', in R. Lee, N. Castree, R. Kithcen, V. Lawson, A. Paasi, C. Philo, S. Radcliffe, S. Roberts, and C. Withers (eds), *The SAGE Handbook of Human Geography* (London: Sage), 69–93.

Nayak, A. (2017) 'Purging the nation: race, conviviality and embodied encounters in the lives of British Bangladeshi Muslim young women', *Transactions of the Institute of British Geographers*, 42:2, 289–302, DOI: 10.1111/tran.12168.

Oosterlynck, S., M. Loopmans, N. Schuermans, J. Vandenabeele, and S. Zemni (2016) 'Putting flesh on the bone: looking for solidarity in diversity, here and now', *Ethnic and Racial Studies*, 39:5, 764–782.

Pastore, F., and I. Ponzo (eds) (2016) *Inter-group Relations and Migrant Integration in European Cities: Changing Neighbourhoods* (London: Springer Open).

Rajkowska, J., and M. Humm (2016) 'The Peterborough Child and Joanna Rajkowska: themes, influences, art', in D. Shaw and M. Humm (eds), *Radical Space: Exploring Politics and Practice* (London: Rowman and Littlefield).

Rogaly, B. (2008) 'Intensification of workplace regimes in British horticulture: the role of migrant workers', *Population, Space and Place*, 14, 497–510.

Rogaly, B. (2016) '"Don't show the play at the football ground, nobody will come": the micro-sociality of co-produced research in an English provincial city', *Sociological Review*, 64:4, 657–680.

Rogaly, B., and K. Qureshi (2013) 'Diversity, urban space and the right to the provincial city', *Identities: Global Studies in Culture and Power*, 20:4, 423–437.

Rogaly, B., and K. Qureshi (2017) '"That's where my perception of it all was shattered": oral histories and moral geographies of food sector workers in an English city region', *Geoforum*, 78, 189–198.

Rogaly, B., and B. Taylor (2010) '"They called them communists then … What d'you call 'em now? Insurgents?" Narratives of British military expatriates in the context of the new imperialism', *Journal of Ethnic and Migration Studies*, 36:8, 1335–1351.

Rutter, J. (2015) *Moving Up and Getting On: Migration, Integration and Social Cohesion in the UK* (Bristol: Policy Press).

Scott, S. (2017) *Labour Exploitation and Work-Based Harm* (Bristol: Policy Press).

Sivanandan, A. (2001) 'Poverty is the new black', *Race and Class*, 43:2, 1–6.

Staeheli, L., P. Ehrkamp, H. Leitner, and C. Nagel (2012) 'Dreaming the ordinary: daily life and the complex geographies of citizenship', *Progress in Human Geography*, 36:5, 628–644.

Stoler, A. (2006) 'On degrees of imperial sovereignty', *Public Culture*, 18:1, 125–146.

Virdee, S., and B. McGeever (2017) 'Racism, crisis, Brexit', *Ethnic and Racial Studies*, 41:10, 1802–1819, DOI: 10.1080/01419870.2017.1361544.

Wise, A., and G. Noble (2016) 'Convivialities: an orientation', *Journal of Intercultural Studies*, 37:5, 423–431.

9

Sanctuary, presence, and the politics of urbanism

Jonathan Darling

Cities are increasingly recognised as important destinations for refugees across the world. Indeed, as the chapters of *Sanctuary cities and urban struggles* have shown, cities play a wide variety of roles within the politics of contemporary migration. They may be orientation points for rights claims and campaigns based on urban diversity and solidarity (Raimondi, this volume), sites of struggle over individual and collective claims to citizenship (Rogaly, this volume), legislative arenas for the incorporation of undocumented migrants through sanctuary ordinances (Bauder, Hudson, and Kuge, this volume), or sites of governance and everyday bordering whereby cities actively impede the rights of migrants (Visser and Simpson, this volume). Of course, as Atak's critical discussion of the practice of sanctuary in Toronto illustrates, cities can occupy each of these multiple roles at different points. Internationally, with more than half of the world's refugees now living in urban areas, humanitarian organisations, such as UNHCR, have moved to develop specific policies for supporting urban refugees (Ward, 2014). The majority of these refugees are hosted informally across cities in the Global South, with the mass displacement of Syrian refugees to cities in Jordan, Lebanon, and Turkey being a significant recent example. In this context, urban environments offer opportunities for employment, autonomy, and access to onward mobility, and at the same time present risks of exploitation, poverty, and repressive policing (Campbell, 2006; Pavanello et al., 2010).

The issues of forced and unauthorised migration are therefore, increasingly urban concerns, both in the context of mass displacements in the Global South and in the ever more restrictive attempts to 'manage migration' that dominate policy in the Global North (Darling, 2017a). In this latter instance, cities have been argued to play a central role in forms of 'local border control' (Lebuhn, 2013: 38), which translate policies and enforcement measures from the nation-state to specific urban contexts, as illustrated through Visser and Simpson's discussion of the emergence and evolution of exclusionary legislation at municipal, county, and state levels in the US. Here cities are often situated as strategic locations for the enforcement of border control through the use of urban networks of police, surveillance, and information infrastructure to trace, detain, and deport asylum seekers and undocumented migrants (see Coleman, 2012; Hynes, 2009; Netto, 2011). Yet, as many of the contributions to this book have illustrated, this is not the only story of refugees and cities. Rather, as Osborne and Rose (1999: 758) suggest, 'cities are complex multiplicities of interests, antagonisms, flows of capital, spatial constructions, moral topographies, forms of authority, and ethical stylisations', and as such they may also be incubators for dissent. Indeed, as Hudson shows in the context of Toronto, and Kuge argues in the context of US sanctuary cities, it is in the complexities of negotiating the practice of sanctuary, and the needs and demands of multiple voices and stakeholders, that a distinctly urban dimension of sanctuary comes to the fore. Thus while efforts to regulate, monitor, and manage society have been argued to reach their peak in urban environments (Graham, 2010), urban features of 'density, size, and diversity' have been argued to provide 'the basic elements for contention to develop' (Uitermark et al., 2012: 2546), as further illustrated by both Raimondi and Rogaly in this volume.

It is in examining these tensions that the contributors to *Sanctuary cities and urban struggles* have foregrounded the power relations at play in diverse imaginaries of sanctuary and urban belonging. In drawing the book to a close, this chapter reflects on some of these power relations to consider how different imaginations of advocacy, activism, and the rights of refugees have been articulated through a specifically urban frame of reference.

In doing so, the chapter develops as follows. I begin by briefly outlining recent work on the 'politics of urbanism' (Magnusson, 2011) that has sought to contest the dominance of a statist perspective in understanding contemporary politics. Building on this urban political focus, I then discuss Derrida's (2001) deconstruction of hospitality and his call to establish 'cities of refuge' that challenge the exclusions of the nation-state system. With this account of hospitality in mind, I then briefly consider the connections between this conceptual framing and the forms of urban sanctuary discussed in detail across this book. Moving beyond this ethical framing, the chapter then considers a political campaign by refugees and asylum seekers that employs cities as strategic sites through which to make claims at national and international levels. Here the city becomes a strategically important conduit for political change, drawing on the discussions of urban struggles and rights claims that have animated the second half of this book. With this relation in mind, and returning to Magnusson's 'politics of urbanism', I conclude by considering the significance of urban presence in offering opportunities for dissent and political organising on the part of asylum seekers, refugees, and unauthorised migrants.

The politics of urbanism

One starting point for such reflection, and for thinking through the debates that have orientated *Sanctuary cities and urban struggles*, is the move to focus discussions around migration, citizenship, and rights away from the nation-state as a dominant or pervasive political actor. Rather, as this book has sought to argue, significant political, practical, and conceptual work is done if we turn an analytical lens to the cities, communities, and neighbourhoods that are engaged in advocating for sanctuary, that are enacting 'everyday borders', and whose role is far more complex than operating as a conduit for sovereign authority (see Darling and Bauder, this volume). A key orientation within this focus is to move from a concern with 'seeing like a state' to 'seeing like a city', as Magnusson (2011) argues. Before moving to consider the application of this lens to discussions of sanctuary, migration, and refugee rights, I first outline its key contours as a way of exploring the complexities of governing mobility.

In putting forward 'the politics of urbanism', Magnusson (2011: 2) argues that our political tendency is to 'see like a state' after James C. Scott, and thus to 'imagine things from the viewpoint of a sovereign government or a sovereign people'. This tendency, deemed 'methodological nationalism' by Wimmer and Glick Schiller (2002), is perhaps most prevalent in work on migration, where the framework of the nation-state and its claims to sovereignty, security, and the right to delineate citizenship have significant prominence. This is a perceptual orientation that attempts to classify and categorise in an effort to ensure coherence, to maintain a hierarchy of authority that is both top-down and neatly arranged. Of course, as Scott (1998) and many others have noted, the realities of state projects are far from such an idealised account. Yet underpinning such realities remains a set of assumptions over where authority resides, how it is expressed, and what it seeks to achieve.

In response, Magnusson (2011) argues for an account of politics that foregrounds what he sees as the practice of politics in everyday life. Drawing on Foucault's discussion of government as the ability to shape the conduct of others through diverse techniques, Magnusson argues that urban life is constituted by a vast array of different, and at times competing, forms of government and self-government. Thus,

> urbanism implies proximate diversity, complicated patterns of government and self-government, a multiplicity of authorities in different registers, the infinite deferral of sovereignty, self-organization and an emergent order that, though chaotic, is by no means anarchic. (Magnusson, 2011: 11)

It is in these facets of urbanism that Magnusson advocates a politics that maintains the contingencies of government. In this way,

> To see like a city is to accept a certain disorderliness, unpredictability, and multiplicity as inevitable, and to pose the problem of politics in relation to that complexity, rather than in relation to the simplicity that sovereignty seeks. (Magnusson, 2011: 120)

The implication is that 'We are not dealing with a simple hierarchical order that can be managed from the top, but rather with a congeries of authorities that collide with one another, sometimes cooperating and sometimes fighting, but none ever in full control' (Magnusson, 2015: 198). In reflecting on the city, it is argued that from this collection of authorities, a fragile and often temporary order does arise. And as such, political questions, when seen 'like a city', are centred on how we deal with this complicated, unpredictable, and often shifting sense of order, rather than wishing for a neatly organised sovereign illusion.

What are the implications of this proposition? First, and perhaps most obviously, it implies that it is not productive to rely upon sovereign claims to authority or to seek in them solutions to political challenges. This is an insight that we can see across a number of the chapters in this book, where claims to sovereign authority have either been contested, or significantly complicated, by the actions of activists, legislators, and policy makers at the municipal level (see Bauder, Atak, Hudson, Kuge, and Raimondi, this volume). Second, it implies that authority is not a zero-sum game, but rather that authority is produced in different collaborations and contexts, and may intensify and diminish at different moments (Allen, 2010), a point in evidence when we consider the work of sanctuary movements in Toronto and their collaborative engagement with municipal governance (Atak and Hudson, this volume). Finally, 'seeing like a city' demands an appreciation of uncertain and unexpected relations of government and authority, of how lives may be ordered and governed in ways unanticipated and perhaps unintended by those assumed to be 'in control'. In this sense, Magnusson (2011: 10) warns that 'we have to be aware that the relevant political actors are not necessarily the ones we have in mind'. We might see these 'unexpected' actors taking the form of the governmental role of church communities in relation to sanctuary (Bauder, this volume), or the (often limited) potential for local law enforcement to offer security to unauthorised migrants (Atak, this volume). In this way, 'the politics of urbanism' involves a call to look beyond the contingencies of the nation-state and to a range of other political actors, as this book has illustrated. More than this, however, the politics of urbanism calls for critical attention to the uncertainties of governance and the impossibility of fully controlling or constraining mobility and the political demands that mobility makes across a range of spatial scales. Again, here we might think of Rogaly's account of the complex urban contestations between different claims to, and modes of, belonging in the city of Peterborough. Seeing 'like a city' thus implies both a focus on urban politics as a site for contesting and critiquing sovereign claims, but also a need to explore the complexities, compromises, and contingencies of urban life as a means to envision alternative approaches to questions of migration, citizenship, and rights. It is with this envisioning of alternatives *through the city* in mind that I explore how cities have been framed in relation to refugee advocacy and the rights of unauthorised migrants.

Hospitality, sanctuary, the city

Derrida's (2001) discussion of the city and its role as a potential refuge emerged as part of a wider deconstruction of hospitality and its ethico-political possibilities (Derrida, 1999). In this work, the city becomes a key context both to imagine a renewed politics of hospitality, and to practically enact such an imagination. For Derrida, hospitality names a constant negotiation between competing demands – for welcome and for regulation at one and the same time. Hospitality is based upon the prerequisite 'that the host ... remains the *patron*, the master of the household, on the condition that he maintains his own authority *in his own house*' (Derrida, 2000: 14, original emphasis). To be hospitable is to claim a particular space as one's own, to assume that one has the right both to welcome a stranger and, conversely, to reject such a stranger. Written into the very constitution of the hospitable are a set of conditions and expectations about who is the 'host', where the limits of this welcome lie, and to whom it may be extended. It is these limits that beset the political practice of hospitality, as Derrida argues that conditional hospitality

> remains a scrutinized hospitality, always under surveillance, parsimonious and protective of its sovereignty ... That is hospitality as it is commonly understood and practiced, a hospitality that gives rise, with certain conditions, to regulated practices, laws, and conventions on a national and international ... scale. (2003: 128)

At the same time, Derrida (1999) argues that the conditions of hospitality are always haunted by the spectre of an unconditional hospitality that marks a welcome to an unanticipated and unidentified guest. Such

> unconditional hospitality is, to be sure, practically impossible to live; one cannot in any case, and by definition, organise it ... this concept of pure hospitality can have no legal or political status. No state can write it into its laws. But without at least the thought of this pure and unconditional hospitality, of hospitality *itself*, we would have no concept of hospitality in general and would not even be able to determine any rules for conditional hospitality. (Derrida, 2003: 129, original emphasis)

The political importance of deconstructing hospitality thus lies not in rejecting or denouncing hospitality as imperfect, but rather in challenging institutions and relations of hospitality, 'calling them to something better, to more just configurations' (Smith, 2005: 67). Derrida's deconstruction of hospitality seeks to focus attention on the fraught and finite negotiations of hospitality as an always imperfectly practised ethic of welcoming the unanticipated stranger, so as to ultimately find ways to 'make laws more hospitable' (Smith, 2005: 70).

In considering how this philosophical account of hospitality relates to the politics of refuge, Derrida (2001) argues that the question of hospitality has too often been cynically employed to promote the conditional inclusion of only those seen as 'worthy' of protection. Thus, at the level of the nation-state a wide array of countries regularly make public statements about their hospitable nature towards refugees and their desire to welcome 'good' migrants (Rosello, 2001). This language is always conditioned by the right to select, classify, and limit hospitality, and it is the exclusivity of conditional hospitality that Derrida (2002) critiques most forcefully in challenging the claim by European governments that asylum seekers and irregular migrants 'abuse' the hospitality of the nation-state.

In response to such concerns, Derrida turns to the city as a site through which to envisage an alternative way of practising hospitality. Derrida argues that cities may offer a path from a conditional framework of limits to a more critical orientation in which 'disruptive narratives' are produced. Derrida (2001: 6) notes: 'If we look to the city, rather than the state, it is because we have given up hope that the state might create a new image for the city.' The example that Derrida draws on is that of the International Cities of Refuge Network (ICORN), a network of cities offering long-term but temporary shelter to writers and artists in need of protection. The Cities of Asylum Network, which went on to become ICORN, was founded in 1993 by the International Parliament of Writers. The network involves over fifty cities across Asia, Europe, and North America, and offers shelter as a means to defend freedom of expression and democratic values. Derrida focuses his account of how cities may 'reorient the politics of the state' in new directions around the model of ICORN as an urban movement offering protection in ways not recognised by the nation-state (Derrida, 2001: 4). He clarifies:

> This is not to suggest that we ought to restore an essentially classical concept of the city by giving it new attributes and powers; neither would it be simply a matter of endowing the old subject we call 'the city' with new predicates. No, we are dreaming of another concept, of another set of rights for the city, of another politics of the city. (Derrida, 2001: 8)

What comes to the fore here is the sense of a renewed appreciation of the urban as a space of political and ethical engagement and experimentation with asylum, as a space that might offer 'another' form of politics, not through simply ascribing greater powers to the city or allowing it further autonomy, but through considering how cities may offer points of rupture and critique in relation to the politics of the nation-state (Critchley, 2011; Darling, 2013). The actions of ICORN, in protecting writers and artists who fall outside the protections of the nation-state, offer an example of this critical position. This is not an unconditional hospitality that welcomes all strangers, nor does it evade limits and constraints, but it does offer an example of how an attempt to 'make laws more hospitable' may be put into practice. Crucially, Derrida (2001) concludes that it is only through the political position of the city, as a space tied to, but not subsumed by, the nation-state, that such experimentation is possible.

A number of theorists have followed Derrida's turn to the city and argued for the need to examine the daily realities of urban life as the grounds on which migrants' rights and claims to citizenship are articulated. Sassen, for example, suggests that the 'last two decades have seen an increasingly *urban* articulation of global logics and struggles, and an escalating use of urban space to make political claims not only by the citizens of a city's country, but also by foreigners' (2013: 70, original emphasis). Cities have thus been argued to remain 'the strategic arena for the development of citizenship' as through their 'concentrations of the nonlocal, the strange, the mixed, and the public, cities engage … processes which decisively expand and erode the rules, meanings, and practices of citizenship' (Appadurai and Holston, 1996: 188). Cities in this imaginary are positioned as complex assemblages that gather together, coordinate, and configure global flows and connections of ideas, people, and materials. Across this book, we have seen a range of examples of this form of urban political imaginary, and in the remainder of this concluding chapter I discuss two of these forms of urban experimentation. In this context, Derrida's discussion of urban hospitality matters, as it speaks to the tensions of refugee advocacy more broadly, between seeking to act on present conditions and limits, while also imagining 'other' forms of political possibility beyond the present (see Bauder, 2016; Darling, 2017b).

Sanctuary and hospitable imperfections

These tensions of advocacy, support, and hospitality have run across a range of the chapters in this book (see Bagelman, Hudson, and Raimondi), and can be illustrated in relation to European sanctuary work. For example, in Sweden, Lundberg and Strange (2017) demonstrate how a range of initiatives to promote values of hospitality have been taken forward by different cities. In Stockholm, groups wanting to align themselves with Refuge Stockholm were given a list of requirements that they had to meet before they were able to be part of the movement. These included providing free or discounted services to undocumented people and not demanding social security numbers for services in an echo of some of the requirements of North American 'sanctuary cities'. This model of gaining support from local organisations relied upon spreading the word about sanctuary events, initiatives, and opportunities through everyday spaces, such as cafés, gyms, cultural associations, and universities. To be part of Refuge Stockholm, organisations were required to offer opportunities for undocumented migrants and refugees to be involved in their activities (Lundberg and Strange, 2017), mirroring some of the practices of the UK's City of Sanctuary movement in Sheffield, where volunteering was seen as a valuable resource to feel part of urban life (Darling and Squire, 2012).

Furthermore, in Sweden we see a model of sanctuary practices that attempted to include both state officials and municipal representatives. For example, in Malmo, city officials worked with sanctuary groups to gain access to the library and ensure that undocumented individuals could borrow books despite lacking formal status. In this context, Lundberg and Strange (2017: 357–358) argue:

> Constructive engagement with city officials complicates a simplistic image of these sanctuary initiatives as pure defiance of the state, presenting a more negotiated character in which they could be both critical of the state's migration policies but equally working with other state-employed bodies at the city level to mitigate the negative effects of the management of migration.

This account of the need for 'constructive engagement' with both urban and state authorities points to a wider concern running through each of these contexts of urban sanctuary, that of the limits of hospitable engagement (Bagelman, 2016). The work of sanctuary movements can be vitally important in trying to promote values of welcoming and hospitality within cities and in offering often piecemeal and yet important concessions to those seeking protection, from the right to borrow books to the ability to seek healthcare without risking deportation. In this way, sanctuary practices have been argued to represent actions that protect against the state (Bauder, 2017; Cunningham, 2012; Yukich, 2012). However, such work has also been critically challenged. First, it has been argued that sanctuary may represent a means of governing through the assertion of humanitarian intentions (Darling, 2013). Thus in legislative terms, Chavin and Garcés-Mascareñas (2012: 244) argue that 'local incorporation practices' reflect 'regulatory imperatives and worries over public safety'. Through enabling undocumented migrants to access services and support, cities can be seen to 'manage' an undocumented population for the wider 'good' of the city, thereby allaying concerns over public health and public order, as Mancina (2012) argues in the case of San Francisco. Seen through this critical lens, the language of the sanctuary city becomes a means of governing the presence of unauthorised migrants and refugees. As a result, the question of who 'deserves' the support of the sanctuary city comes to the fore in debating the limits of urban hospitality (Houston and Morse, 2017; Marrow, 2012; Yukich, 2013). Furthermore, the temporal horizon of hospitality associated with Derrida (2000), of a state of sanctuary that is always 'to come', may do little to promote a more assertive and agential political role for asylum seekers and refugees whereby rights are claimed *by*, and not *for*, those seeking refuge (Squire and Darling, 2013; Nyers, 2003).

The varied examples of urban sanctuary discussed across this book each reflect different political contexts and opportunity structures. Yet what they hold in common is a focus on re-imagining the role of the city as a place that can offer protection in some form. Such forms of welcome may assuage the effects of repressive immigration controls. However, as noted above, the claims of sanctuary cities are also limited, most notably in that they risk the reiteration of categorical assumptions over who is 'deserving' of welcome. Distinctions such as these are central to the categorising processes that shape ideals of hospitality (Derrida, 2001), and illustrate how progressive imaginaries of the city may be enfolded into state-centric logics of citizenship. The constraints of hospitality as a conditional politics still abound here, but sanctuary practices do gesture towards making such conditions 'better' in a reflection of Derrida's hopes for the city. Building on these discussions, I now consider a movement that attempts to use the city as a terrain to make claims for rights, reflecting further some of the dynamics of urban contestation and struggle foregrounded in the second half of *Sanctuary cities and urban struggles*.

Activism and urban networks

The 'Dignity not Destitution' campaign in the UK seeks to challenge existing government policy on the support of asylum seekers, and in doing so enrols urban authorities as key conduits in calling for political change. In the UK, asylum seekers have, since 2004, been denied the right to work while awaiting refugee status and provided with a weekly cash support capped significantly below other forms of social welfare. The 'Dignity not Destitution' campaign calls on the government to change the policy of withdrawing asylum support after decisions on status have been taken, regardless of whether or not an individual can be returned to their country of origin. As some countries do not have deportation agreements with the UK, and therefore refuse to accept returnees, this places refused asylum seekers from these countries in a legal limbo between the official refusal of status in the UK and an inability to return to the country from which they have fled. In such cases, refused asylum seekers are forced to rely on charities and friends for survival. Destitution, in this context, is less an accidental or procedural gap within the asylum system and more an intentional and insecure position imposed on those no longer wanted by the state (Darling, 2009).

In opposing the use of destitution as a deterrent within the asylum system, the 'Dignity not Destitution' campaign argues that asylum seekers who would otherwise be destitute should be provided with sufficient support so that they can meet their essential living needs and be given permission to work if their case hasn't been resolved within six months. The campaign was started in 2009 in Bristol and Glasgow by a mixture of asylum advocates, support groups, and asylum seekers, who together attempted to gain local political support for the opposition of government policy on destitution. Following this example, the model of focusing on urban authorities was transferred to a series of other cities as local activists, social movements, and support networks became aware of the 'Dignity not Destitution' campaign. The campaign not only evoked human rights claims for equality and justice via demands for basic living needs, but addressed these demands to national government *through the city* as a conduit for advancing a refugee rights agenda. Through public demonstrations, lobbying of councillors, public petitions, and encouraging the public to send postcards to their elected representatives demanding 'Dignity not Destitution' for asylum seekers, the campaign was intended to encourage urban authorities to pass motions of opposition to government policy.

To date, twelve local authorities have debated and passed motions to oppose asylum destitution and to call for changes in asylum policy. The challenge beyond these local motions of support is clearly to effect an impact on central government policy. However, the importance of local authorities supporting such a cause should not be underestimated. Indeed, one of the key aims of this form of political mobilisation was to utilise multiple urban publics in order to push for change through drawing varied audiences into an awareness of destitution. In this sense, the campaign reflects how 'movements emanate from cities but also stretch outwards' (Uitermark et al., 2012: 2546).

'Dignity not Destitution' is therefore an example of a wider range of social movements and organisations around migrants' rights that have sought to strategically employ the city as a context from which to form networks of advocacy, dissent, and campaigning (see also Raimondi, this volume). The UK's Right to Remain movement of anti-deportation activism often seeks to articulate anti-deportation struggles in a context of localised connections to specific cities and their communities, and the international No One Is Illegal movement grounds its no-borders activism in the production of a network of urban activism reaching from Berlin to Vancouver (Vrasti and Dayal, 2016). In these cases, the city is imagined not simply as a target of interventions and campaigns, but as a location from which to make political claims beyond the city, be that to the nation-state, to diverse and spatially distant publics, or to networks of activists and distant campaigns. The role of the city here is both as a strategic stage for political contention (Uitermark et al., 2012), one that takes advantage of how cities are located in networks of power and influence (Allen, 2010; Sassen, 2013), and as a site in which asylum seekers and refugees can find support from advocacy organisations and diverse groups of supporters. It is this mix of activism that speaks beyond the city and the piecemeal provision of support in the here and now, that might be argued to define how asylum seekers, refugees, and unauthorised migrants are rewriting the role of the city as a space of politics. Such an imaginary is, however, still limited to specific campaigns and movements, and is often concerned with ameliorating exclusions and improving conditions, rather than with undermining the sovereign claim of establishing normative categories of 'worthy' and 'unworthy' migrants. To explore a more radical horizon, I want to turn to claims centred on urban presence itself to argue that these might offer the alternative openings envisaged through a 'politics of urbanism' (Magnusson, 2011).

The politics of presence

In referring to the politics of presence, I discuss claims made through the interweaving of rights to both mobility and political participation within the city. To start with an example, we might look to Fernandez and Olson's (2011) discussion of the claims made by undocumented migrants in Flagstaff, Arizona. In working with migrant rights' campaigns, Fernandez and Olson argue that many of those without legal status are in fact 'fighting for the right to *come and go* more than they are for the right to *come and stay*' (2011: 415, original emphasis). Focusing on how migrants organised to push the city council to file an injunction against the anti-immigrant Arizona Senate Bill 1070, they highlight the insistence that city officials 'hear their collective voice and represent their interests' (Fernandez and Olson, 2011: 412). In illustrating the multiple communities and mobile networks that these migrants are engaged in, Fernandez and Olson (2011: 415) argue that they make demands to both 'movement and place', as 'they are demanding the freedom to live, raise families and work across borders, and insisting on the right to participate in whatever public they are presently in', thereby asserting that 'the right to belong and participate in a public realm, should be less a matter of where you *were* (born) than where you *are*' (2011: 417, original emphasis; see also Bauder, 2014). The politics of presence is therefore an articulation of an openness to mobility alongside the 'ability to participate in local affairs' (Fernandez and Olson, 2011: 418) that has often framed concerns with the right to the city (Harvey, 2008; Purcell, 2003; Rogaly, this volume). As such, it reflects a demand for *both participation and mobility* that may be enhanced *through* the negotiations of urban life.

Drawing from this example, we might note two orientation points for the politics of presence. The first is in returning to those sanctuary ordinances that seek to protect undocumented migrants and refugees. While such ordinances may have a regulatory function, they have nevertheless been argued to present openings for forms of 'local citizenship' that draw on the 'right to the city' (Varsanyi, 2008; Lefebvre, 1996). Reading sanctuary ordinances through the right to the city suggests that the legal and social protection of sanctuary may offer a framework on which claims to rights for services, protection, and political participation are made. However, the right to the city is often tied to the notion of inhabitance (Purcell, 2003), such that those able to exercise such rights are residents. By contrast, the value of presence may be in critiquing this requirement of residency, and connecting to wider discussions around rights based on domicile and rights based within a legal and discursive framework of human rights (Bauder, 2014; Oomen et al., 2016). Presence is about the temporary fixing of mobilities, rather than their capture within a given spatial form. Thus while many urban sanctuary movements advocate rights based on 'the need to prove one's residency' (Nyers, 2010: 137), a number seek to 'articulate ideas of membership based on physical presence' (Nyers, 2010: 137). It is here that a politics of presence draws on a second orientation point.

As noted in Raimondi's contribution to this book, the 'autonomy of migration' approach views migration as a constituent force in social life (Mezzadra, 2011). In doing so, it seeks to reframe migration as having 'the capacity to develop its own logics, its own motivation, its own trajectories that control comes later to respond to, not the other way round' (Papadopoulos and Tsianos, 2013: 184). In this sense, the 'autonomy' of migration reflects a challenge to the perceptual 'policing' of migration as a 'problem' to be managed in particular ways. In focusing on 'autonomy', Papadopoulos and Tsianos (2013: 188) argue for a concern with the social transformations 'sustained and nurtured silently through the everyday and seemingly non-political experiences and actions of people'. Building on and moving beyond a focus on the right to the city as noted by Raimondi and Rogaly in this volume, the politics of presence therefore reflects a concern with a mobile politics of everyday critique. Presence in this context becomes 'a matter of social fact rather than legal status' (Nyers, 2010: 137), and opens up to challenge the categorisations of membership associated with citizenship, residency, and formal rights to services and belonging. Asking on what basis rights and services are denied to those present in the city, as in the demands made by undocumented migrants in Flagstaff, the politics of presence names alternative 'ideas of political membership' at the urban level as a way to influence 'ideas of security and citizenship' at the level of the nation-state (Ridgley, 2008: 65).

Presence as an orientation point for political claims is not necessarily or inherently urban. However, it has been argued that we see in the urban the political possibilities of presence most readily. For Sassen (2010: 9), this value emerges from the fact that in cities 'the localization of the global creates a set of objective conditions of engagement' through which presence may be politicised by irregular migrants, refugees, and asylum seekers. This 'engagement' is twofold, reflecting both a presence to power and a presence 'vis-à-vis each other' (Sassen, 2006: 317). Presence, in its urban manifestation, might thus denote a point of political potential that can be mobilised by different causes and concerns in drawing on an engagement with authority localised in the city, as we saw in the work of the 'Dignity not Destitution' campaign.

This approach is, of course, not without failings. Most notably, there is a need to be wary of positioning presence as a straightforward claim to visibility. In some cases, as May (2010) argues, visibility may offer a valuable means of demonstrating the political identification of a group positioned outside the remit of citizenship rights. Yet there is a danger in visibility. As noted in discussions of the ubiquity of urban borders, being visibly present can invite the increased 'policing' of forced and unauthorised migrants. Similarly, there is also a significant distinction to be made here between the forms of group visibility and collective identification that May (2010) valorises, and the risks of visibility for the individual. The politics of presence in this sense is not equally distributed or in any sense universal. Rather, it may reflect a potential resource to be tactically and carefully employed in the practice of negotiating claims to rightfulness. In this context, a claim to political presence centred on the city demands a more nuanced engagement with the informalities and insecurities of non-citizen subjectivity, and demands attentiveness to the strategic use of presence as a political tool in given urban contexts, some of which may produce the visible articulation of a collective identity, some of which may seek to avert, resist, or avoid such visibility.

Linked to such concerns, there is the question of how practical a focus on presence may be. The value of presence may be in offering a different starting point for discussion – one emergent from the relations of urban life rather than the imposition of sovereign authority. Thinking through the value of presence as a social fact, and of the frames of justice and injustice to which it may be connected, means viewing presence as an orientation point in exploring 'new scripts' on migration (Isin, 2012: 148). A politics of urban presence might be seen as an unlikely political shift in many contexts, yet its exploration may have the potential to shape solidarities centred on the city as a stage of political and social connection.

Viewing rights within the city as tied only to presence may thus disrupt governmental assumptions that rights have to be tied to citizenship and the state. Crucially, a focus on presence foregrounds the possibility of political solidarities centred on common experiences of the urban across otherwise distanciated constituencies. For example, in the Latin American context the Cities of Solidarity initiative has focused on building urban solidarity through positioning refugee resettlement as an opportunity to improve urban services for all (Varoli, 2010). Similarly, Phillimore and Goodson (2006) argue that urban refugee resettlement can be a means of regeneration when detached from the exclusionary binaries of rights that distinguish 'host' from 'guest' communities. To focus on presence is therefore to examine 'the hard work of ... repositioning the immigrant and the citizen as urban subjects, rather than essentially different subjects' (Sassen, 2013: 69). Urban presence may unite individuals across status and re-imagine the city not as a bounded object to be welcomed to or excluded from, but rather as a relational and collaborative production of those present at any given point. In this sense, presence and its political possibilities draws on the sense of multiple, and at times conflicting, articulations of urban belonging, evocatively articulated in Rogaly's account (this volume) of struggles for *particular* 'rights to the city'.

This is not to suggest that a focus on presence may overtake a concern with citizenship status and rights bestowed by the nation-state. It is to argue that we may see a range of alternatives if we move away from a frame of reference that is concerned only with the hospitable accommodation of difference. Just as 'the deployment of exclusionary city ordinances are not only about shaping an *urban* public, but about shaping a *national* public as well' (Varsanyi, 2008: 47, original emphasis), so too might we think of the kinds of rights claims enacted through cities as not simply affecting urban imaginaries but also affecting transnational publics. In this context, the potential role of urban contestations and rights claims in shaping a transnational politics of migration, rather than a necessarily national one, offers one avenue for future consideration, both academically and politically. From the potentials, and dangers, of urban networks of transnational collaboration and policy-transfer (Barber, 2013; McCann and Ward, 2011) to the formation of transnational solidarities of mobile activism and campaigning (Featherstone, 2012), the urban politics of presence may resonate with a range of debates beyond the limits of the nation-state as a political arena and a powerful sovereign actor (Magnusson, 2011).

Conclusion

In this chapter, I have highlighted the varied ways in which cities have been narrated through the agency and activism of asylum seekers, refugees, unauthorised migrants, and their supporters. From the promise of hospitality enshrined in biblical 'cities of refuge' to the contemporary vision of 'sanctuary cities', an image of the city as a site of refuge has been a powerful part of progressive and utopian urban imaginaries. Yet alongside this desire to link the city to ethical values of hospitality and sanctuary has been a recent turn by activists and advocates to employ the strategic possibilities of the city as a conduit for political change (see Bauder and Raimondi, this volume). Such activism is, of course, not without response, for just as Uitermark et al. (2012: 2546) argue that cities are places of contention, they also note that such practices inevitably produce new means of control as 'local states and their partners develop strategies and techniques to direct the ebbs and flows of contentiousness constantly bubbling up from the urban grassroots'. By focusing on cities as sites that often throw up the lived realities of displacement, and that place refugees in relation to other residents, activists and advocates have begun to explore how the negotiations of everyday urban life might be made more hospitable, and at the same time how the politics of presence might assert claims to rights that undermine the very nature of hospitality itself.

There are, of course, limits to the potentials of the city. As Vrasti and Dayal (2016: 998) highlight, sanctuary politics often entail a tendency to reproduce 'host' and 'guest' positions in problematic ways, a potential to view access to services as the end point of migrant justice, and 'the possibility that sanctuary eases and normalizes undocumented life'. Yet it is indicative of the tensions running through accounts of sanctuary that at the same time Vrasti and Dayal argue that modalities of sanctuary 'whether legislative or esthetic, can offer a temporary reprieve from marginalization' (Vrasti and Dayal, 2016: 1008). Similarly, as I have argued throughout this chapter, campaigns such as 'Dignity not Destitution' provide examples of how connections have been forged in the hope of affecting government policy through incremental processes of critique, awareness raising, and garnering public support. These may offer only momentary reprieves in the present, but are nevertheless important as political orientation points for further campaigns and for forging solidarities with other causes. In this way, perceptions and policies on asylum, support, and entitlements are altered not immediately but incrementally, as critical questions are posed in and through the political opportunities and limits that cities provide (Darling, 2017a). In this context, the role of an ethics focused on hospitality can never be to assert a politics of rights based around urban presence, as such an ethics can never fully escape its association with a model of 'care' and support. However, such an ethics may be significant in shaping the public and political context in which assertive claims for rights and political voice are responded to differently. This is to view the role of sanctuary and hospitality as more than simply piecemeal reprieves for those suffering the violence of the state, but as opportunities to influence the tenor and tone of debate around refuge. It is also to see the politics of advocacy, campaigning, and assertion around migration as necessarily comprised of multiple, and at times inconsistent and contradictory, political claims and positions. Within the complex mix of moral and political positions that marks contemporary advocacy, in focusing on the claims made through cities, advocates have increasingly begun the task that Derrida (2001) envisaged in writing of how cities could 'reorient the state'. In this sense, while limited and imperfect, what we see here and across this book are important attempts to reflect upon, and experiment with, the role of the city. As such, they keep alive the utopian imaginary of the city as 'a place for reflection – for reflection on the questions of asylum and hospitality – and for a new order of law and democracy to come to be put to the test' (Derrida, 2001: 23).

Acknowledgements

Thanks to Helen Wilson for her continued support and generous discussion of all things urban. The discussion of the politics of presence here draws on J. Darling, 'Forced migration and the city: irregularity, informality, and the politics of presence', *Progress in Human Geography*, 41:2 (2017), 178–198.

References

Allen, J. (2010) 'Powerful city networks: more than connections, less than domination and control', *Urban Studies*, 47:13, 2895–2911.
Appadurai, A., and J. Holston (1996) 'Cities and citizenship', *Public Culture*, 8:1, 187–204.

Bagelman, J. (2016) *Sanctuary City: A Suspended State* (New York: Palgrave Macmillan).

Barber, B. (2013) *If Mayors Ruled the World: Dysfunctional Nations, Rising Cities* (New Haven, CT: Yale University Press).

Bauder, H. (2014) 'Domicile citizenship, human mobility and territoriality', *Progress in Human Geography*, 38:1, 91–106.

Bauder, H. (2016) 'Possibilities of urban belonging', *Antipode*, 48:2, 252–271.

Bauder, H. (2017) 'Sanctuary cities: policies and practices in international perspective', *International Migration*, 55:2, 174–187.

Campbell, E. H. (2006) 'Urban refugees in Nairobi: problems of protection, mechanisms of survival, and possibilities for integration', *Journal of Refugee Studies*, 19:2, 396–413.

Chavin, S., and B. Garcés-Mascareñas (2012) 'Beyond informal citizenship: the new moral economy of migrant illegality', *International Political Sociology*, 6, 241–259.

Coleman, M. (2012) 'The "local" migration state: the site-specific devolution of immigration enforcement in the US South', *Law & Policy*, 34:1, 159–190.

Critchley, S. (2011) *Impossible Objects* (Cambridge: Polity).

Cunningham, H. (2012) 'The emergence of the Ontario Sanctuary Coalition', in R. K. Lippert and S. Rehaag (eds), *Sanctuary Practices in International Perspectives: Migration, Citizenship and Social Movements* (Abingdon: Routledge), 162–174.

Darling, J. (2009) 'Becoming bare life: asylum, hospitality, and the politics of encampment', *Environment and Planning D: Society and Space*, 27:4, 649–665.

Darling, J. (2013) 'Moral urbanism, asylum and the politics of critique', *Environment and Planning A*, 45:8, 1785–1801.

Darling, J. (2017a) 'Forced migration and the city: irregularity, informality, and the politics of presence', *Progress in Human Geography*, 41:2, 178–198.

Darling, J. (2017b) 'Acts, ambiguities, and the labour of contesting citizenship', *Citizenship Studies*, 21:6, 727–736.

Darling J., and V. Squire (2012) 'Everyday enactments of sanctuary: the UK City of Sanctuary movement', in R. K. Lippert and S. Rehaag (eds), *Sanctuary Practices in International Perspectives: Migration, Citizenship and Social Movements* (Abingdon: Routledge), 191–204.

Derrida, J. (1999) *Adieu to Emmanuel Levinas*, trans. P.-A. Brault and M. Nass (Stanford, CA: Stanford University Press).

Derrida, J. (2000) 'Hostipitality', trans. B. Stocker and F. Morlock, *Angelaki*, 5:3, 3–18.

Derrida, J. (2001) *On Cosmopolitanism and Forgiveness*, trans. M. Dooley and M. Hughes (London: Routledge).

Derrida, J. (2002) *Negotiations: Interventions and Interviews, 1971–2001*, trans. E. Rottenberg (Stanford, CA: Stanford University Press).

Derrida, J. (2003) 'Autoimmunity: real and symbolic suicides', in G. Borradori (ed.), *Philosophy in a Time of Terror: Dialogues with Jürgen Habermas and Jacques Derrida* (Chicago: University of Chicago Press).

Featherstone, D. (2012) *Solidarity: Hidden Histories and Geographies of Internationalism* (London: Zed Books).

Fernandez, L., and J. Olson (2011) 'To live, love and work anywhere you please: critical exchange on Arizona and the struggle for locomotion', *Contemporary Political Theory*, 10, 415–417.

Graham, S. (2010) *Cities Under Siege: The New Military Urbanism* (London: Verso).

Harvey, D. (2008) 'The right to the city', *New Left Review*, 53, 23–40.

Houston, S. D., and C. Morse (2017) 'The ordinary and extraordinary: producing migrant inclusion and exclusion in US sanctuary movements', *Studies in Social Justice*, 11:1, 27–47.

Hynes, P. (2009) 'Contemporary compulsory dispersal and the absence of space for the restoration of trust', *Journal of Refugee Studies*, 22:1, 97–121.

Isin, E. F. (2012) *Citizens without Frontiers* (London: Bloomsbury).

Lebuhn, H. (2013) 'Local border practices and urban citizenship in Europe: exploring urban borderlands', *City*, 17:1, 37–51.

Lefebvre, H. (1996) 'The right to the city', trans. E. Kofman and E. Lebas, in E. Kofman and E. Lebas (eds), *Writing on Cities* (Oxford: Blackwell), 147–159.

Lippert, R. K., and S. Rehaag (eds) (2012) *Sanctuary Practices in International Perspectives: Migration, Citizenship and Social Movements* (Abingdon: Routledge).

Lundberg, A., and M. Strange (2017) 'Who provides the conditions for human life? Sanctuary movements in Sweden as both contesting and working with state agencies', *Politics*, 37:3, 347–362.

Magnusson, W. (2011) *Politics of Urbanism: Seeing Like a City* (London: Routledge).

Magnusson, W. (2015) *Local Self-Government and the Right to the City* (Montreal: McGill-Queen's University Press).

Mancina, P. (2012) 'The birth of a sanctuary city: a history of governmental sanctuary in San Francisco', in R. K. Lippert and S. Rehaag (eds), *Sanctuary Practices in International Perspectives: Migration, Citizenship and Social Movements* (Abingdon: Routledge), 205–218.

Marrow, H. B. (2012) 'Deserving to a point: unauthorized immigrants in San Francisco's universal access healthcare model', *Social Science & Medicine*, 74:6, 846–854.

May, T. (2010) *Contemporary Political Movements and the Thought of Jacques Rancière: Equality in Action* (Edinburgh: Edinburgh University Press).

McCann, E., and K. Ward (eds) (2011) *Mobile Urbanism: Cities and Policymaking in the Global Age* (Minneapolis, MN: University of Minnesota Press).

Mezzadra, S. (2011) 'The gaze of autonomy: capitalism, migration and social struggles', in V. Squire (ed), *The Contested Politics of Mobility: Borderzones and Irregularity* (London: Routledge), 121–142.

Netto, G. (2011) 'Strangers in the city: addressing challenges to the protection, housing and settlement of refugees', *International Journal of Housing Policy*, 11:3, 285–303.

Nyers, P. (2003) 'Abject cosmopolitanism: the politics of protection in the anti-deportation movement', *Third World Quarterly*, 24:6, 1069–1093.

Nyers, P. (2010) 'No One Is Illegal between city and nation', *Studies in Social Justice*, 4:2, 127–143.

Oomen, B., M. F. Davis, and M. Grigolo (eds) (2016) *Global Urban Justice: The Rise of Human Rights Cities* (Oxford: Oxford University Press).

Osborne, T., and N. Rose (1999) 'Governing cities: notes on the spatialisation of virtue', *Environment and Planning D: Society and Space*, 17:4, 737–760.

Papadopoulos, D., and V. S. Tsianos (2013) 'After citizenship: autonomy of migration, organisational ontology and mobile commons', *Citizenship Studies*, 17:2, 178–196.

Pavanello, S. S., S. Elhawary, and S. Pantuliano (2010) *Hidden and Exposed: Urban Refugees in Nairobi, Kenya* (London: Overseas Development Institute).

Phillimore, J., and L. Goodson (2006) 'Problem or opportunity? Asylum seekers, refugees, employment and social exclusion in deprived urban areas', *Urban Studies*, 43, 1715–1736.

Purcell, M. (2003) 'Citizenship and the right to the global city: reimagining the capitalist world order', *International Journal of Urban and Regional Research*, 27:3, 564–590.

Ridgley, J. (2008) 'Cities of refuge: immigration enforcement, police, and the insurgent genealogies of citizenship in US sanctuary cities', *Urban Geography*, 29:1, 53–77.

Rosello, M. (2001) *Postcolonial Hospitality: The Immigrant as Guest* (Stanford, CA: Stanford University Press).

Sassen, S. (2006) *Territory, Authority, Rights: From Medieval to Global Assemblages* (Princeton, NJ: Princeton University Press).

Sassen, S. (2010) 'The city: its return as a lens for social theory', *City, Culture and Society*, 1, 3–11.

Sassen, S. (2013) 'When the center no longer holds: cities as frontier zones', *Cities*, 34:1, 67–70.

Scott, J. C. (1998) *Seeing Like a State: How Certain Schemes to Improve the Human Condition Have Failed* (New Haven, CT: Yale University Press).

Smith, J. (2005) *Jacques Derrida: Live Theory* (London: Continuum).

Squire, V., and J. Darling (2013) 'The "minor" politics of rightful presence: justice and relationality in City of Sanctuary', *International Political Sociology*, 7:1, 59–74.

Uitermark, J., W. Nicholls, and M. Loopmans (2012) 'Cities and social movements: theorizing beyond the right to the city', *Environment and Planning A*, 44:11, 2546–2554.

Varoli, F. (2010) 'Cities of solidarity: local integration in Latin America', *Forced Migration Review*, 34, 44–46.

Varsanyi, M. W. (2008) 'Immigration policing through the backdoor: city ordinances, the "right to the city," and the exclusion of undocumented day laborers', *Urban Geography*, 29:1, 29–52.

Vrasti, W., and S. Dayal (2016) 'Cityzenship: rightful presence and the urban commons', *Citizenship Studies*, 20:8, 994–1011.

Ward, P. (2014) 'Refugee cities: reflections on the development and impact of UNHCR urban refugee policy in the Middle East', *Refugee Survey Quarterly*, 33:1, 77–93.

Wimmer, A., and N. Glick Schiller (2002) 'Methodological nationalism and beyond: nation-state building, migration and the social sciences', *Global Networks*, 2:4, 301–334.

Yukich, G. (2012) 'I didn't know if this was sanctuary: strategic adaptation in the New Sanctuary Movement', in R. K. Lippert and S. Rehaag (eds), *Sanctuary Practices in International Perspectives: Migration, Citizenship and Social Movements* (Abingdon: Routledge), 106–118.

Yukich, G. (2013) 'Constructing the model immigrant: movement strategy and immigrant deservingness in the New Sanctuary Movement', *Social Problems*, 60:3, 302–320.

Index

EU authorised representative for GPSR:
Easy Access System Europe, Mustamäe tee 50,
10621 Tallinn, Estonia
gpsr.requests@easproject.com